CORK CITY REFLECTIONS

Kieran McCarthy & Daniel Breen

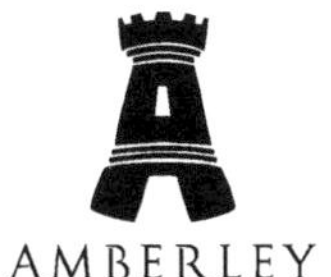

AMBERLEY

Dedicated to all the former staff and patrons of Cork Public Museum over the past 75 years

First published 2021

Amberley Publishing
The Hill, Stroud, Gloucestershire, GL5 4EP
www.amberley-books.com

ISBN 978 1 3981 0458 7 (print)
ISBN 978 1 3981 0459 4 (ebook)

British Library Cataloguing in Publication Data.
A catalogue record for this book is available from the
British Library.

Typesetting by SJmagic DESIGN SERVICES, India.
Printed in Great Britain.

Appointed GPSR EU Representative: Easy Access System
Europe Oü, 16879218
Address: Mustamäe tee 50, 10621, Tallinn, Estonia
Contact Details: gpsr.requests@easproject.com, +358 40
500 3575

Contents

Introduction

Landscape is differentiated. It resembles a network of related places, some revealed through our habitual actions, some through familiarity and affinity and some through particular moments and events stored in communal memory ... the environment is itself pregnant with the past – as we walk it, we not only remember our own past – that is after all how we get around – but we also enact the activities of those who have gone before. Places do not have locations but histories (M. Pearson, 2006, *In Comes I, Performance, Memory and Landscape*)

People have been sending, receiving and collecting postcards for well over 150 years. They have always come in a variety of forms including plain, comedic, memorial, and of course topographical. Their popularity reached its zenith in the two decades before the outbreak of the First World War when people used postcards for a variety of everyday reasons, from ordering shopping to making appointments. Postcards have been described as the 'social media' of the Edwardian period as it is estimated that around one billion penny postcards were sold annually in the United States alone between 1907 and 1915.

Since 1992, Cork Public Museum has actively sourced and collected postcards of Cork interest. The majority of postcards are topographical in nature and cover towns and villages throughout County Cork. Presently, the collection numbers in the thousands but the museum is constantly on the lookout for rarer and unique examples or gems. In an age where digital photography and the internet have made capturing and sharing images so effortless, it is easy to forget that in the decades before the camera became popular and affordable, postcards were the only photographic souvenirs of the landscape available to ordinary people.

In this book, which builds on our *Cork City Through Time* (2012), we continue to explore Cork Public Museum's extensive collection of postcards. They are of times and places that Corkonians are familiar with. There is a power in these images – they all have multiple interpretations; they are a window into the place, neighbourhood, people, their lives and identity.

Old postcards show the city of Cork to be a place of scenic contrasts. The city as a visually bright world with all its shapes and contours challenges the photographer to take the best photograph, to capture the best of the city. Many of the postcards show or frame the River Lee and the tidal estuary and the intersection of the city and the water. The postcards show how rich the city is in its traces of its history. The variety of postcards also reflects upon how the city has developed in a piecemeal sense, with each century bringing another addition to the city's landscape.

For the photographer, it took time and patience to set up the picture. One had to wait for the people, weather, order and symmetry to be right. The gathering of memory, life, energy, the city's beat, its light and shape had to be considered. The same challenges were present when trying to retake old photographs in the present day.

In more depth, the postcards show people's relationship to their world – continuity and familiarity crossing past and present. They record a person, an event, a social phenomenon, and attempt to reconstruct a sense of place. The postcards let moments linger, reflect on life and showcase the the city as a work of art. The tinting or colouring of postcards adds more subtlety and weight to the image and to the concept of the city as a work of art. The tinting adds more to the romanticisation of the landscape.

Some public spaces are well represented, emphasised, and are created and arranged in a sequence to convey particular meanings. Buildings such as a City Hall, a courthouse or a theatre symbolise the theatrics of power. Indeed, one hundred years ago in Ireland was a time of change; the continuous rise of an Irish cultural revival, debates over home rule and the idea of Irish identity were continuously negotiated by all classes of society. Just like the tinting of the postcards, what the viewer sees is a world which is being contested, refined and reworked. Behind the images presented is a story of change – complex and multi-faceted.

The postcards freeze the action, conceptualise society and civil expressions – from the city's links with the natural world such as rivers and tide to its transportation networks, commerce and social networks. Places of Cork pride, heritage and popular culture are depicted and are validated, communicating the ideas of those places. Indeed, some of the postcards have personal comments written on the back. All types of emotion are represented, from happiness in visiting Cork to comments on how the addressee was missed.

We have grouped the postcards under thematic headings like Main Streets, Public Buildings, Transport, and Industry. The highlight of Edwardian Cork was the hosting of an International Exhibition in 1902 and 1903 and through the souvenir postcards we can get a glimpse of this momentous event. We hope that any reader of this book will not only appreciate how Cork City has evolved and grown over the last century but also how invaluable postcards can be in understanding the nuances and complexities of studying images and their history.

Dan Breen & Kieran McCarthy

The Evolution of People & Place

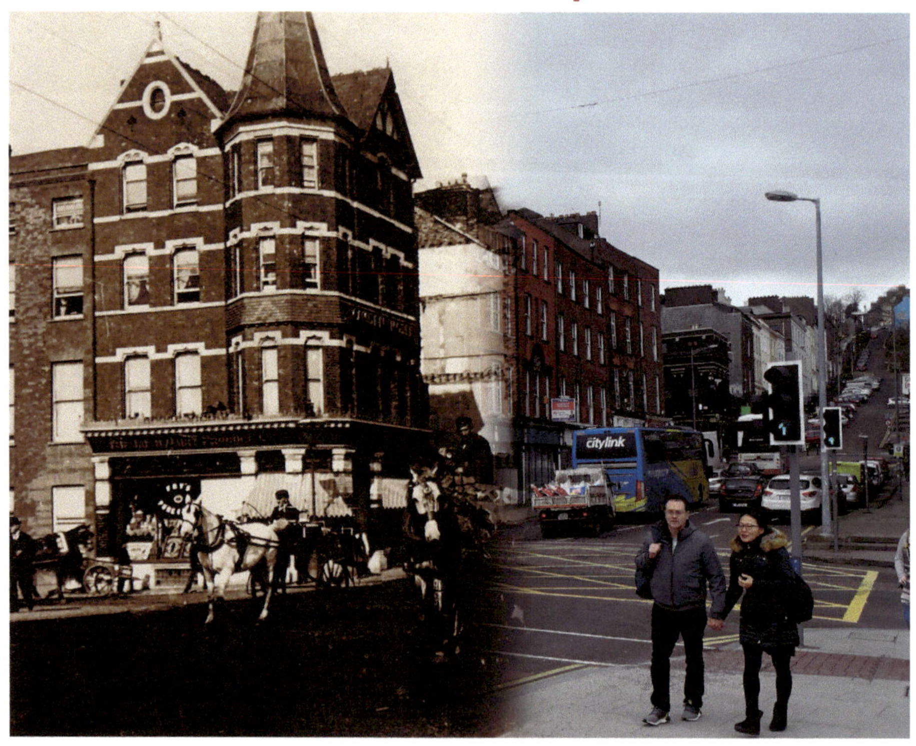

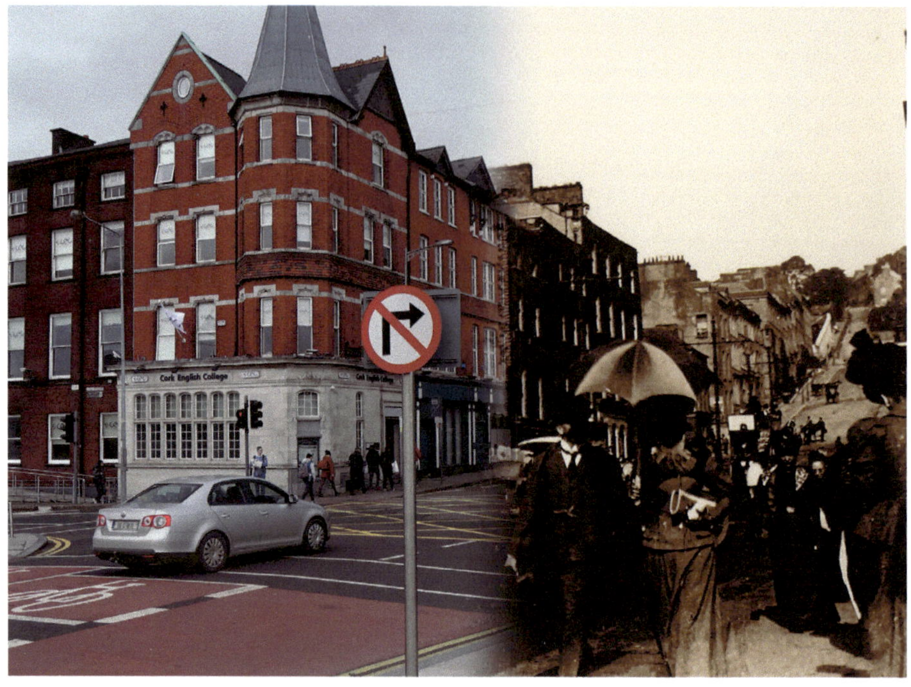

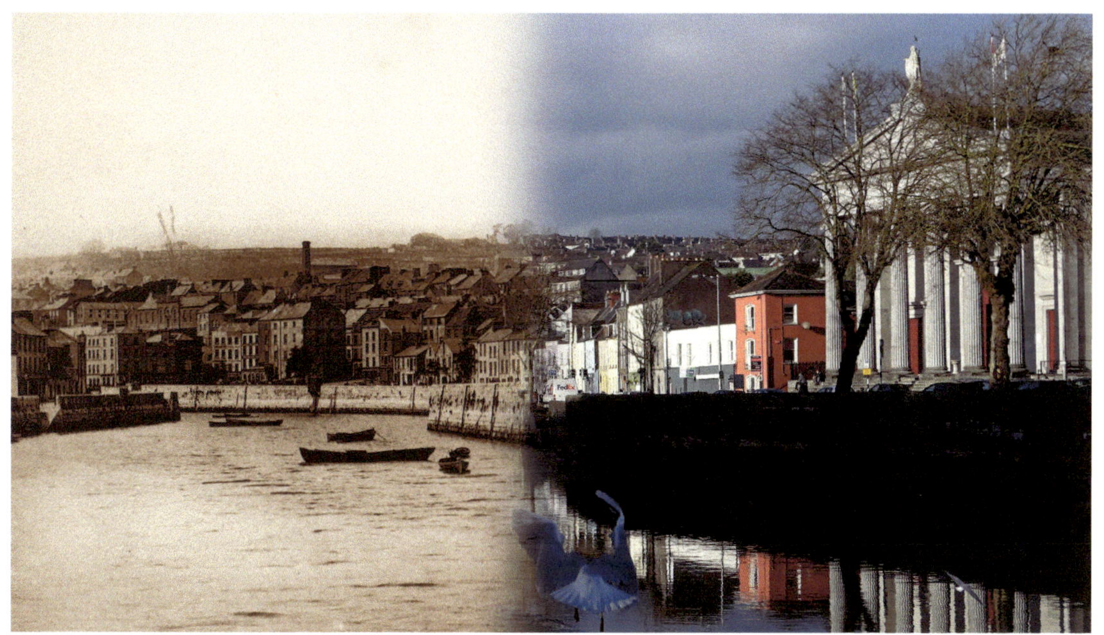

View of Pope's Quay

The most important influence on the city's development was and is the River Lee, which has witnessed the city's growth from a monastic centre to a cosmopolitan twenty-first-century city. The main urban centre was built on a series of marshy islands at the lowest crossing point of the river, where it meets the sea. The Irish for the city is Corcaigh, which means 'marshes'. The image of the North Channel, shows the city's notable hilly topography, its built landscape and the associated myriad of different architectural styles. By the early twentieth century, the population of the city was 75,000. The middle classes lived in the expanding suburbs whilst the majority of the working classes lived in slum conditions within the inner city. Unemployment and emigration were high. The city today still boasts extensive views from its quays and bridges.

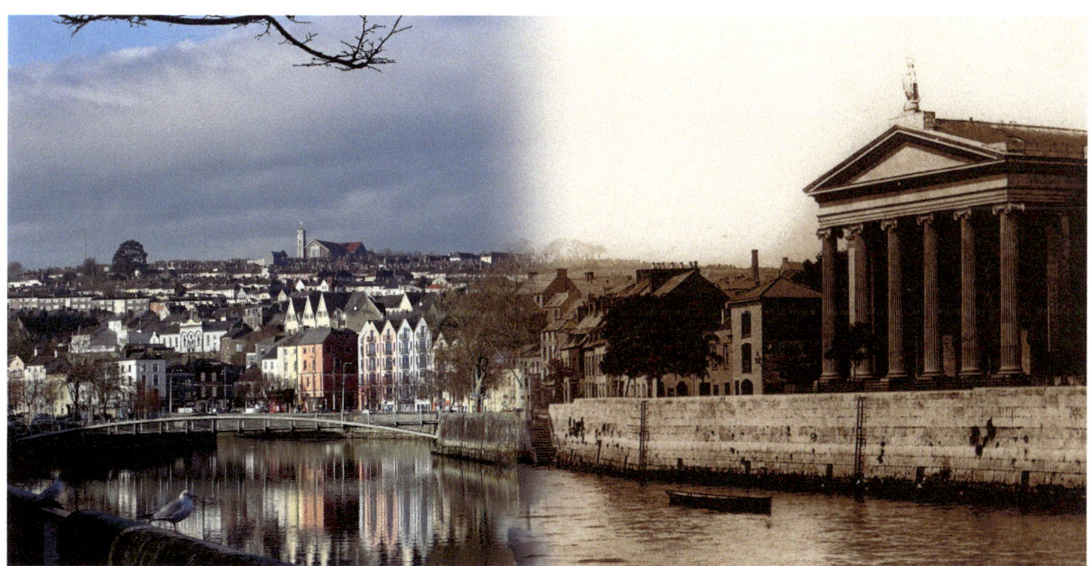

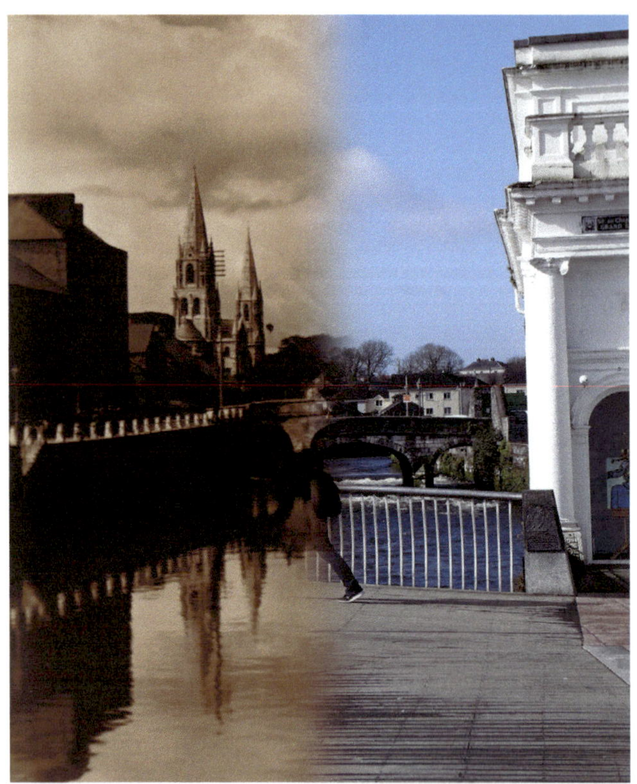

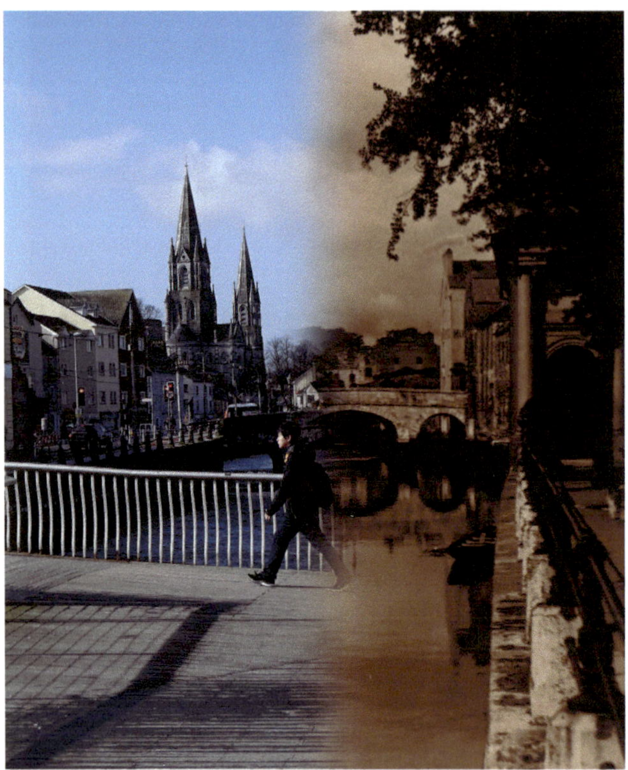

Marshy Origins

The first known settlement at Cork began as a monastic centre in the seventh century, founded by St Finbarre. This is now marked by the late nineteenth-century structure of St Finbarre's Cathedral. The Vikings were the first to develop a basic timber bridge spanning from the valley side to one of the marshes, now marked by South Gate Bridge. This was the start of a rich maritime history and a strong identification as a port town. In the time of the Anglo-Normans, who established a fortified walled settlement and a trading centre in Cork around AD 1200, South Gate Drawbridge formed one of the three entrances. In May 1711, agreement was reached by the council of the city that North Gate Bridge would be rebuilt in stone in 1712 while in 1713, South Gate Bridge would be replaced with stone arched structures. Both North and South Gate Drawbridges were designed and built by a George Coltsman, a Cork City stonemason/architect. South Gate Bridge still stands today in its past form apart from some minor restructuring and strengthening

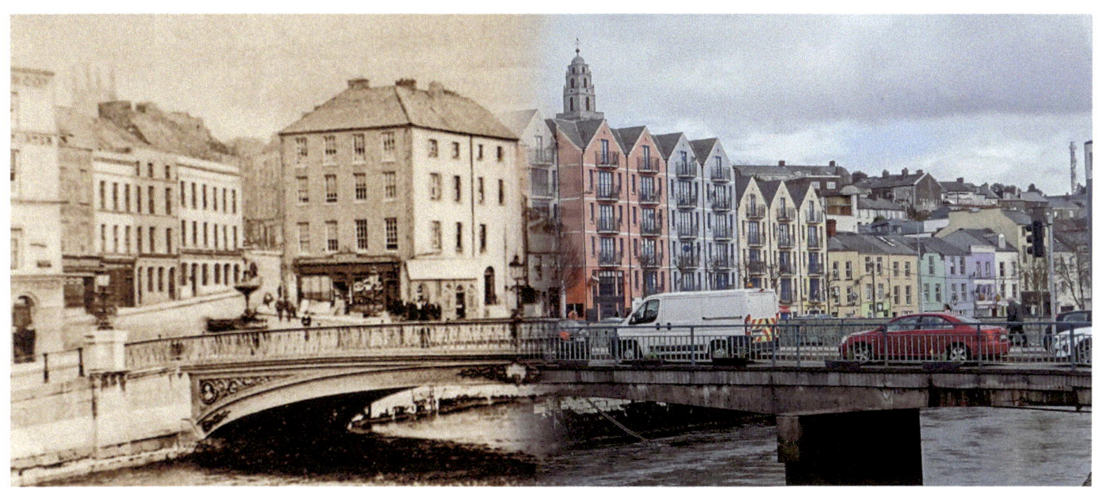

North Gate Bridge

The foundation stone for the fourth bridge, known North Gate Bridge, was laid in April 1863. The new bridge was to be a cast-iron structure with the ironwork completed by Ranking & Co. of Liverpool. An ornate Victorian style was incorporated into the new structure with features such as ornamental lamp posts and iron medallions depicting Queen Victoria; Albert the Prince Consort; Daniel O'Connell, the Irish champion of Catholic emancipation; Sir Thomas Moore, designer; and Barry McMullen, contractor. Nearly 100 years later in 1961, the bridge would have to be reconstructed again due to increased road traffic and heavier vehicles.

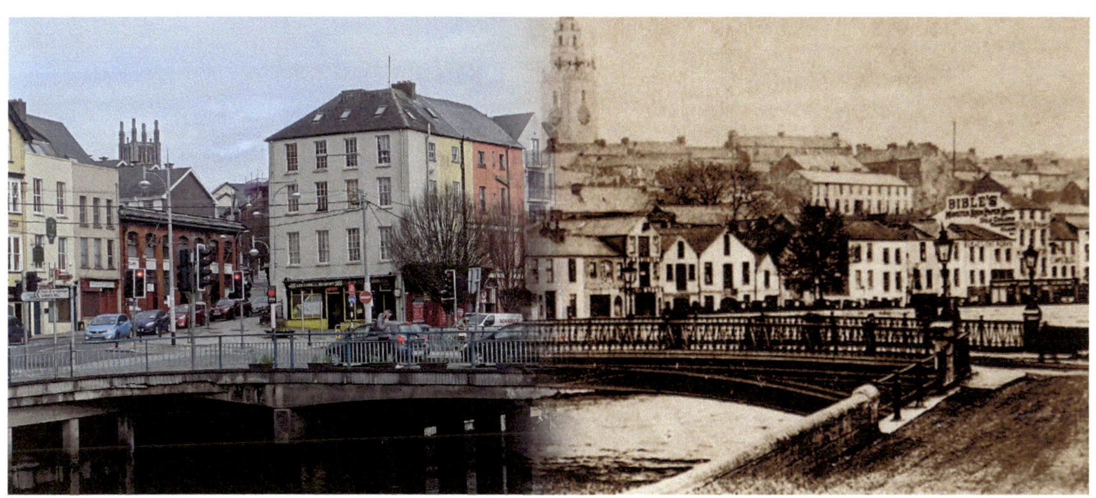

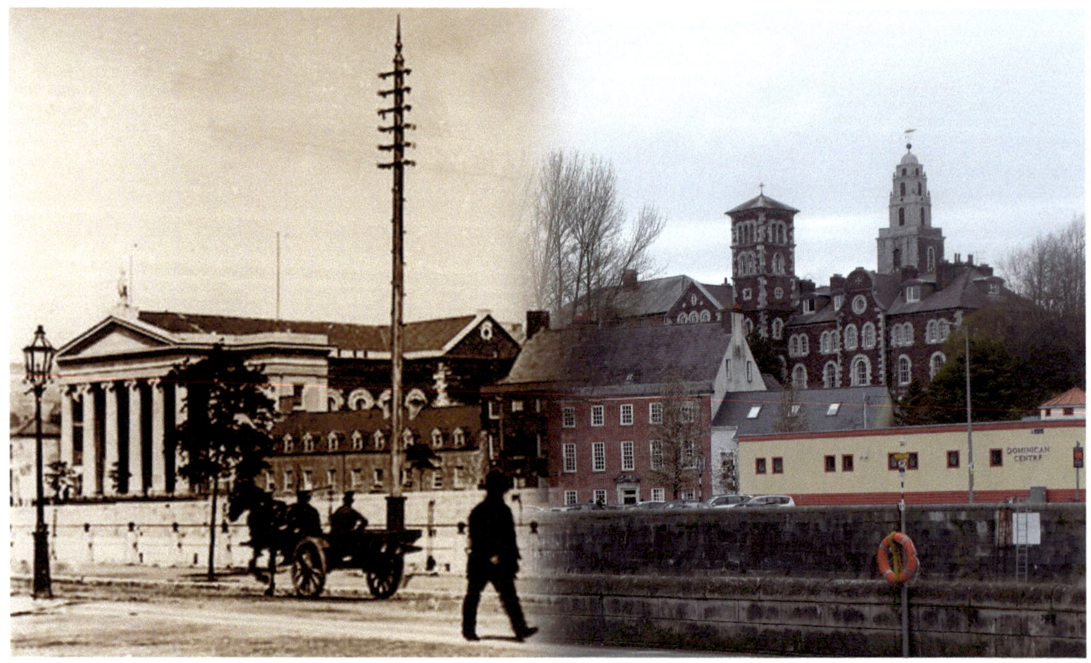

Lavitt's Quay

In the early eighteenth century, large portions of marshland to the west and east of the walled town (of which North and South Main Streets were the principal thoroughfares) were to be reclaimed by Cork Corporation and two influential religious groups who were of the Corporation: the Huguenots and the Quakers. One of the first Huguenot families to develop property was Joseph Lavitt, whose family were primarily involved in overseas trade and sugar refining. Lavitt's Quay, as seen in this photograph, was initially constructed in 1704 and echoes the Huguenots' past presence in the area. The areas of present-day French Church Street, Carey's Lane and Academy Street in the city centre are located at the core of the Huguenot quarter.

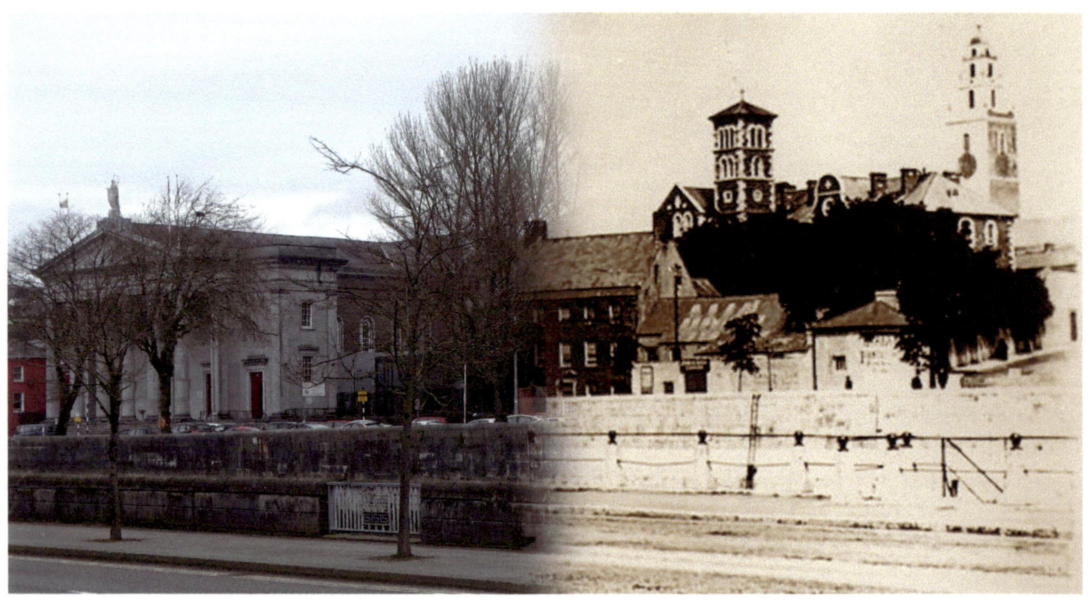

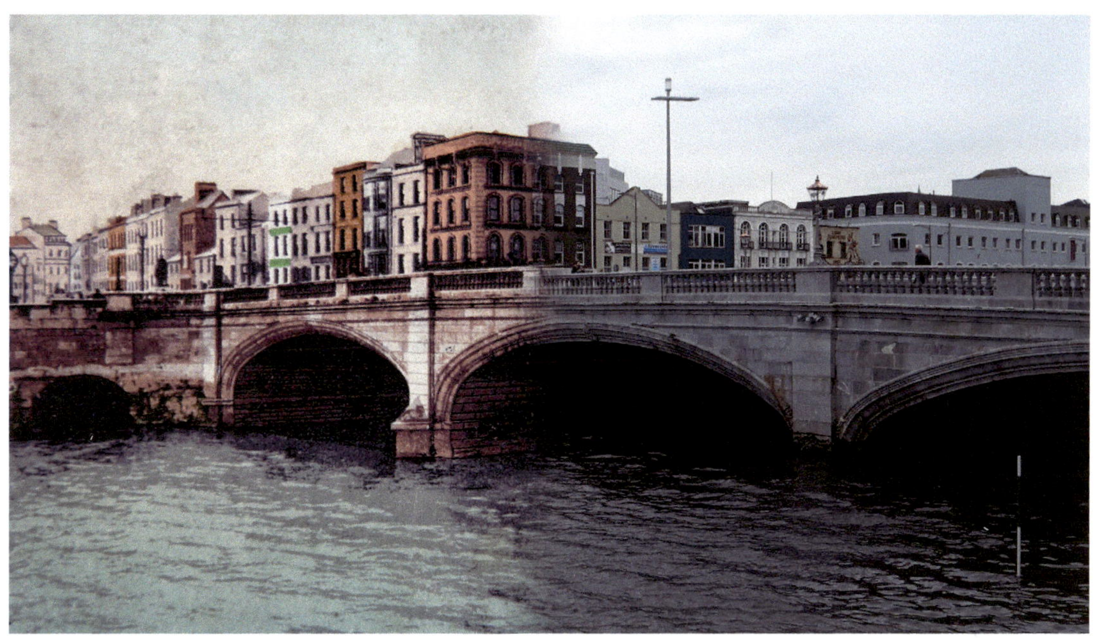

St Patrick's Bridge

Prior to the 1700s, the area around this bridge site was just marshland. As the city's trading fortunes increased vastly in its British and overseas markets in the eighteenth century, the knock-on population growth demanded more housing, streets, canals and warehouses. A curving channel of the River Lee was turned into a canal with quays, shops and warehouses on both sides of it. *Circa* 1780, the canal was filled, which created the wide and elegant thoroughfare of St Patrick's Street. To improve access into its eastern section, in 1787, St Patrick's Bridge was created to connect the new street to the adjacent steep hill to be named St Patrick's Hill. The hill can boast being one of the city's steepest hills to climb.

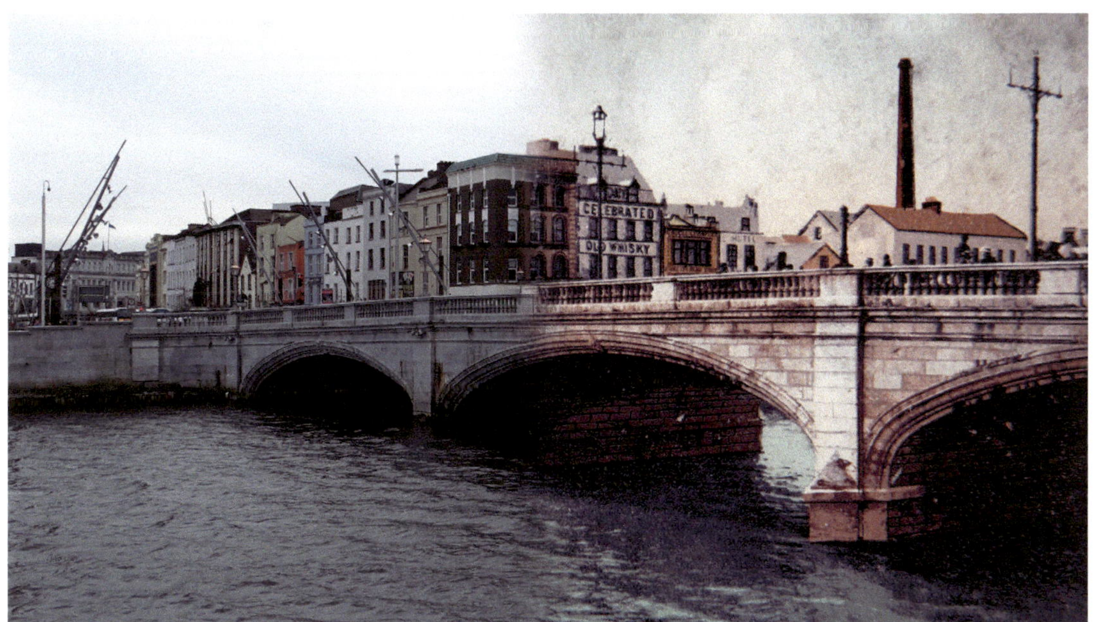

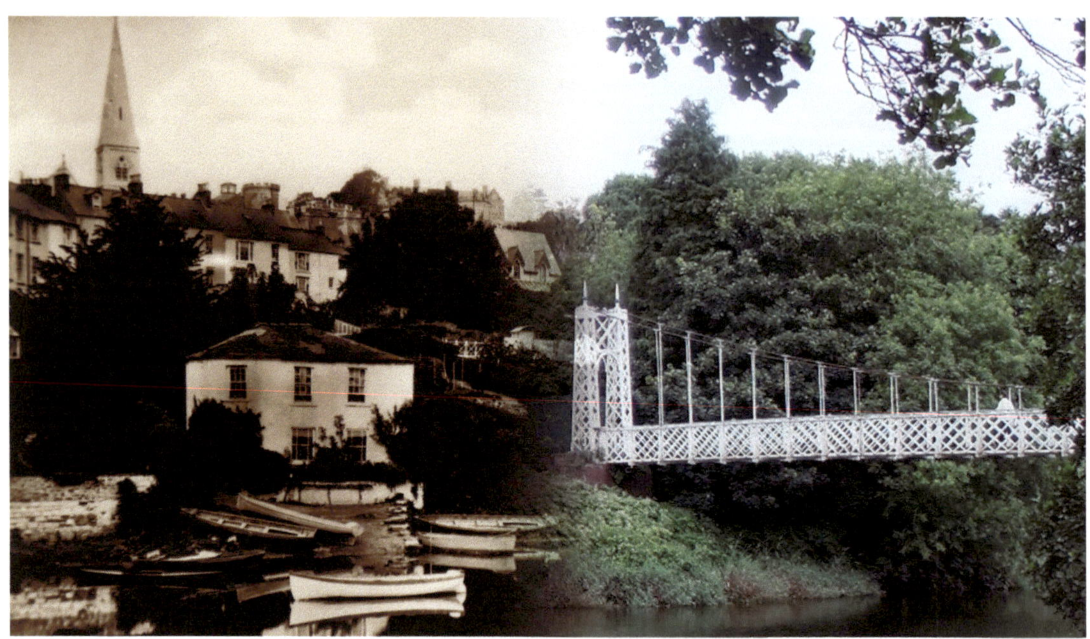

Sunday's Well

In 1750, Charles Smith, writing in his *History of Cork*, compares the banks of the River Lee to those of the River Seine and the River Thames, remarking their very similar features on a smaller scale. He describes that overlooking the city on the hills are 'neat houses, gardens and plantations' of the middle classes as shown above in the beautiful postcard of Sunday's Well. To this day similar scenes can still be viewed adjacent to Daly's Bridge (opened in 1927) – or more affectionately known by Corkonians as the Shakey Bridge – and from the paths of the walkways along the river.

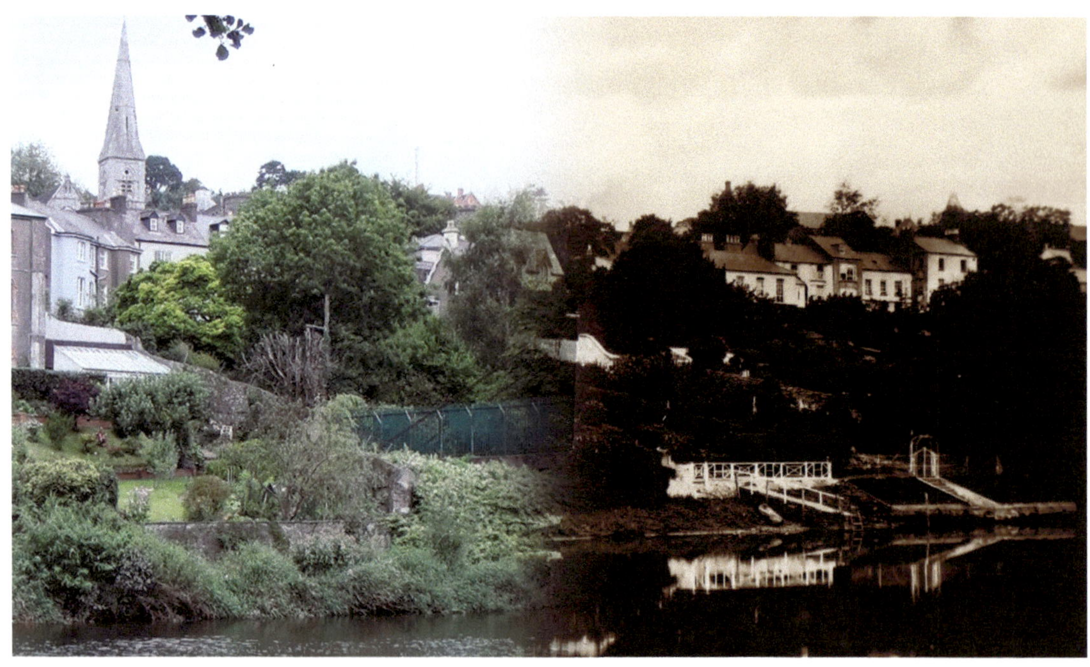

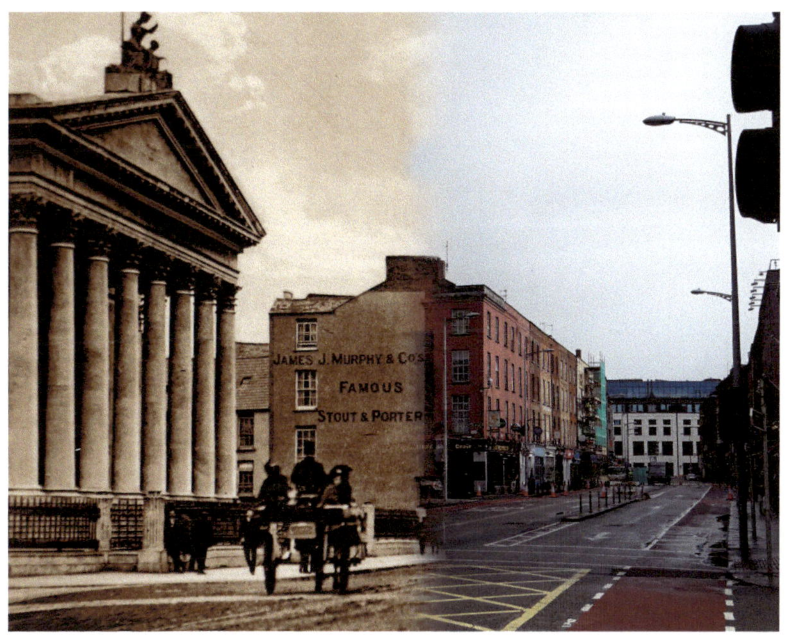

Great George's Street

In 1765, the Cork Wide Street Commission was set up to deal with the problems of an expanding city, especially in improving the health conditions of the people living in Cork. The commission aimed to improve public health in the city by widening old and dilapidated medieval laneways. Sixteen commissioners were appointed in Cork in 1765, but due to financial problems, it was really only in the early 1800s that the commission made an impact. Around this time, streets such as South Terrace, Dunbar Street and Great George's Street (opened November 1824 and now called Washington Street) were laid out.

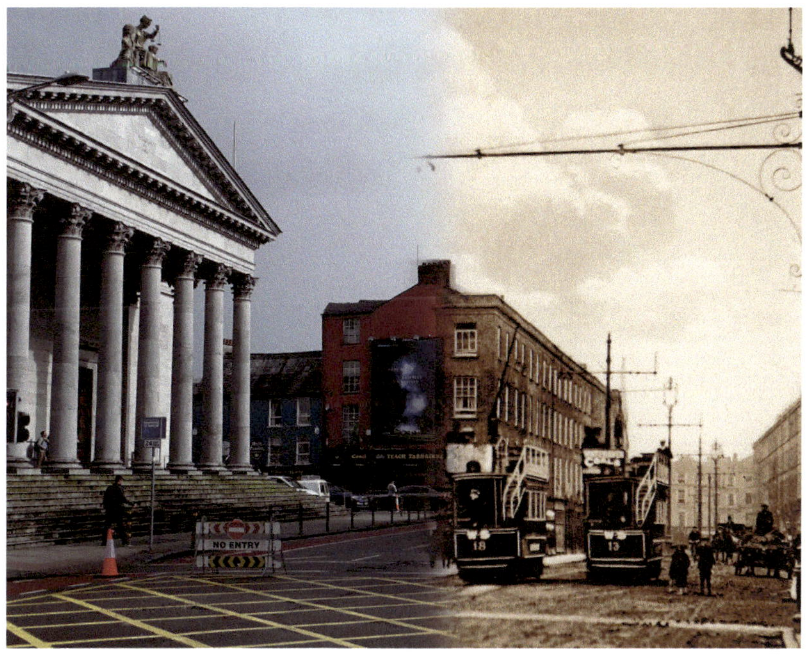

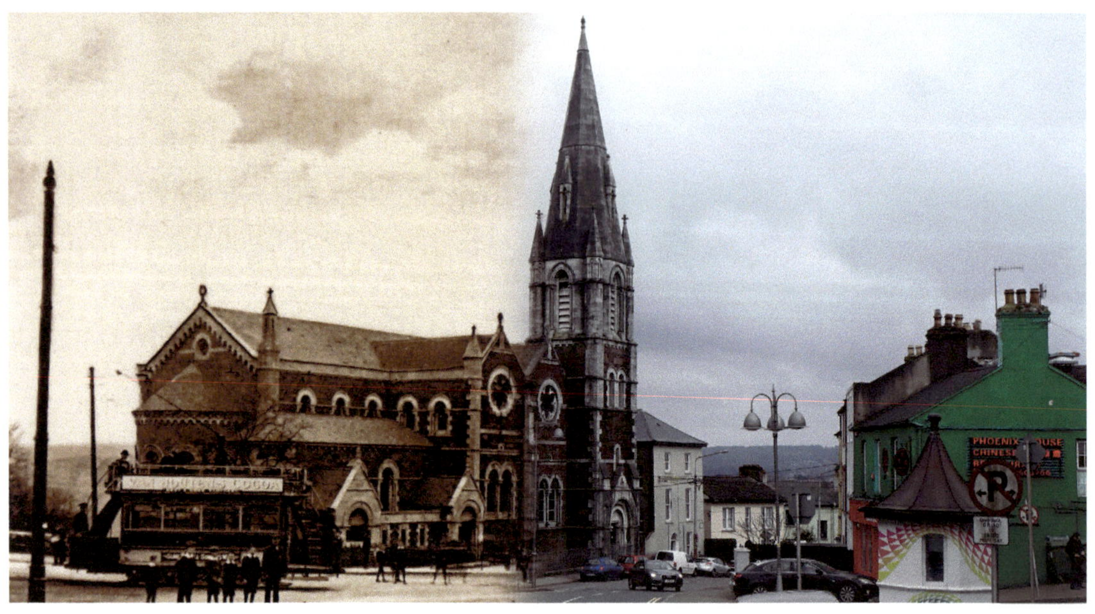

View of St Luke's Church

An increase in inner-city population in the early nineteenth century led more middle- and upper-class citizens to move out and invest in housing construction in undeveloped suburbs – some close to the city and some further out, such as Summerhill North, Montenotte, Ballintemple, Blackrock and the Mahon Peninsula. Summerhill Road (North) was laid out between 1801 and 1832 as well as a myriad of new residences. Such housing provided the catalyst for the creation of St Patrick's Church and the first of three incarnations of St Luke's church (see postcard) – St Patrick's and St Luke's had their foundation stones laid in the 1830s. St Luke's Church was consecrated in 1837 whilst St Patrick's Church opened in 1848.

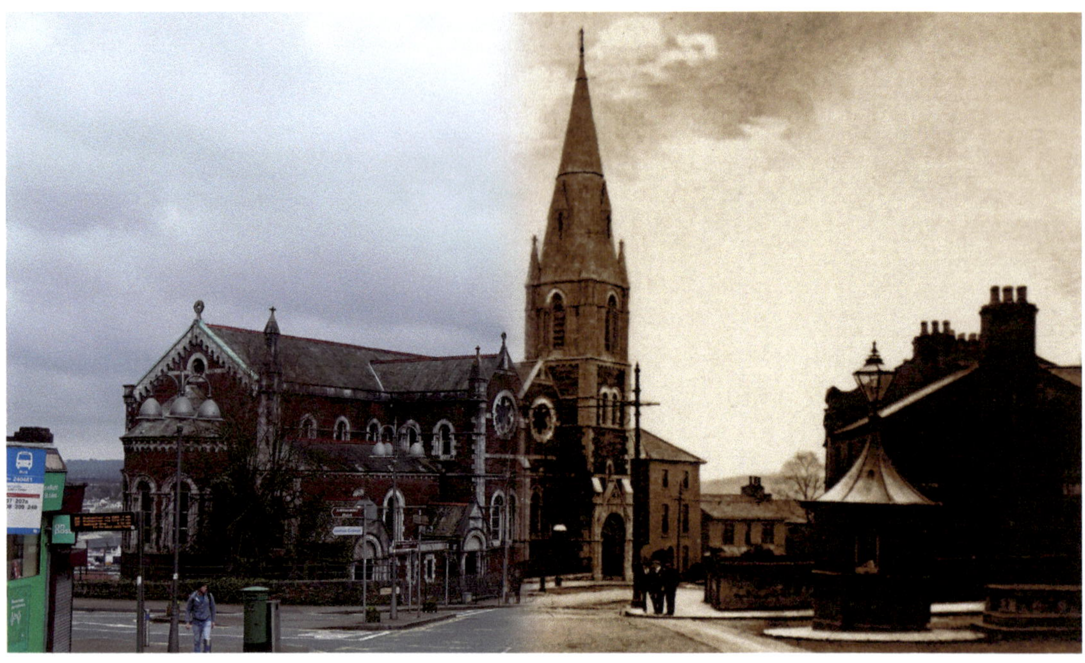

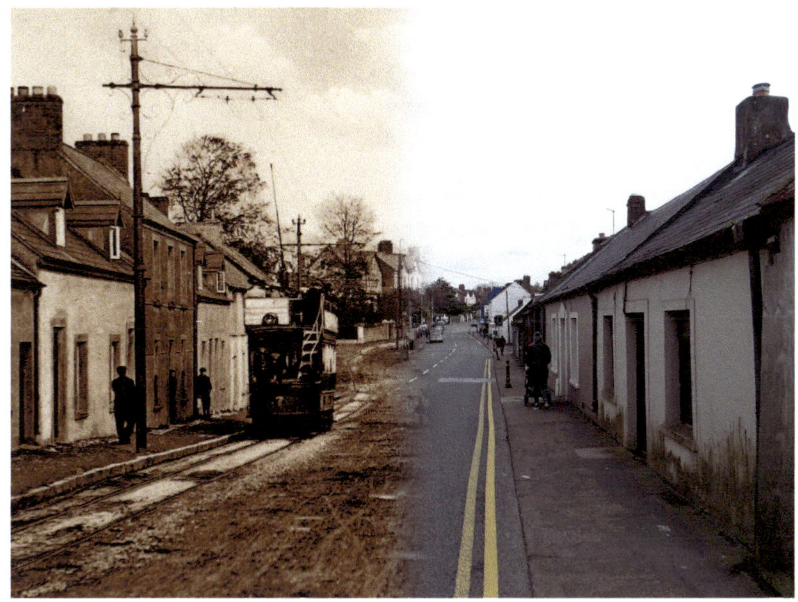

Ballintemple

Urban legend describes how the Knights Templar had a church in Ballintemple from 1392, the first parish church of Blackrock. The church is long gone but an old graveyard and a historic village street have survived the test of time. Today along Blackrock Road one can see the various late nineteenth-century Victorian architectural styles such as Norman, Gothic, Renaissance, Georgian, Victorian, Italianate, French, and Oriental. The houses can boast such architects such as Brother Michael Riordan, Sir John Benson, Richard Brash, and the Deanes, Morrisons, Hargraves, Walkers, and Hills. The architectural DNA comprises local stone, sand, brick, slates from Killaloe, Rosscarbery and Wales, timber from Canada and Scandinavia, cement from Portland in England and ironwork for railings obtained from Scottish foundries.

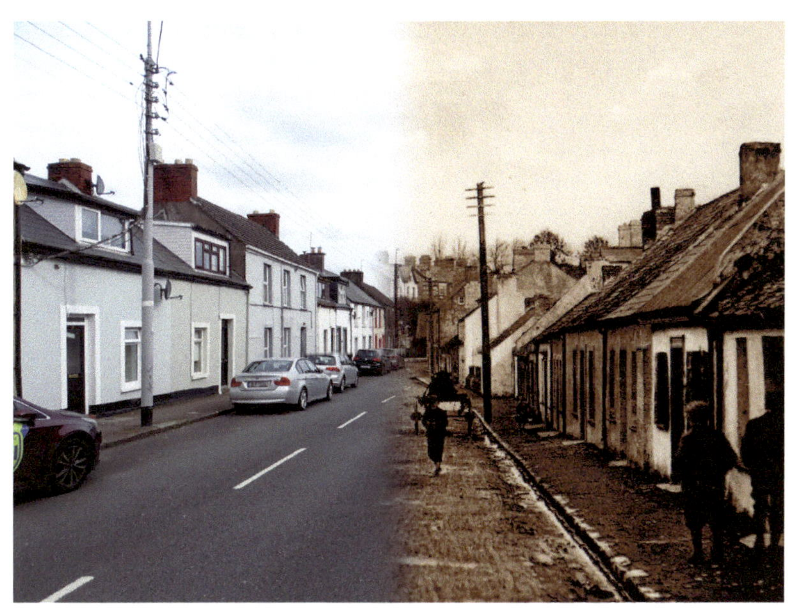

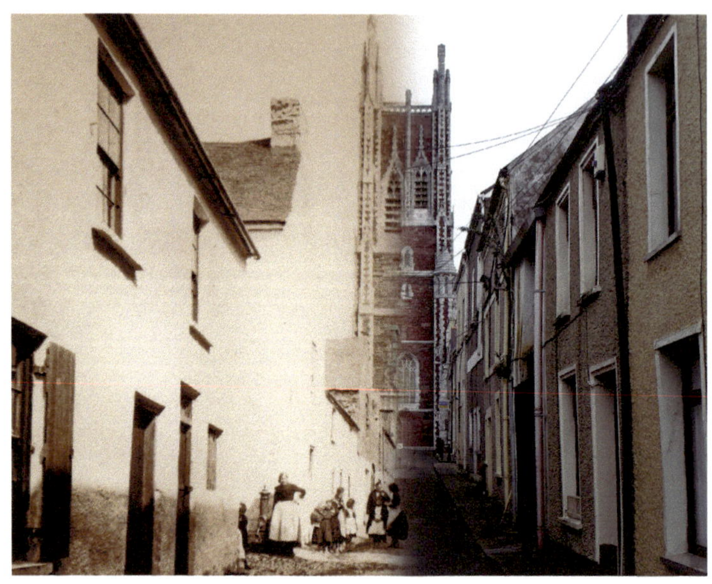

Cathedral Avenue/Former Eason's Lane

On Cork's north side, just north of the butter market place which provided the foundations of Cork's economic growth, were located around 400 tenement houses. In the first week of December 1917, Mr D. J. Coakley, Principal of the Cork School of Commerce, delivered a lecture entitled 'General Principles of Housing and Town Planning', with a specific focus on Cork City. Mr Coakley painted a stark picture of housing stock in the city. There was a very large proportion of unsanitary houses which he described 'not quite suitable for human beings to live in'. In referring to the tenement houses he stated that some of them were so old and dilapidated, and so structurally bad, that repairing them was out of the question, and, consequently, almost forty houses had been closed off some years previously because of being unfit for human habitation. Coakley made the case that accommodation was urgently needed for 115 families whose houses need to demolished as they were in such a poor state.

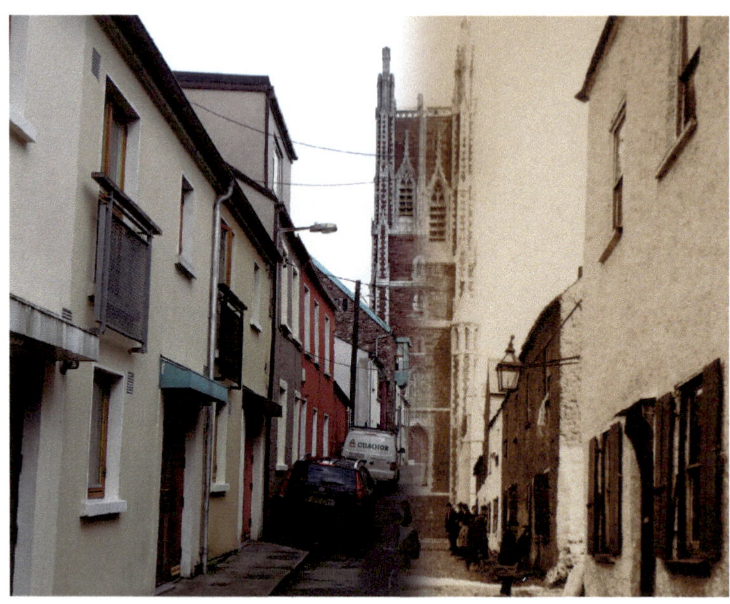

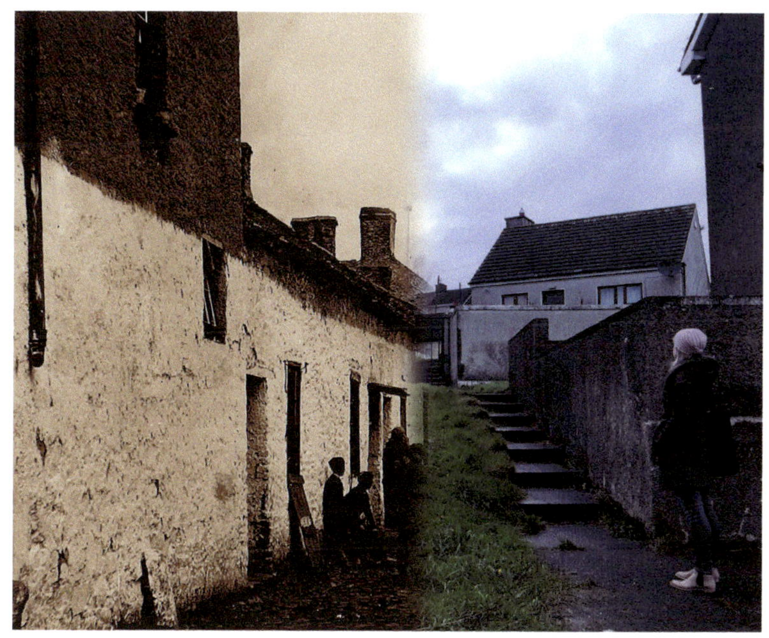

In Mr D. J. Coakley's lecture on 'General Principles of Housing and Town Planning', he highlighted the large challenge that was overcrowding. In 719 tenement houses 726 cases of overcrowding were discovered. ln some cases the cubic space of the sleeping apartments amounted to only 72 cubic feet for each person. There were several instances where a father and mother with sons and daughters over twenty years of age all slept in the same small apartment. Of the 12,850 houses in Cork, 1,500 didn't have backyards and nearly half were situated in the centre on the flat of the city. The habitations varied from cabins to cellars, all in a poor and run-down state.

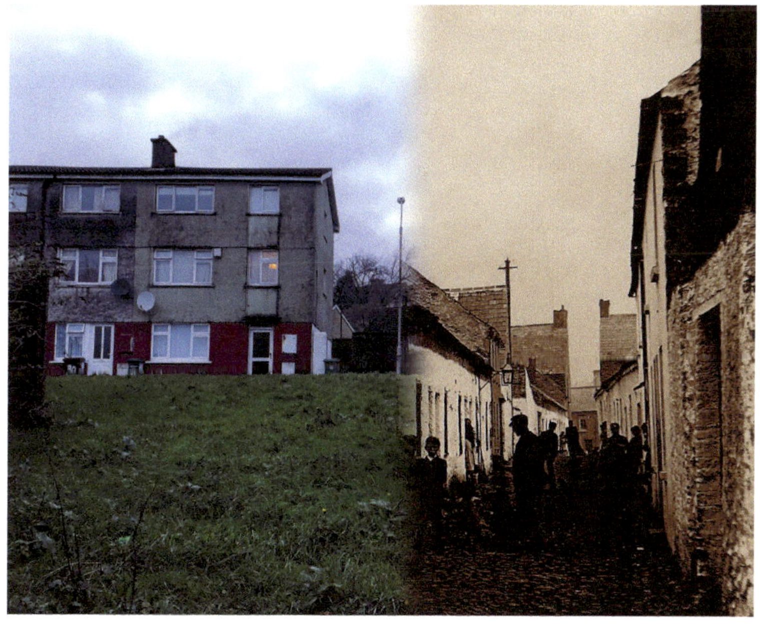

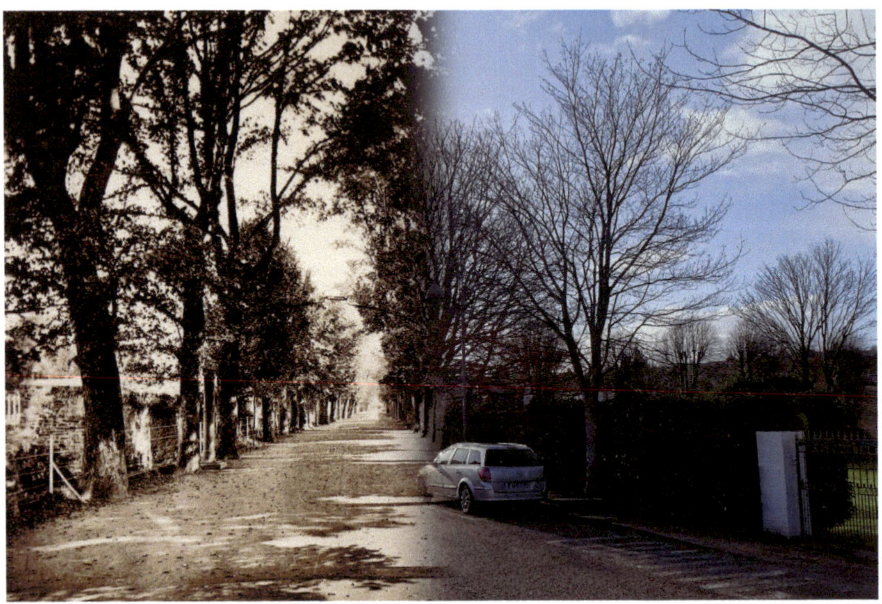

In 1719 a large section of marshy land, now the area of Fitzgerald Park, was bought by Cork Corporation's town clerk, Edward Webber. Webber, a Dutchman, decided to build a raised walkway across some undeveloped marshy islands, at his own expense. He named it after a famous promenade in Amsterdam, the Meer-Dyke, which translates roughly as an embankment to protect the land from the sea. In time it became a fashionable meeting place for the middle to upper classes of the city. Between 1795 and 1850, the gardens and tea house were used as a summer residence for the Lord Mayor of Cork. At one stage people were employed to build an elegant pond and to take care of his grounds. In the early 1830s people again started to use the walk. The renewed interest from the public led the Corporation to make the promenade more attractive by erecting a slate-covered bandstand.

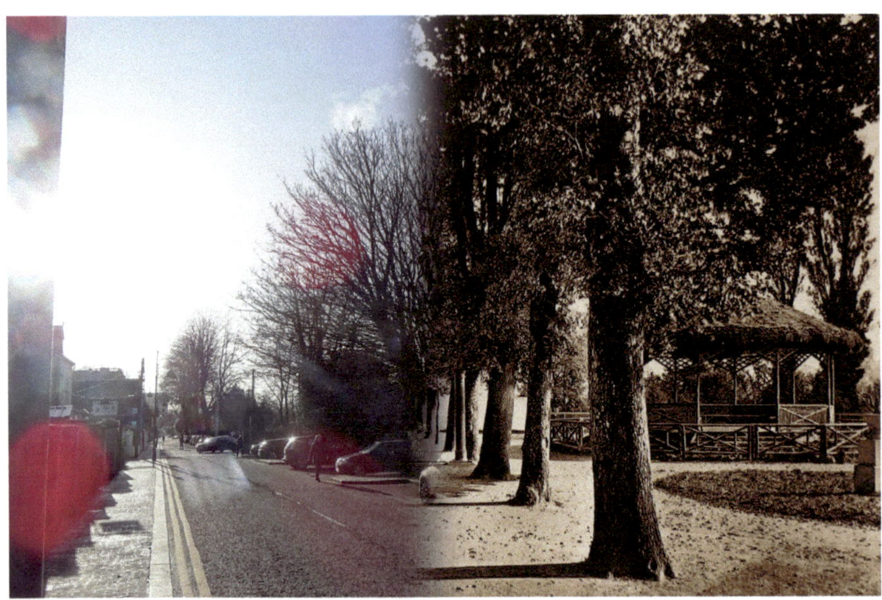

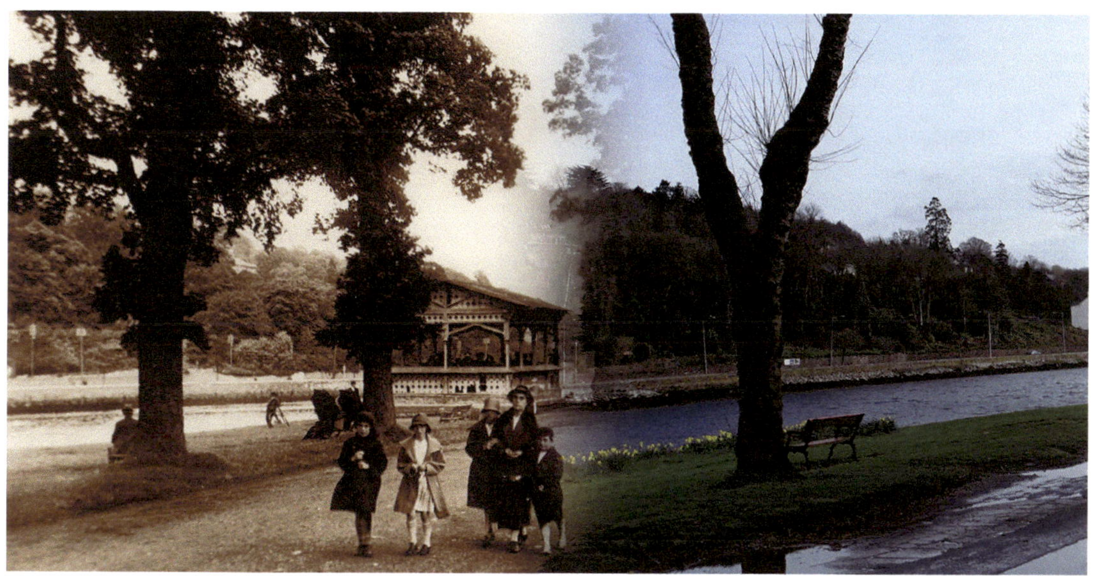

The Marina

The Marina was a Victorian walkway funded by Cork Corporation but the original designer is unknown. Originally, the walkway was a dock called the Navigation Wall, which was a narrow wall constructed in the 1780s and which jutted out into the river. The Navigation Wall acted as an extension to the city's docks. Later in time, gravel and mud were dredged from the river to reclaim the adjacent slobland and create the very popular 'Marina Walk'. One prominent feature of the city's interaction with time and British imperialism was the time cannon gun on Cork's Marina. Put in place in 1876, as recorded in the minutes of the meetings of the Cork Harbour Commissioners, the gun – an 18 pounder – stood on a platform built for it at the city end of the Marina. It fired daily at 12.35 p.m. – as up to 20 May 1916 the time difference between Ireland and the UK was twenty-five minutes and twenty-two seconds behind Greenwich Mean Time.

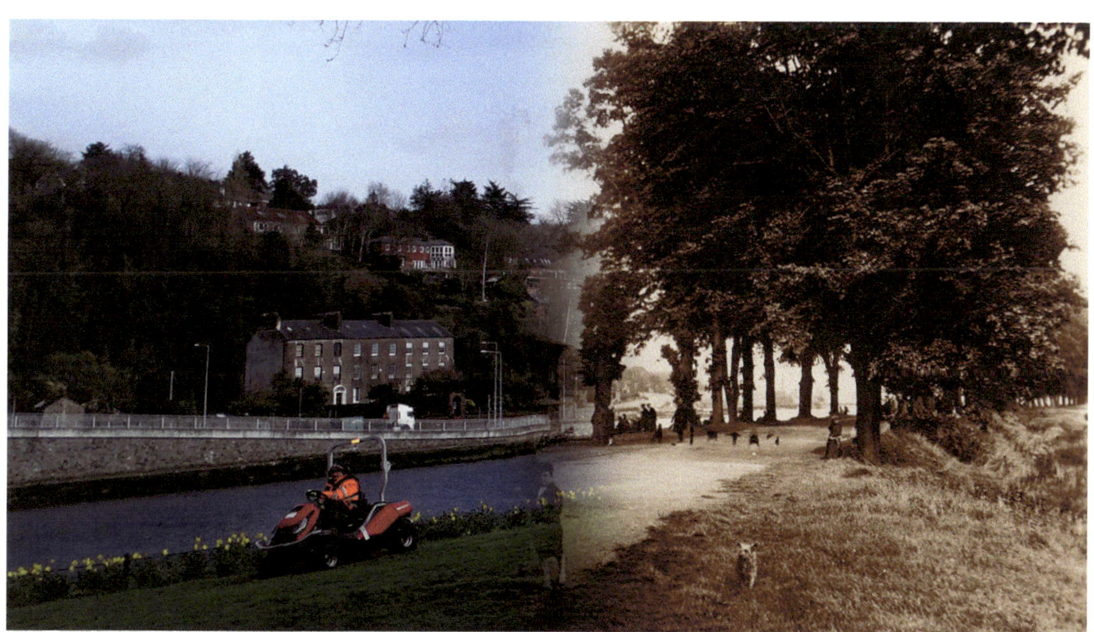

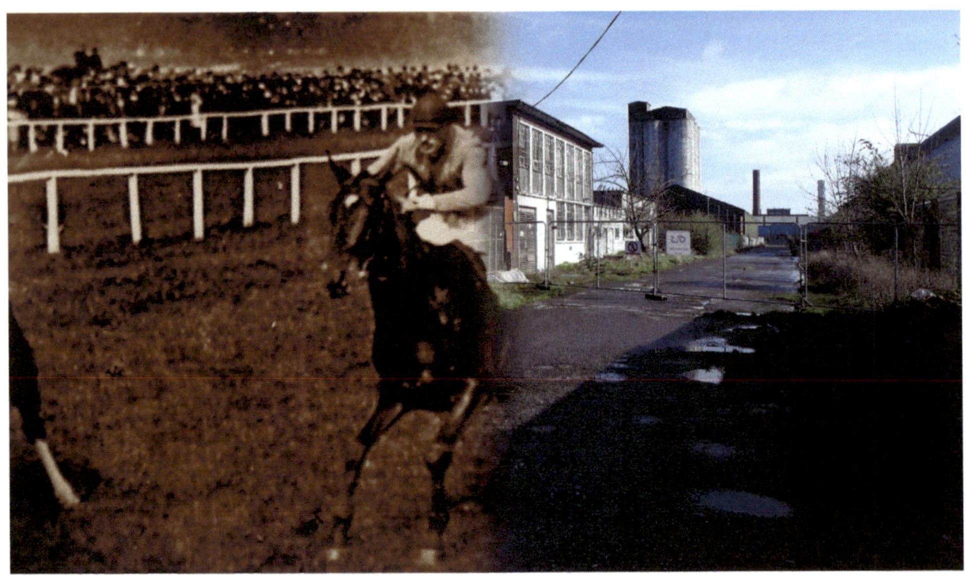

Cork Park Racecourse

In March 1869, Cork Corporation leased to Sir John Arnott and others slobland for a term of five years and for the purpose of establishing a racecourse. There were no systematic attempts at drainage, so races were held in mud and slush on many occasions. The first races were held on 17 and 18 May 1869, and a total of 30,000 people attended. In 1892, the City and County of Cork Agricultural Society leased space from Cork Corporation in the eastern section of the Cork Park, which later became the Cork Showgrounds. In November 1916, Fords made an offer to purchase the freehold of the Cork Park grounds and considerable land adjoining the river near the Marina. Fords, Cork Corporation and the Harbour Commissioners entered into formal negotiations. The company acquired approximately 130 acres of land, which also had a river frontage. The tractor factory gave employment to at least 1,000 adult males and paid the minimum wage of one shilling per hour.

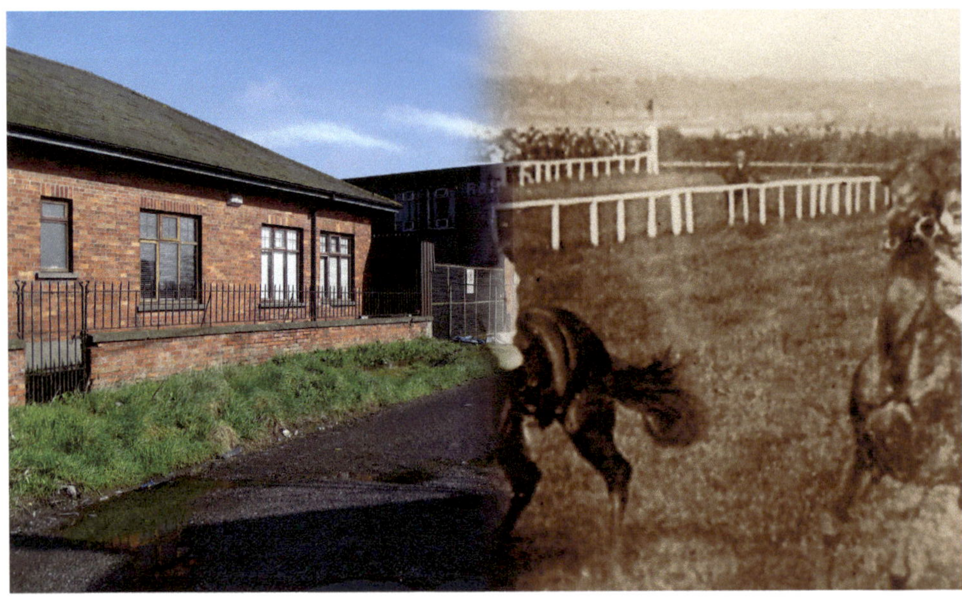

The Industrious City

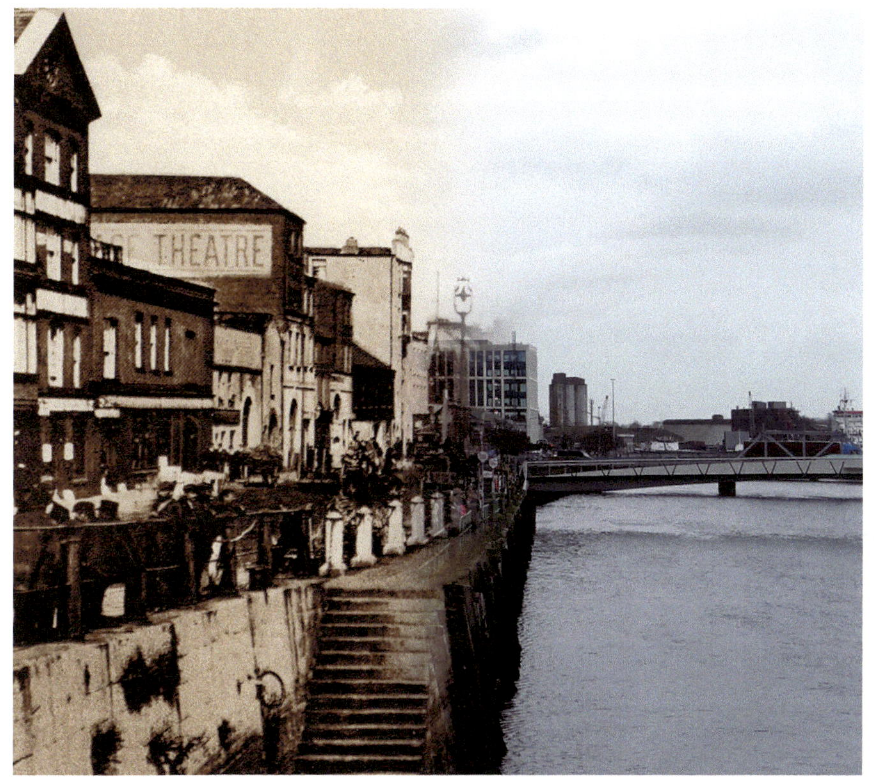

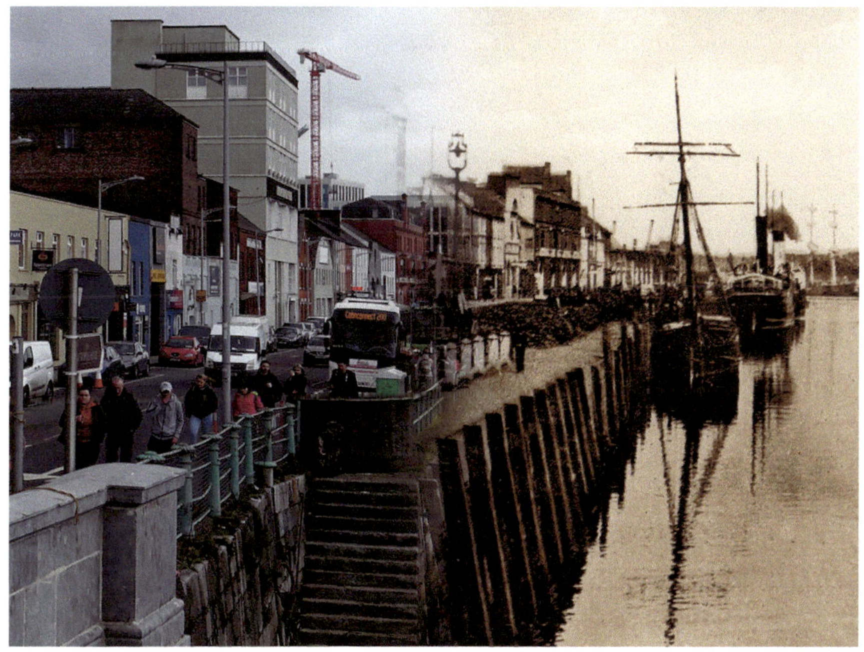

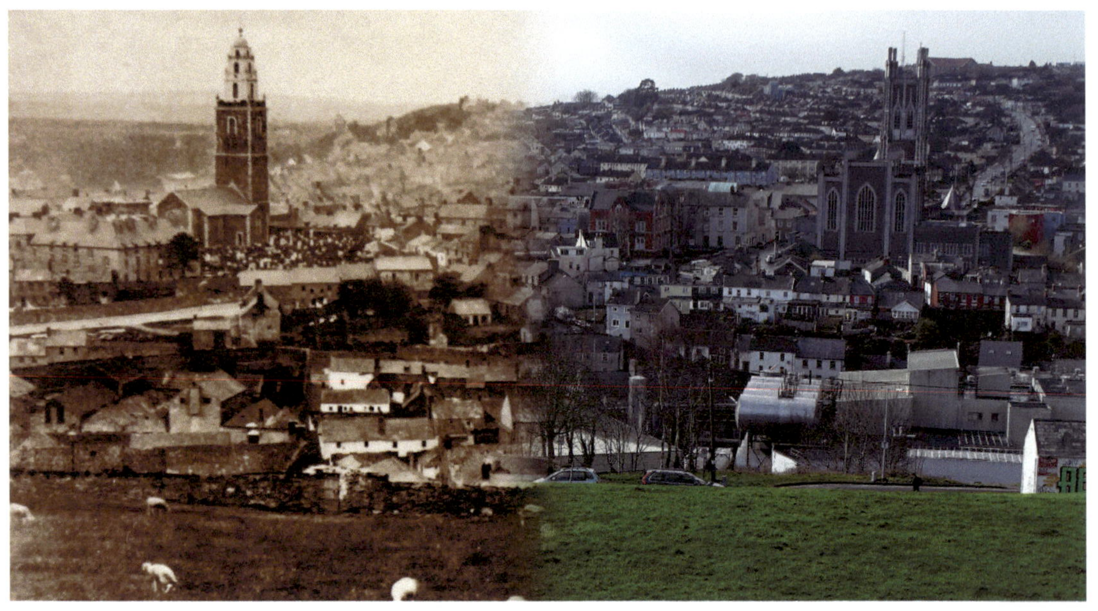

Atop St Patrick's Hill

The postcard captures a view of the city from the perspective of the visiting farmers to Cork. In the eighteenth and early nineteenth centuries, Cork was a great centre for the export of livestock. Old Youghal Road into St Patrick's Hill, below, provided one of the principal routeways into the city's cattle markets from the north-east side of the city. In 1748, two English gentlemen touring Ireland noted that 90,000 black cattle were killed for export purposes between August and December in the city's cattle market near Shandon Street. In the western hemisphere, the West Indies provided the greatest market for provisions. Other export areas were Barbados, Carolina, Georgia, Jamaica, Newfoundland and Britain. The sheep in this early twentieth-century postcard remind the viewer of the city's closeness to the surrounding agricultural hinterland.

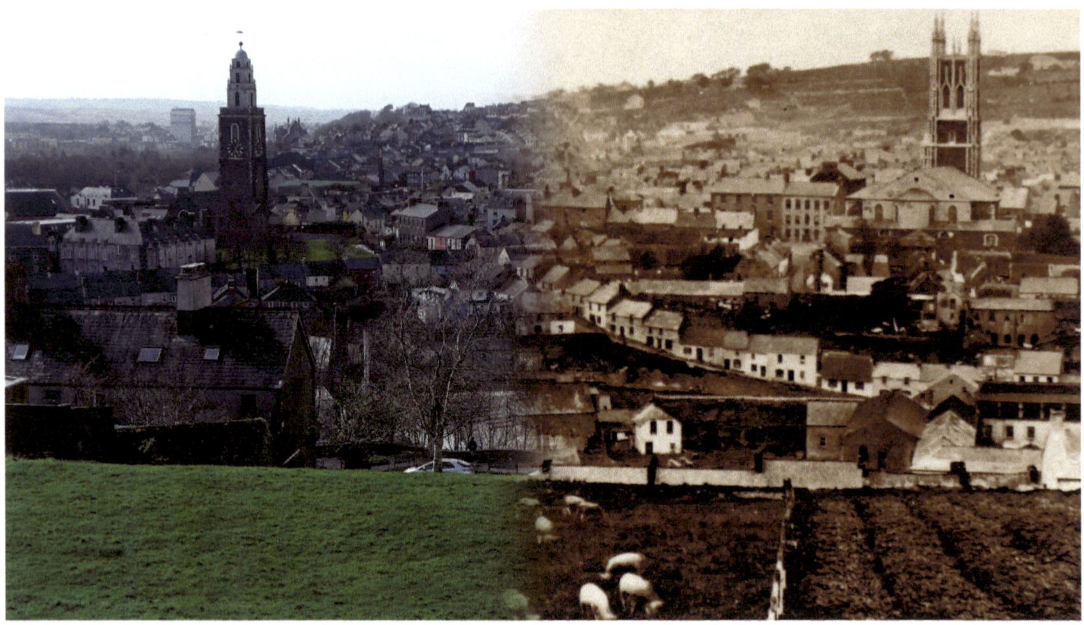

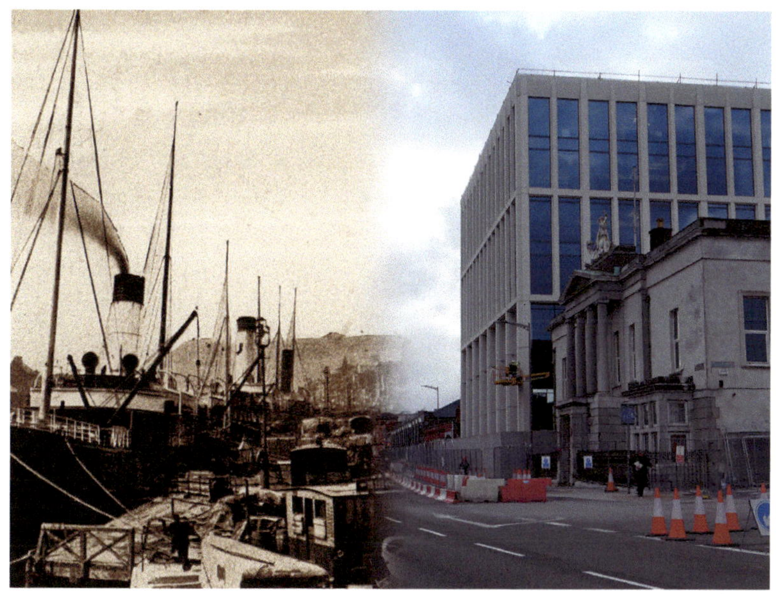

Penrose Quay

The Cork Steamship Company was established in 1843 under the direction of Ebenezer Pike. The principal building, as seen in the right of the postcard, still survives today and the statue of St George slaying a dragon still adorns the top of the building. In the beginning, the Cork Steamship Company bought older steamships and as well new ones. In 1903, it is recorded that there were sixteen vessels, varying from 1,000 to 2,400 tons. Across the newspapers of spring and autumn 1918, references are regularly made of subscriptions being made to the Cork Sailors' Widows and Orphans Fund. It was established to relieve the impact on families who lost their breadwinners on six Cork-owned torpedoed steamships during the First World War. Ninety-six lives were lost on the six Cork steamers and applications for relief from the fund were received for ninety-five households.

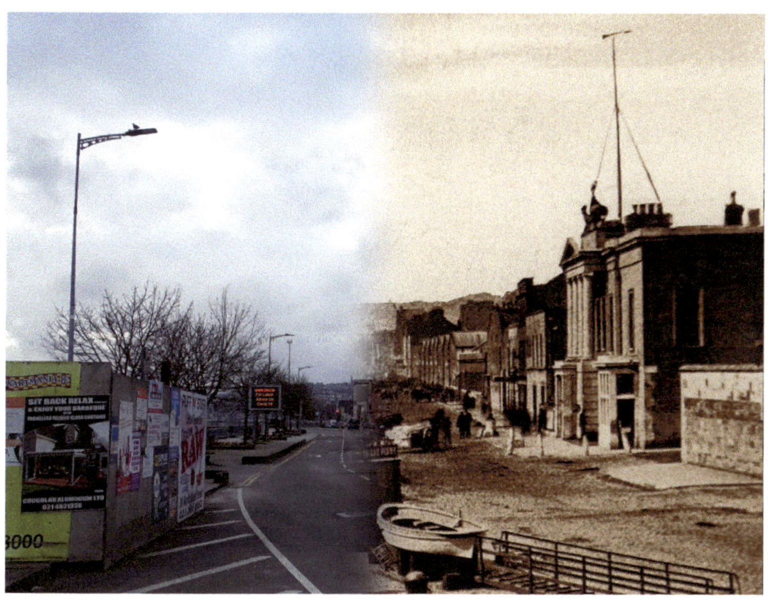

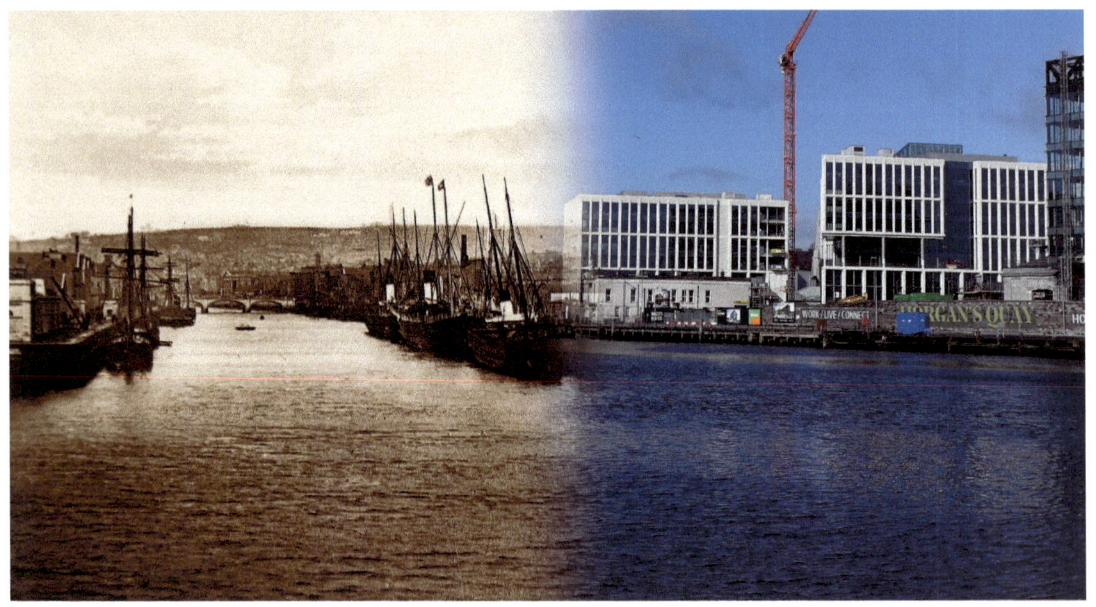

Penrose Quay

Port trade was the engine in Cork's development throughout many centuries. One hundred years ago, considerable tonnage could navigate the North Channel as far as St Patrick's Bridge, and on the South Channel as far as Parliament Bridge. St Patrick's Bridge and Merchant's Quay were the busiest areas, being almost lined daily with sailing ships and steamships. Such was the importance of the steamship industry, the Register of Members of the City of Cork Steam Packet Company reveals that from 14 September 1918, the British and Irish Steam Packet Company Ltd is recorded as owning Cork aggregate shares totalling 125,474, out of a total of 140,000. Further purchases brought that company's holding to 136,417.

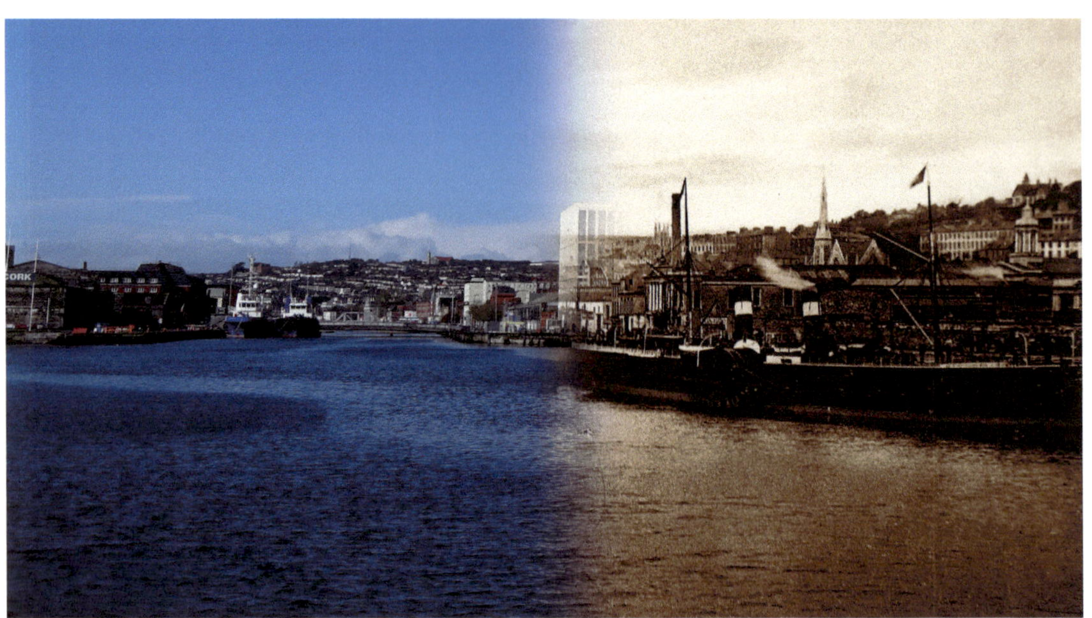

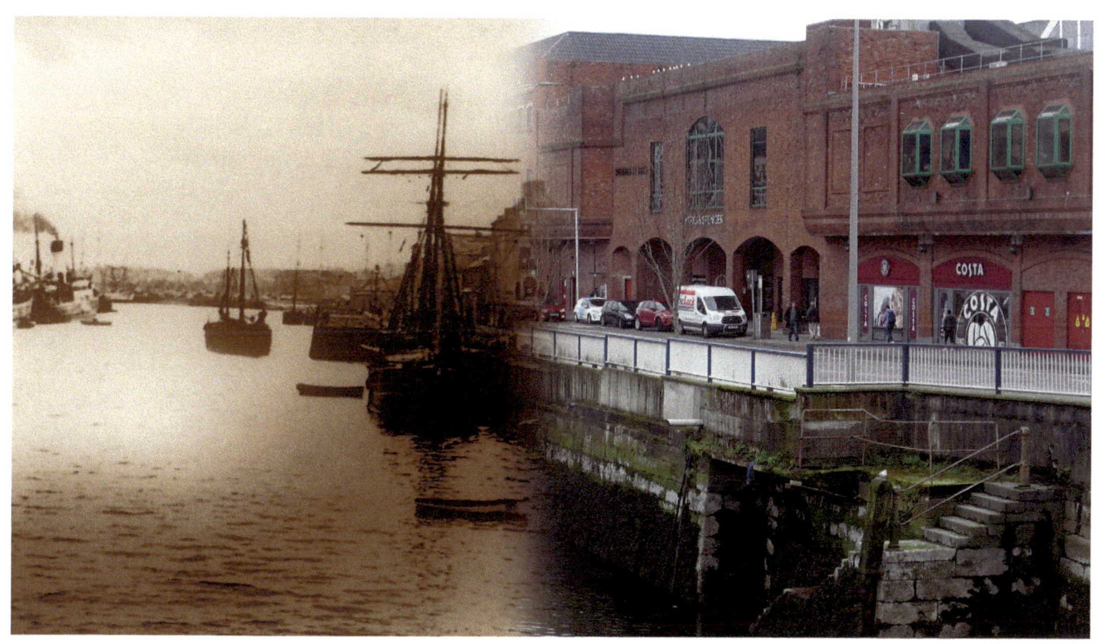

Merchant's Quay

Being the leading commercial port of Ireland, Cork's exports were considerable – cattle, pickled pork, bacon, butter, corn, fowl, porter, eggs and spirits such as and whiskey. Exports were principally pewter, whiskey, butter provisions, cattle, fowl, and eggs. Butter was the staple trade. Merchant's Quay comprised such businesses as Daly and Foley Ship Agents, Swedish and Italian Vice-Consuls, McBride Engineering, Lee Motor Company, as well as the Royal Sailors' Home. Since its foundation in 1852, the principal mission of the Home was to lobby the British Admiralty for accommodation for sailors of the Royal Navy and of the mercantile community. During 1919 the Cork Sailors' Home was visited by 2,956 seamen. Today where ships once moored and sailors once embarked is the large 1990s-built Merchants Quay Shopping Centre.

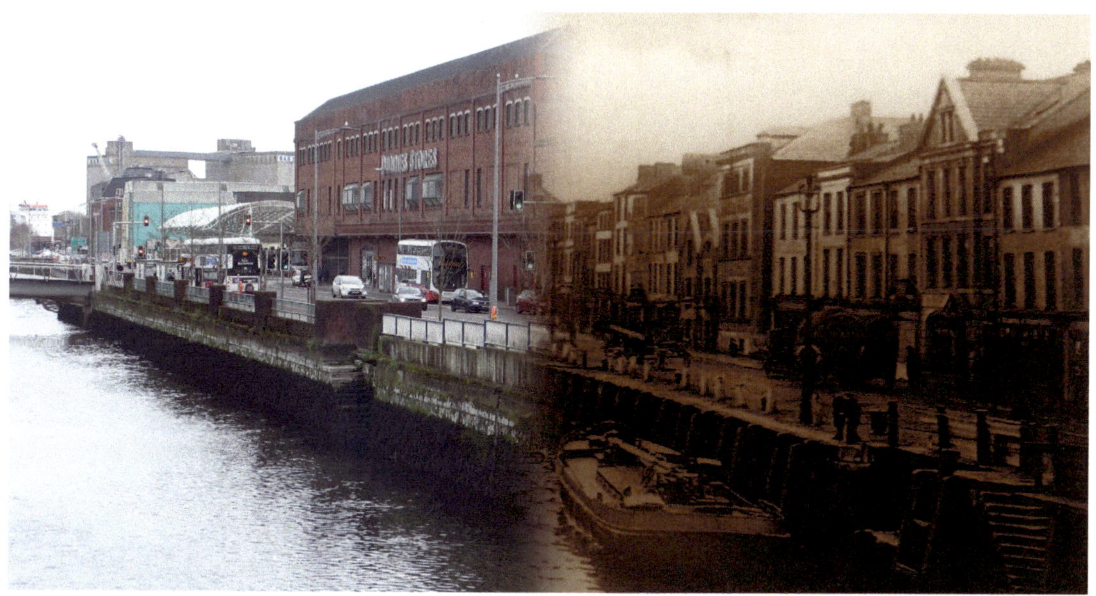

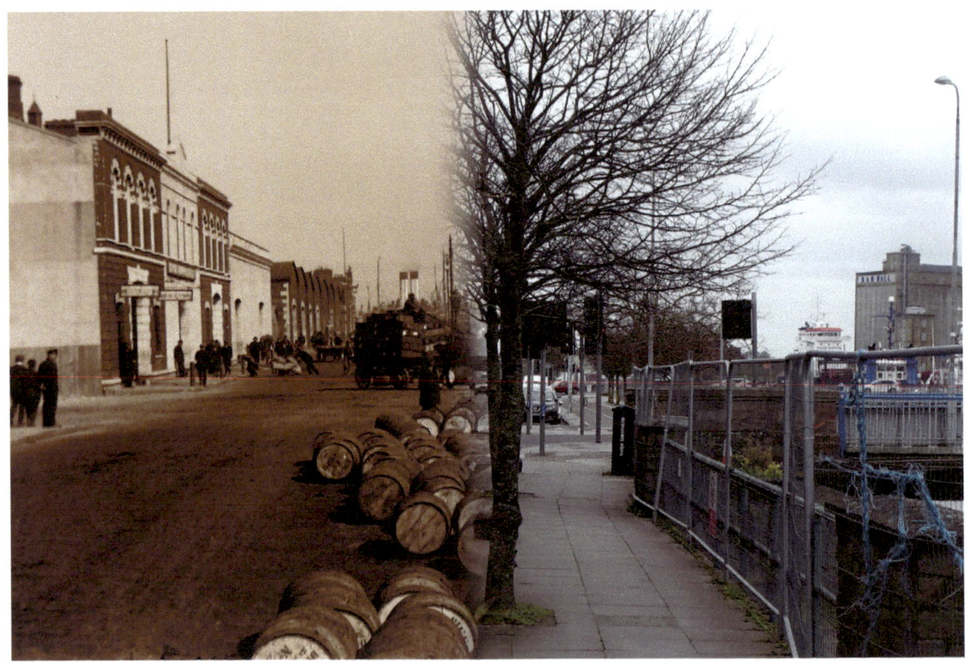

St Patrick's Quay

The imports at the turn of the twentieth century consisted of maize and wheat from various ports of Europe and America, timber from Canada and the Baltic, and fish from the Newfoundland and Labrador regions. Bark, valonia, shumac, brimstone, sweet oil, raisins, currants, lemons, oranges and other fruit, wine, salt, and marble were imported from the Mediterranean. Tallow, hemp and flaxseed came from St Petersburg, Riga and Archangel. Sugar arrived from the West Indies with tea from China, and coal and slate from Wales.

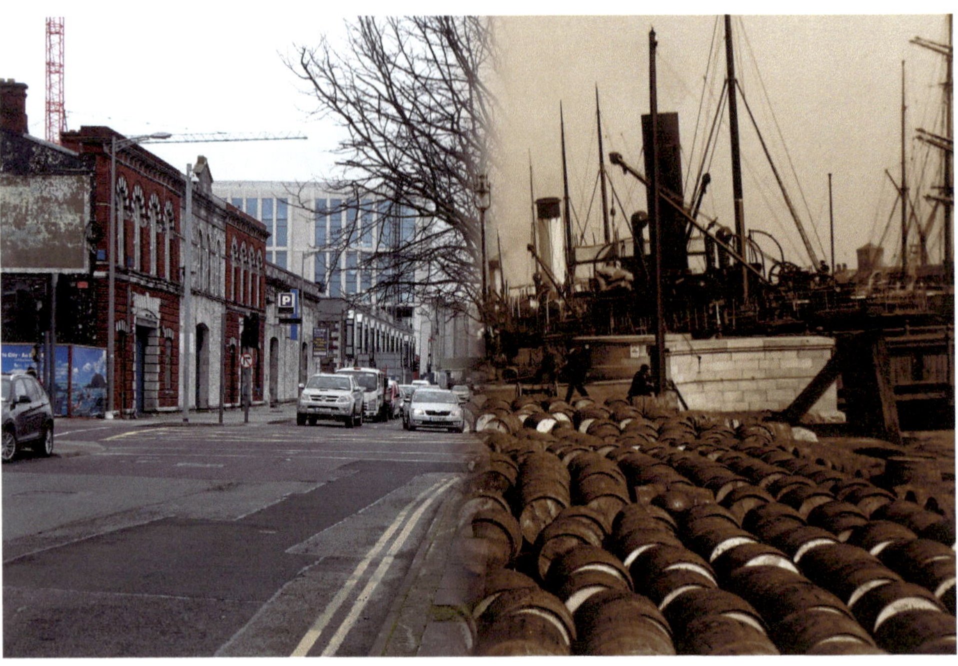

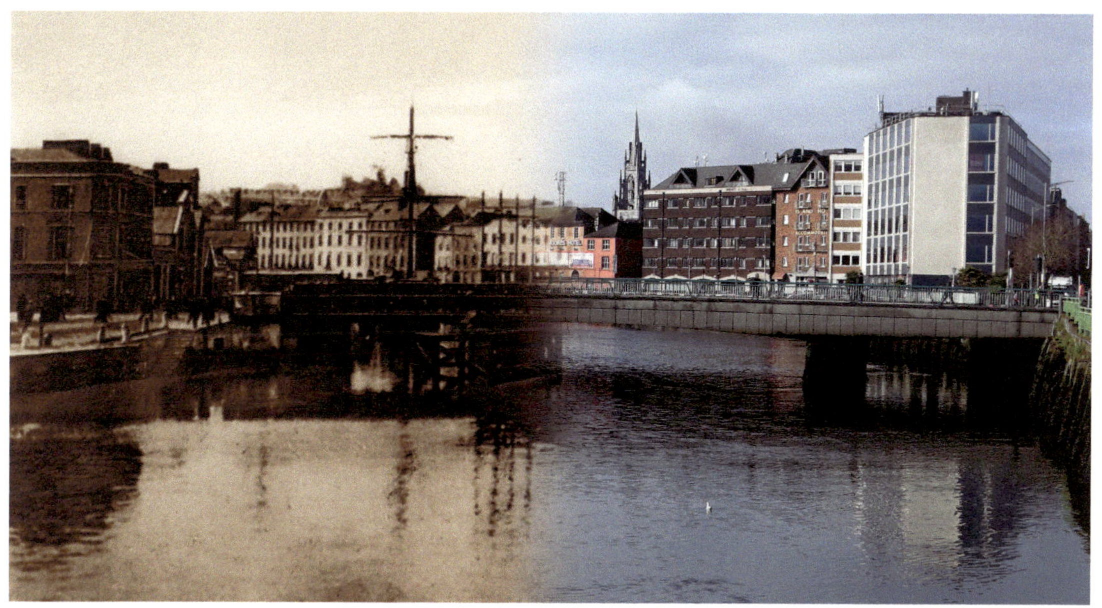

Parnell Bridge

The old Anglesea Bridge, built in the 1830s, could not cope with the volume of traffic using the bridge by the 1870s. Cork Corporation decided to replace the old bridge in 1875. It chose a swing bridge designed by T. Claxton Fiddler in 1877. The building of the new bridge was delayed due to contractual and legal disputes. It was finally opened on 18 November 1882 and named Parnell Bridge after Charles Stewart Parnell, who was active MP for Cork City in campaigning for fair rents and tenure. During the general election campaign of 1885, Parnell emphasised the intention of his party to secure home rule and gave some indications of the sort of scheme he would accept. In May 1886, he supported Gladstone's First Home Rule Bill and called for land reform, the development of Irish manufacturing industry and the restoration of an Irish Parliament.

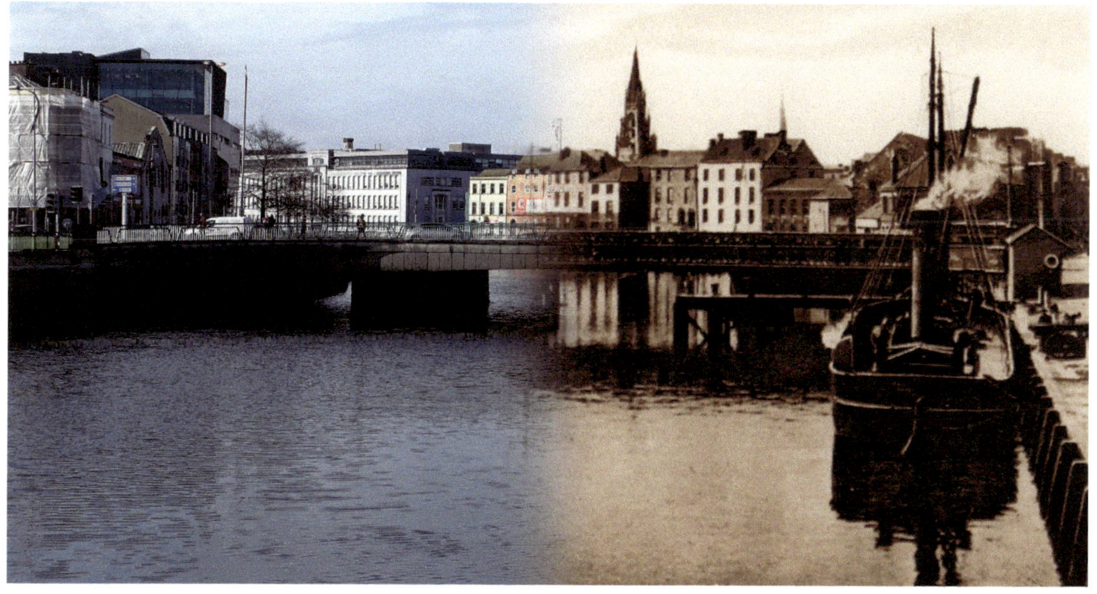

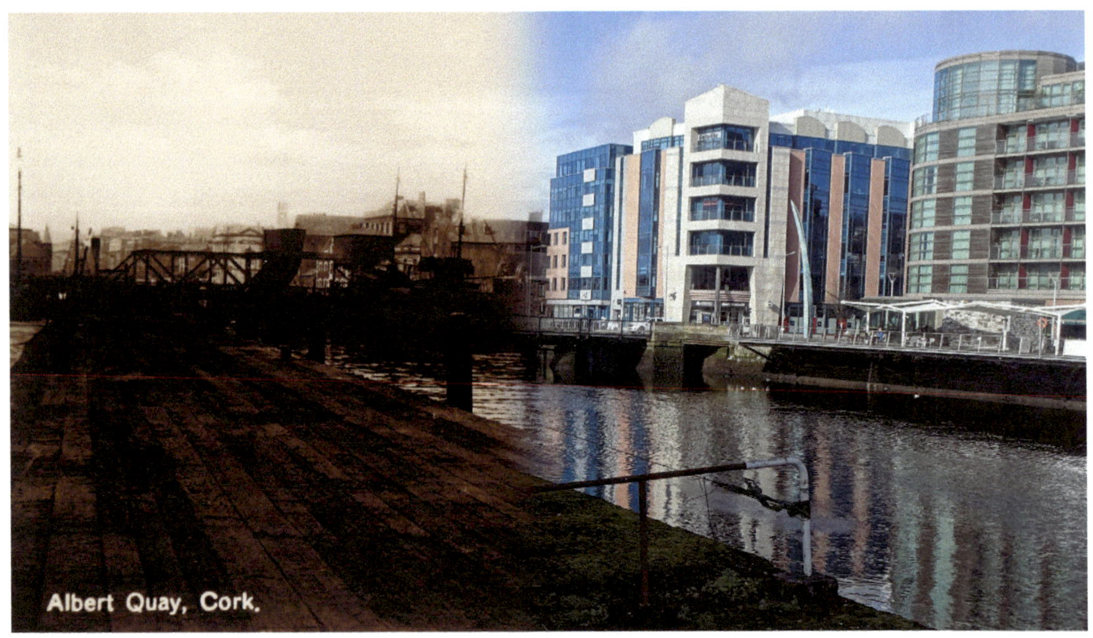

Albert Quay

Suttons Coals, coal merchants, can be viewed below of this photograph. One hundred years ago, their main premises were on the South Mall and apart from coal they also sold seeds, manure and agricultural implements. In the city they had warehouse spaces, below in Lapp's Quay, and also at St Patrick's Quay, New Street and King Street. In the county of Cork they had eleven centres with a further fourteen centres scattered across the southern half of the country. During Ireland's economic boom of the 2000s, the then derelict site was redeveloped by Howard Holdings Ltd and now contains a number of offices block units, the Clayton Hotel and a popular boardwalk.

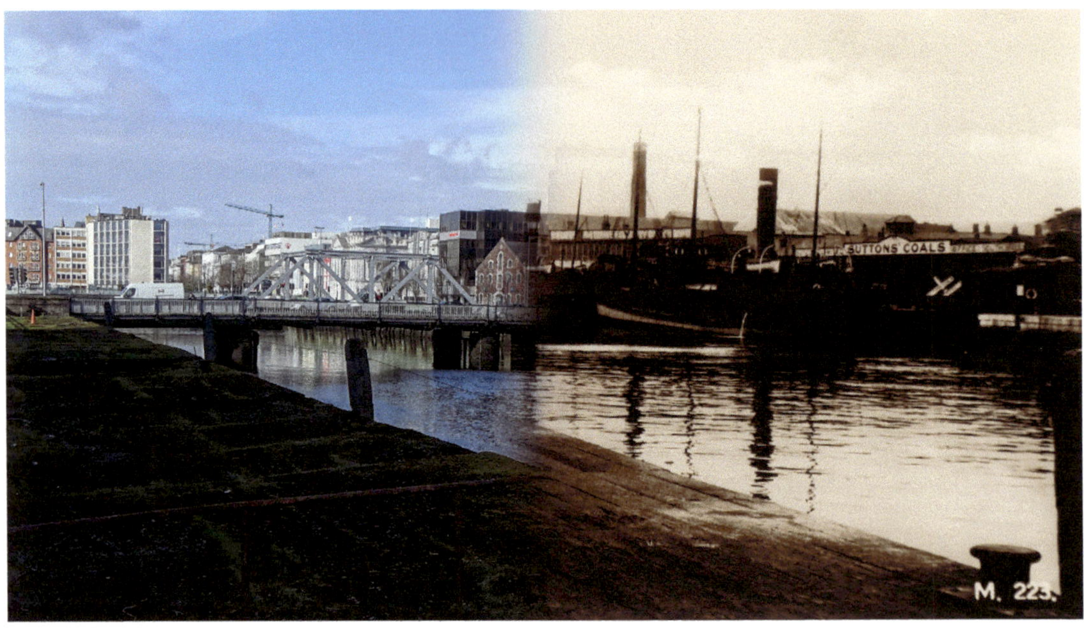

Cork Butter Market

In 1858, 428,000 firkins of butter were being exported per annum but by 1891, this had reduced to 170,000 firkins. Competitive European prices out-competed the prices set by the butter market at Cork. In addition, the city's best consumer, the British citizen, favoured neater packaging, smaller more exact weights, improved colour, texture and taste – qualities that Cork butter did not possess. The quantity of butter exported continued to decrease. Cork butter had been locally inspected and graded for over 150 years and therefore additional regulations and controls of the market were not welcome. Despite the protestations of Irish producers and dealers, a new grading system was put into place in 1918, with the grading work being carried out in England.

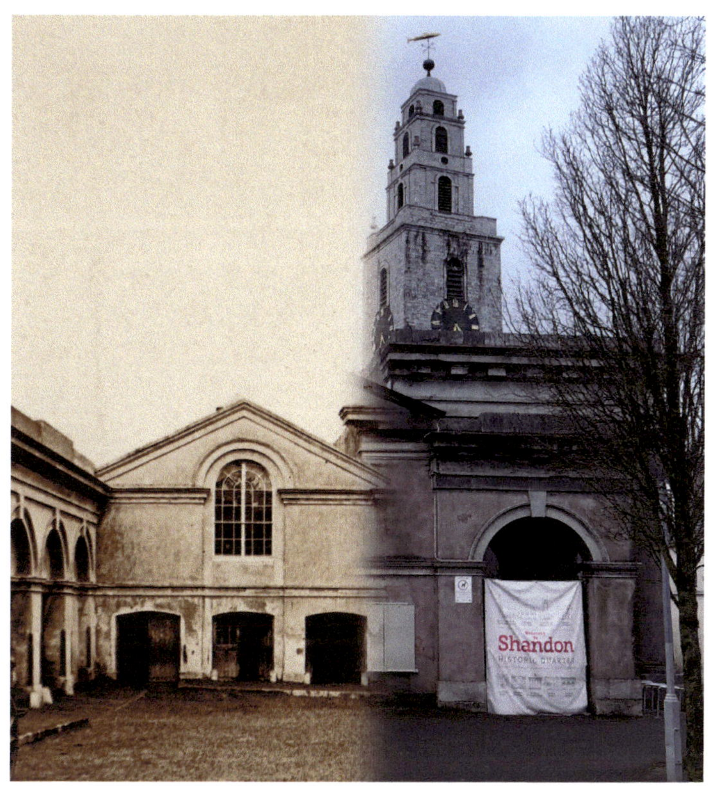

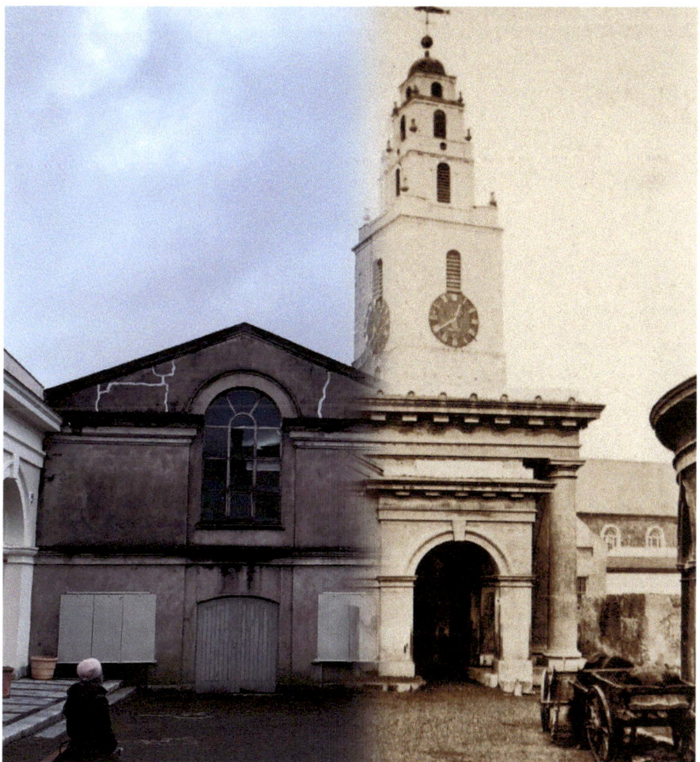

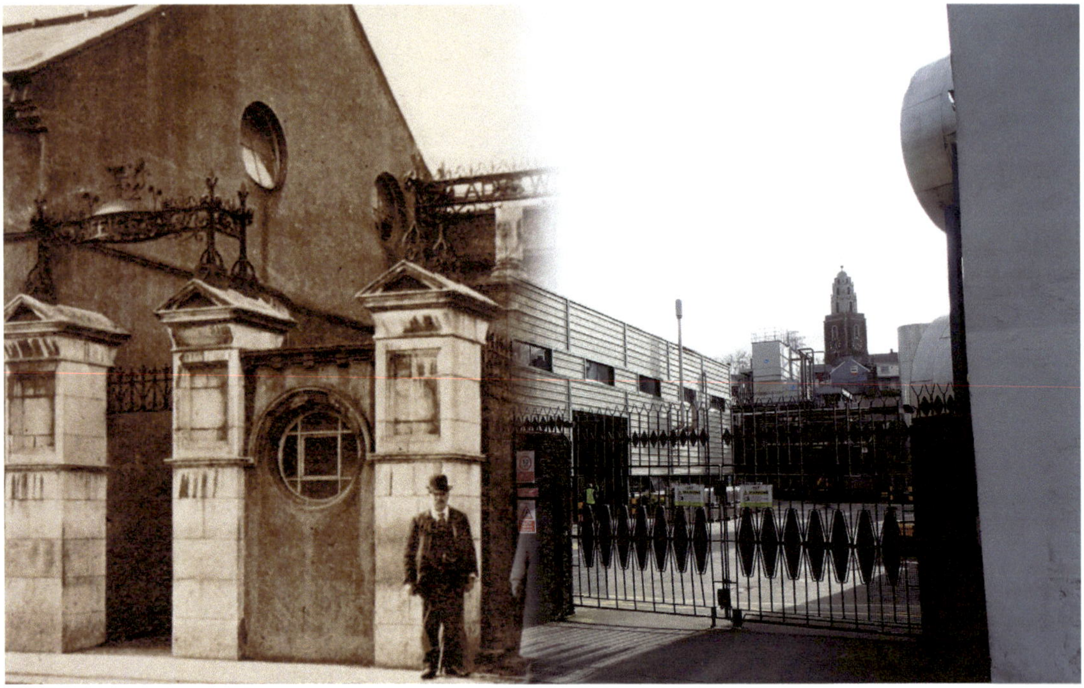

Our Lady's Well Brewery

The manufacturing industries of the city in the late nineteenth century were brewing, distilling and coach-building, which were all carried on extensively. The river provided the water power for many industries in Blackpool. Our Lady's Well Brewery, which takes its name from a famous holy well nearby, was founded in 1854 by Messrs James, William, Jerome and Francis Murphy. The firm had a steady trade with the British Colonies, London, Manchester and other parts of England. The business is now owned and operated by Heineken Ireland.

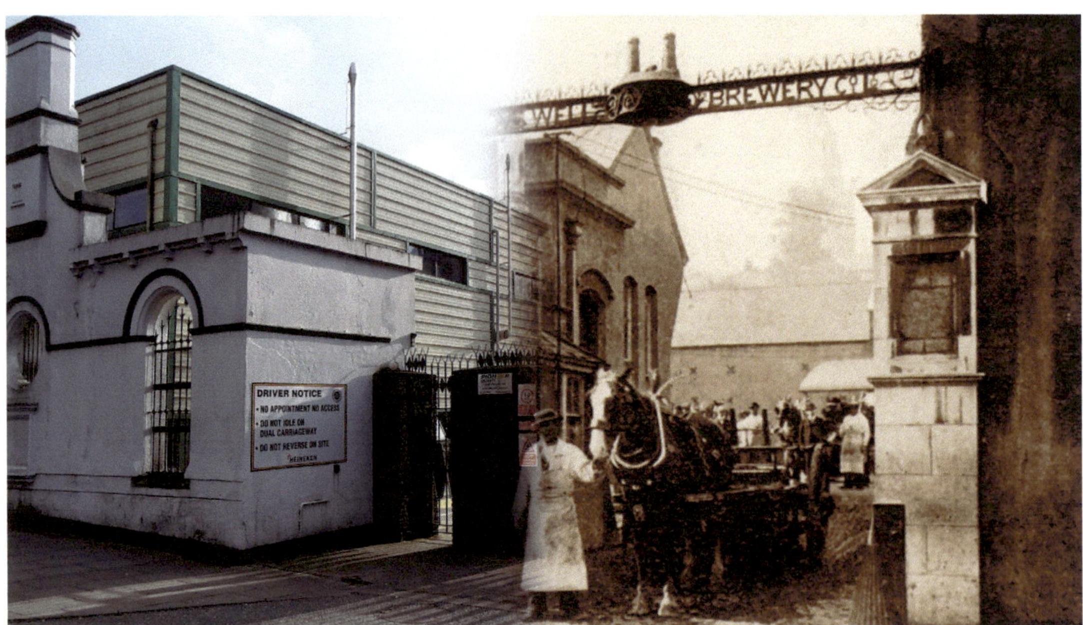

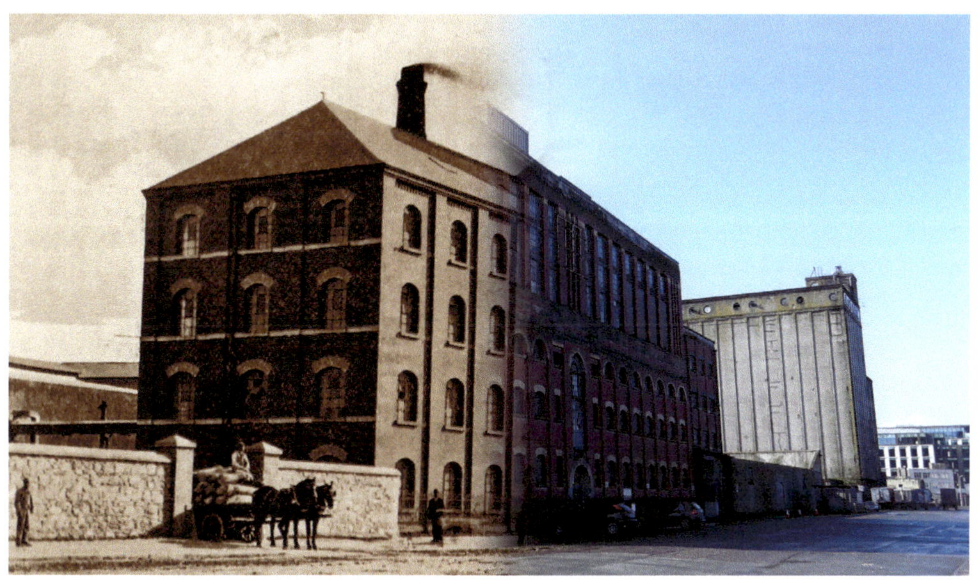

Cork National Flour Mills

By 1810 Cork had become a big market for flour, especially with brewers and distillers. Up to the years 1875 to 1880, the only method of manufacturing flour was grinding by millstones – wheat being ground between two flat circular stones. Between 1875 and 1880 Cork became one of the first milling centres in Ireland to adopt the roller process, and a number of well-equipped mills in the city and county were constructed, in which some 70,000 tons of wheat was milled annually, and, in addition, close on 90,000 tons of maize was ground. A large and landmark mill and warehouse complex known as the Cork National Flour Mills on Cork's South Docks was built in 1892 and remodelled in 1934. Odlums operated their flour mills venture there from 1965 for a time. The building now awaits a new purpose in the present-day re-configuration of Cork's South Docks.

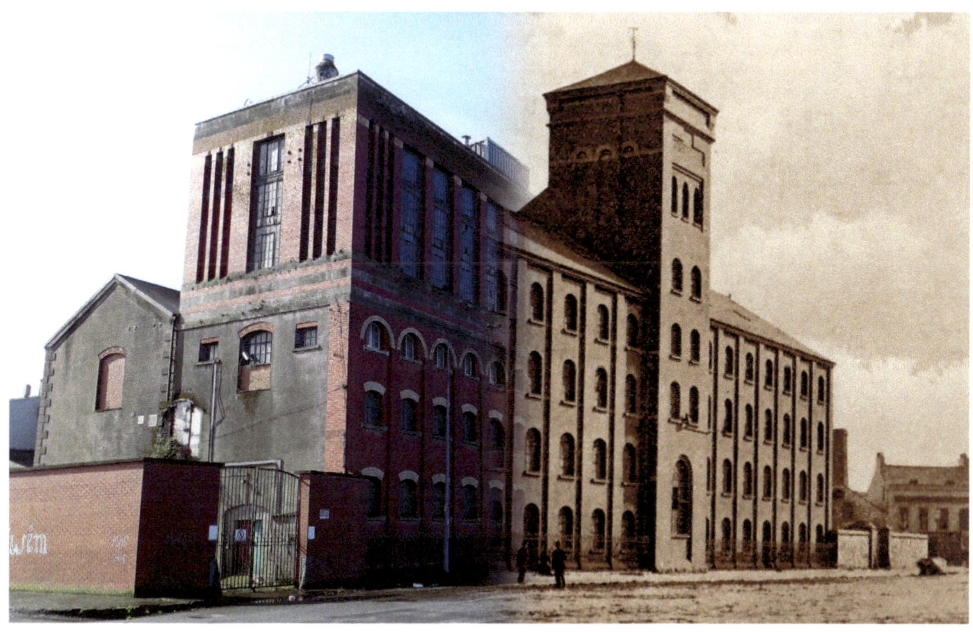

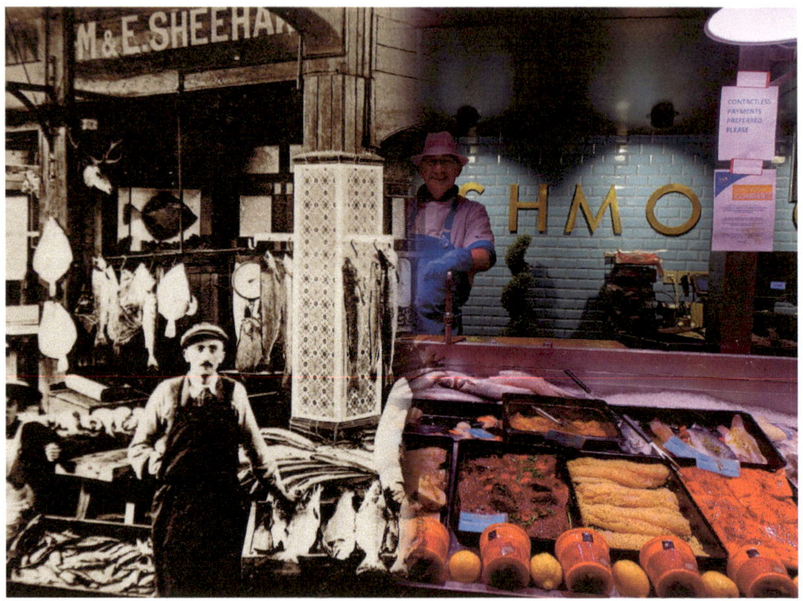

English Market

The market was opened in 1788 and was known then as the Root Market. Today Corkonians know the market under several names: the Princes Street Market, the English Market, and the Grand Parade market. A characteristic of the market is the selling of tripe and drisheen, which are both traditional foods which have been eaten in Cork for centuries. Drisheen is extra special as it is indigenous to Cork. Nearly all stalls are food stalls. There are many butchers, fishmongers, a couple of bakers and numerous other stalls selling food from near and far away. This was part of a historic first visit to the Republic Ireland by Queen Elizabeth II, reflecting a changing Anglo-Irish relationship. In May 2011, the UK's Queen Elizabeth II visited the market and chatted to many stallholders.

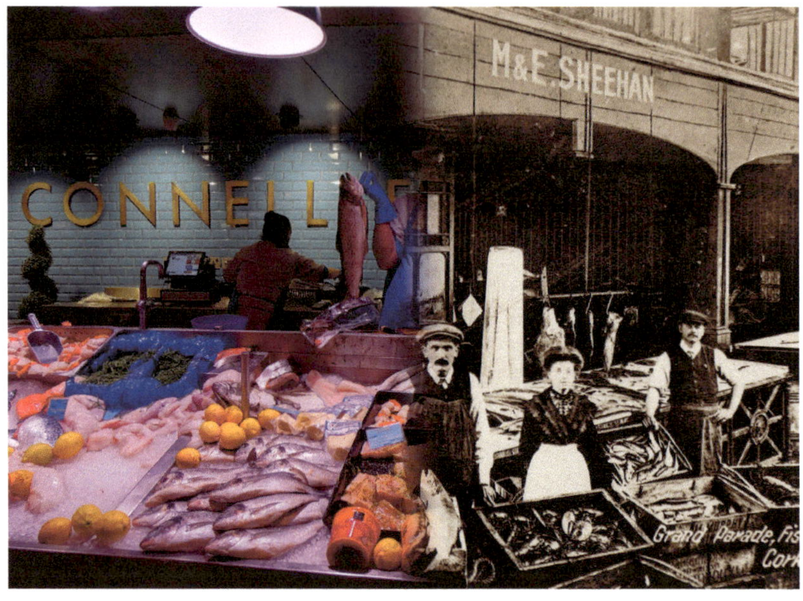

Cornmarket Street

The first municipal corn market was constructed in 1719 overlooking a square that was located on a filled-in portion of a channel of the River Lee (Coal Quay). Unfortunately, the name of this square is not recorded, but it was located on what is now Cornmarket Street. Over the centuries, the square grew to be the traditional central market area of the city. It would have been thronged with dealers and customers, purchasing anything from a needle to an anchor. Several stalls still operate here today. The second incarnation of the Cornmarket building also still exists Initially constructed in the 1740s, this building is reputed to be the work of Italian architect Allesandro Callileo. One hundred years later, the building was remodelled, and reopened in 1843 as a corporation bazaar. The quality of the masonry is a core characteristic in the streetscape and was expertly carried out by skilled stone cutters and masons.

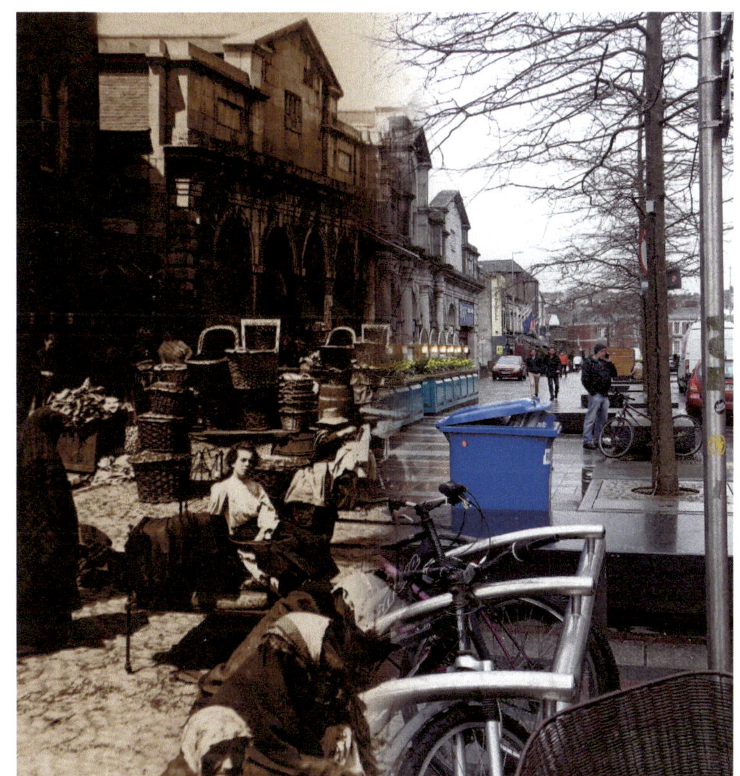

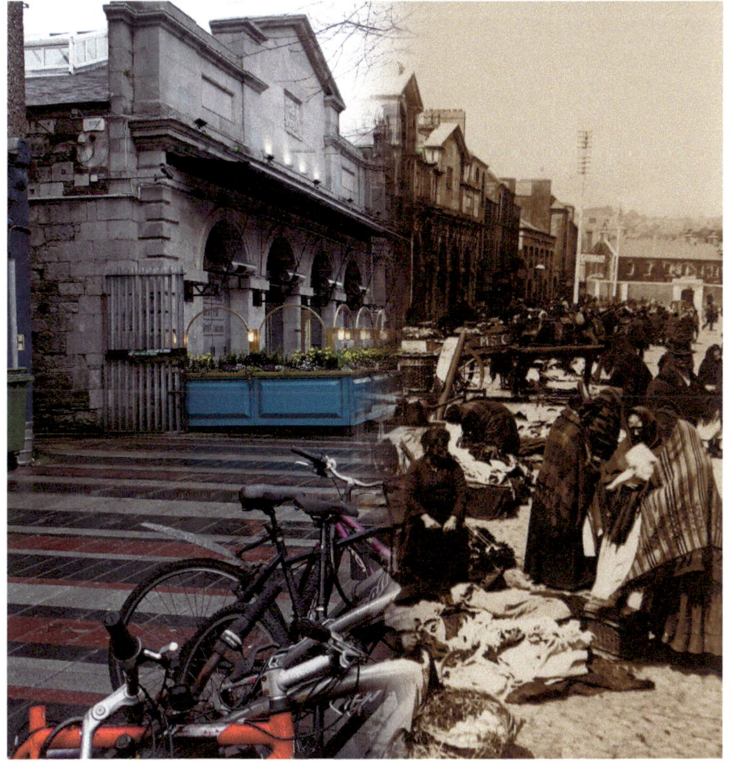

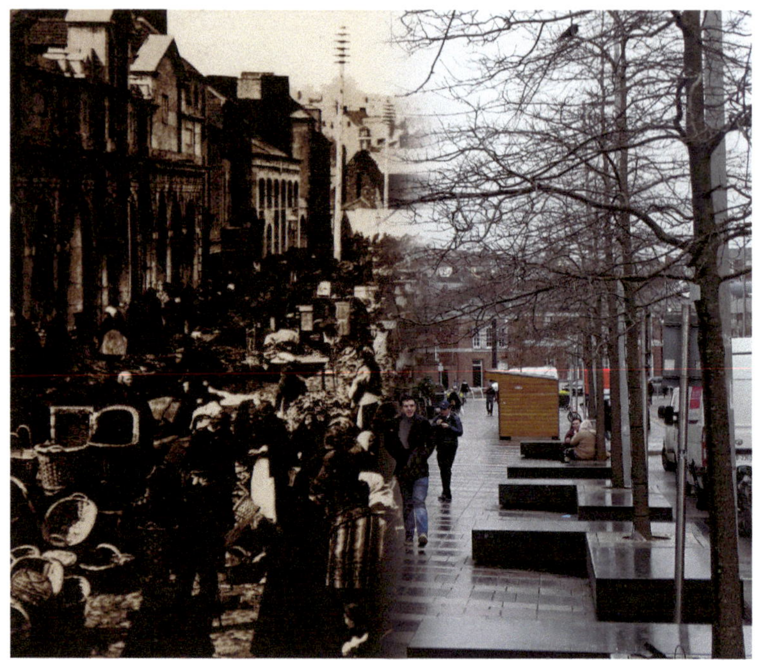

Cornmarket Street

During 2011–12, over €1 million was allocated by Cork City Council with the help of European Structural Funds for the refurbishment of Cornmarket Street. The street underwent a massive facelift to give it the feel of a European outdoor market. Existing stalls were modernised. Conscious of the effects of change on tradition, an annual festival has been organised by the Cork Middle Parish and the Coal Quay Historical Society from 2012 onwards.

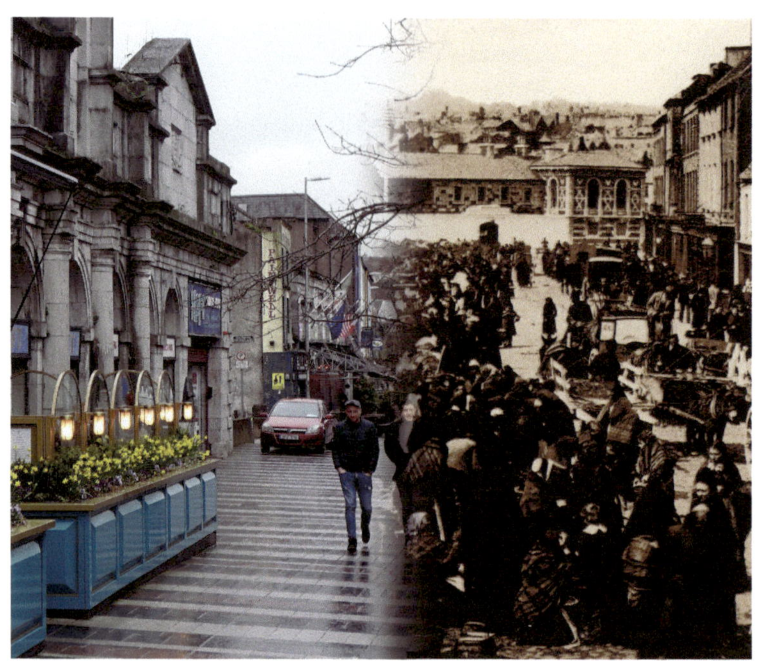

Branding a City

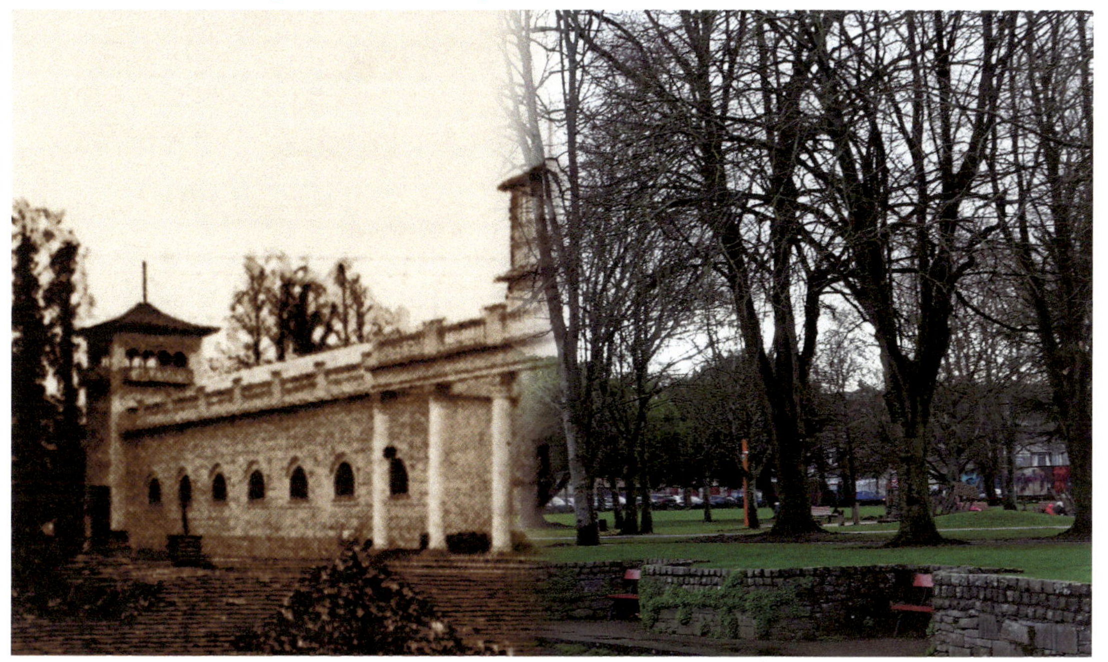

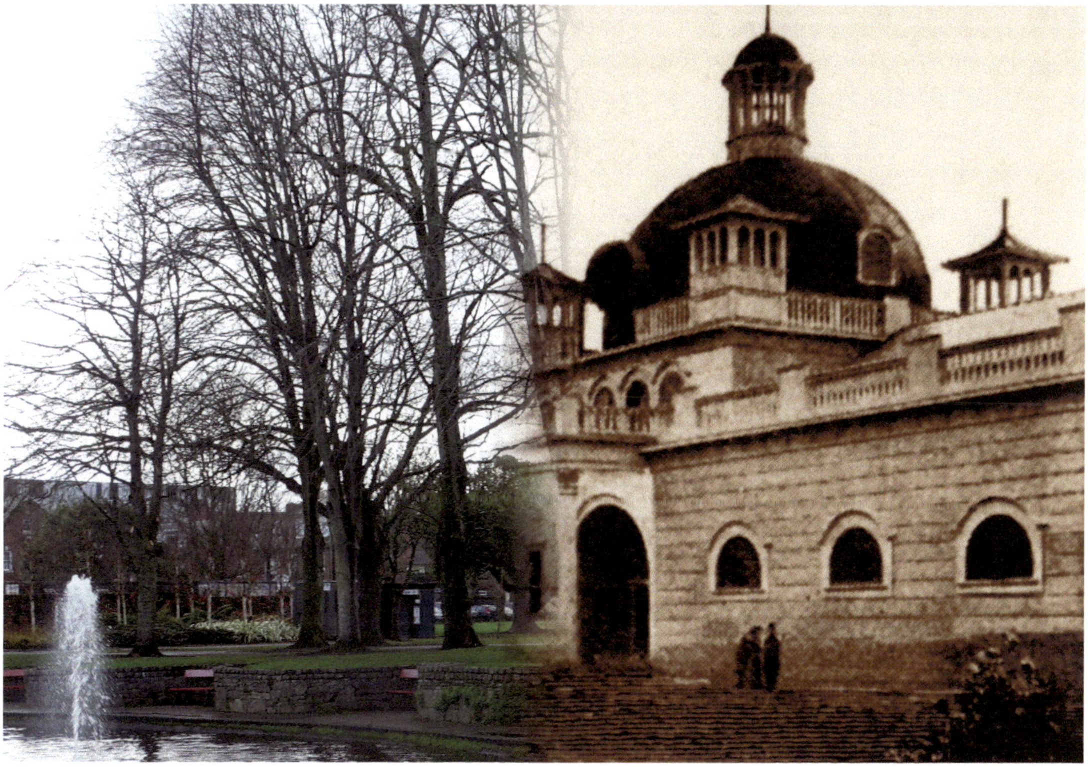

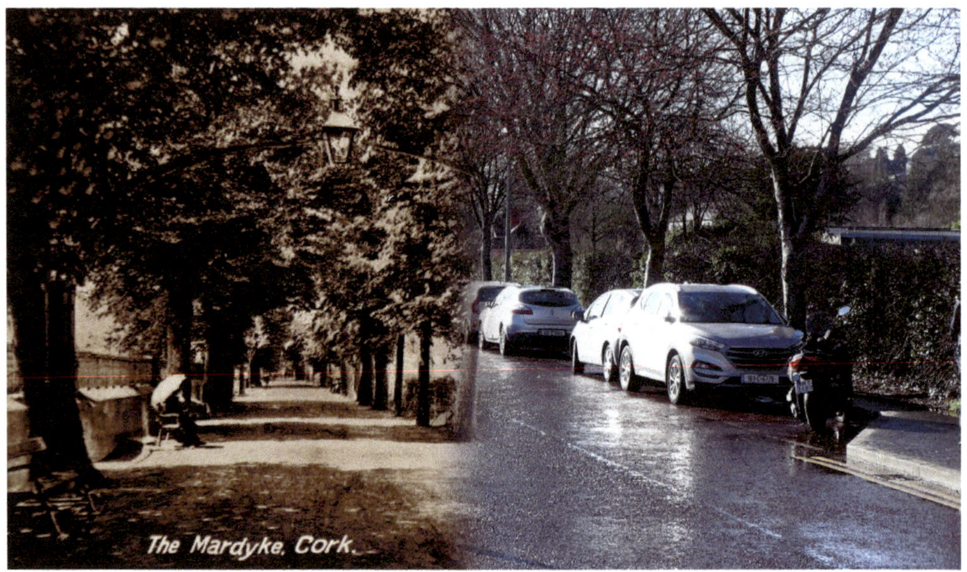

Origins of an International Exhibition

The exhibition or world fair movement in Ireland is an underestimated and often-forgotten mode that was used to advance Irish society in the late nineteenth century and early twentieth century. Exhibitions in Cork were held in the years 1852, 1883, 1902/1903 and 1932. All were highly visible spaces in public life and grasped the popular imagination of contemporaneous society. Inspired by the Paris International Exhibition of 1900, it was intended originally to host an exhibition of industrial goods at the rear of Cork City Hall, on the site of the exhibition of 1883, but the project grew so successfully and with such rapidity that the ground space was found totally insufficient. A site in the Mardyke was then selected and the various owners, which included the Cork Cricket Club, the Sunday's Well Boating & Tennis Club, Captain Jennings and Mr Cornelius Desmond, placed their grounds at the disposal of the Executive Committee of the exhibition.

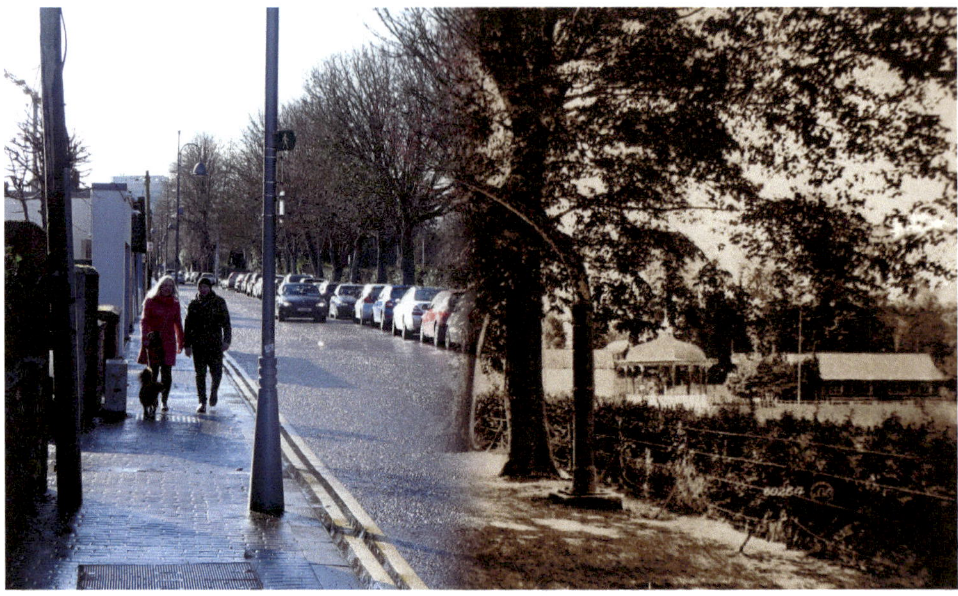

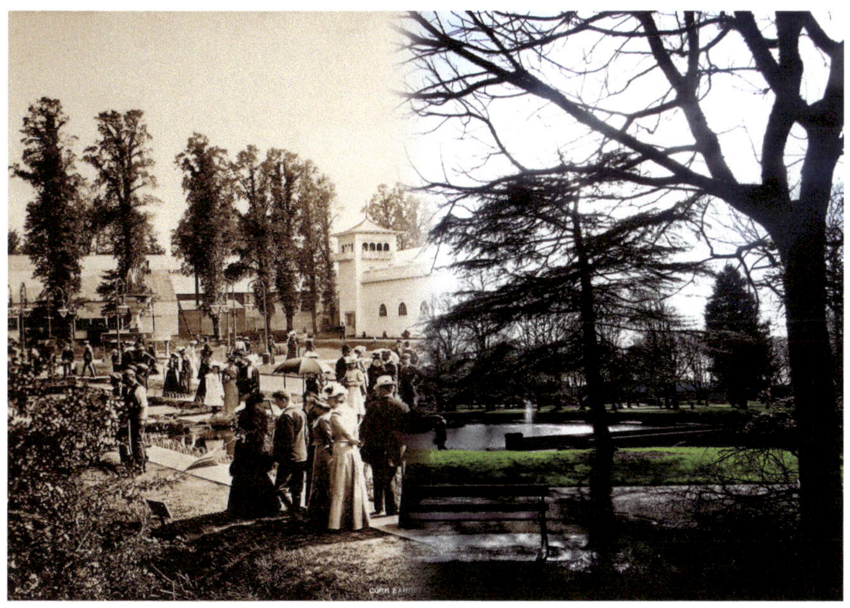

The Exhibition Grounds

From May to November 1902, the Cork International Exhibition spanned a 44-acre site not far from the city centre encompassing an area on the Mardyke that now includes the Cork Cricket Club, the Sunday's Well Boating & Tennis Club, Fitzgerald Park, and the university's sports arena. The exhibition grounds were elaborately laid out and had several large exhibiting halls and pavilions as well as an assortment of smaller buildings including tea houses, restaurants and kiosks. Irish and foreign exhibitors, some from 'exotic' locations such as China, Russia, and Turkey, filled these halls and pavilions with exhibits and demonstrations for all to see. The exhibition was visited by over a million people. The industrial hall, made of fibrous plaster, had a floor space of 170,000 feet and comprised seven parallel avenues and one avenue at right angles. It was lit and ventilated from the roof, front and sides.

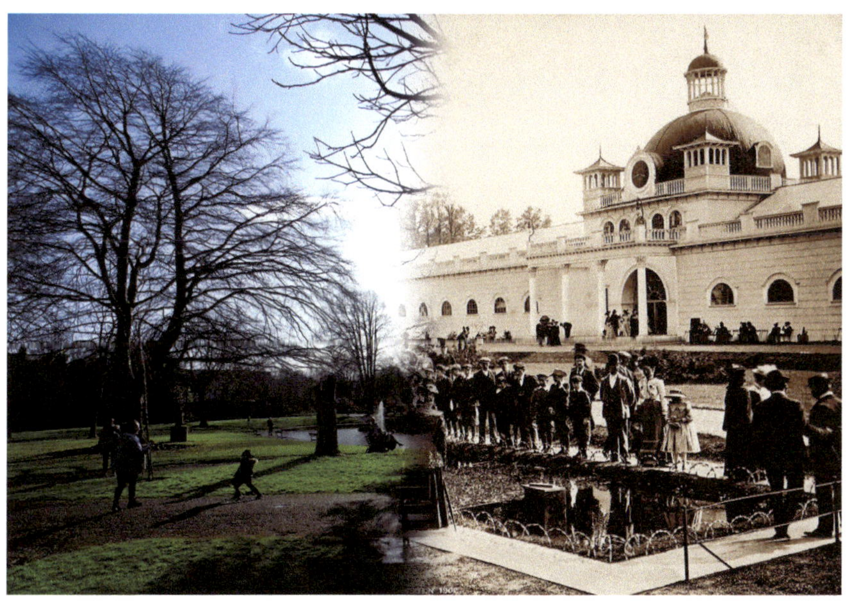

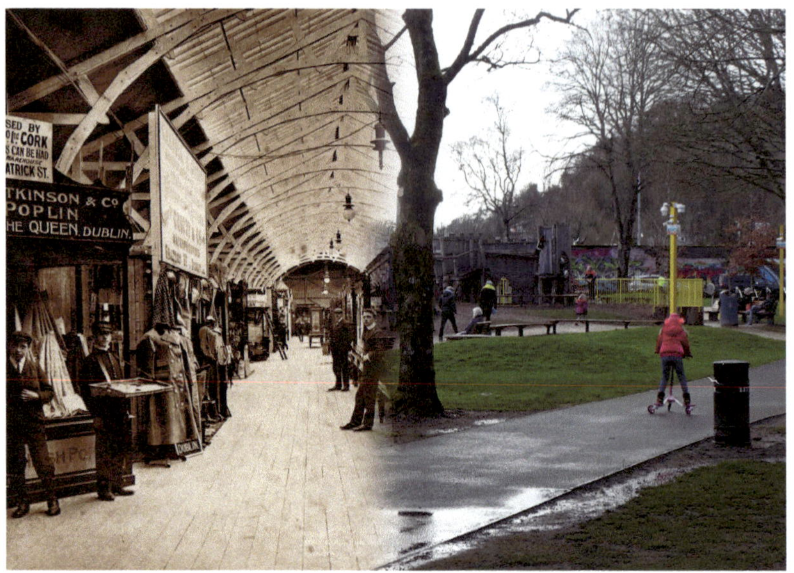

Exhibits

Corkman Mr Henry A. Cutler designed the General Exhibition Buildings. The Honorary Architect was Mr William O'Connell, Hanover Street, Cork, a well-known local builder who constructed the whole of the buildings. Several hundred exhibits were on display in 1902 from May to October. With such a display, extensive regulations existed for exhibitors. The charge inside the building was two shillings per square foot. Exhibits were not admitted until payment for space had been made in full. Spaces not occupied seven days previous to the exhibition opening were re-allotted and all payments already made forfeited. Application for space and for power had to be made by 31 October 1901 to the Honorary Secretary, R. A. Atkins. No exhibit or part of could be removed from the exhibition. Exhibits not removed within fifteen days after the close of the exhibition were to be put in warehouses at the cost and risk of the owners, and to be auctioned off after three months.

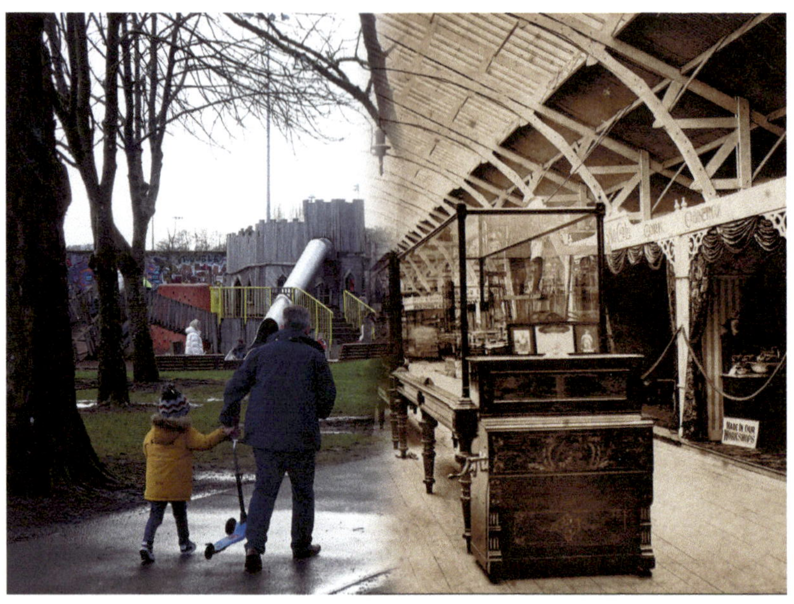

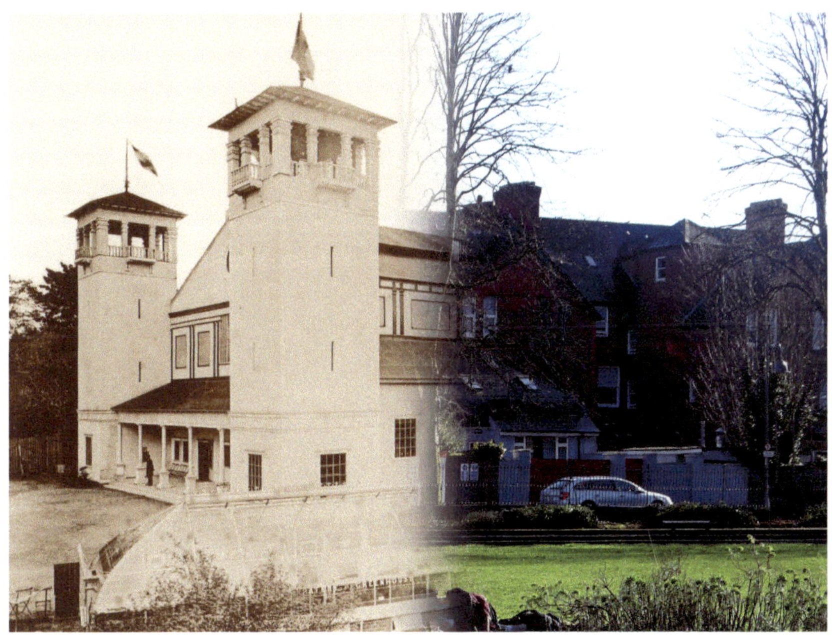

Exhibition Concert Hall

The concert hall possessed comfortable seating accommodation in the auditorium for 2,000 people, while the organ loft afforded ample room. Regular concerts were held here over the period of the exhibition. It was also the space where opening speeches by dignitaries on 1 May 1902 set out the vision of the exhibition, embracing forward-looking sentiments, a creative entrepreneurialism and the quest to adopt technological innovation whilst engaging an Irish national past – all subtly challenging the demands for home rule and championing the retention of direct rule by Britain.

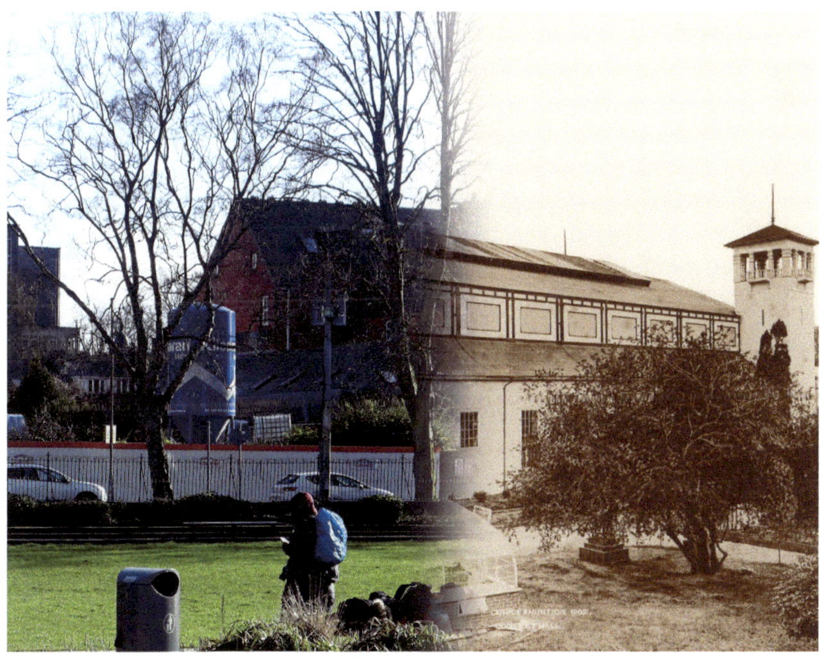

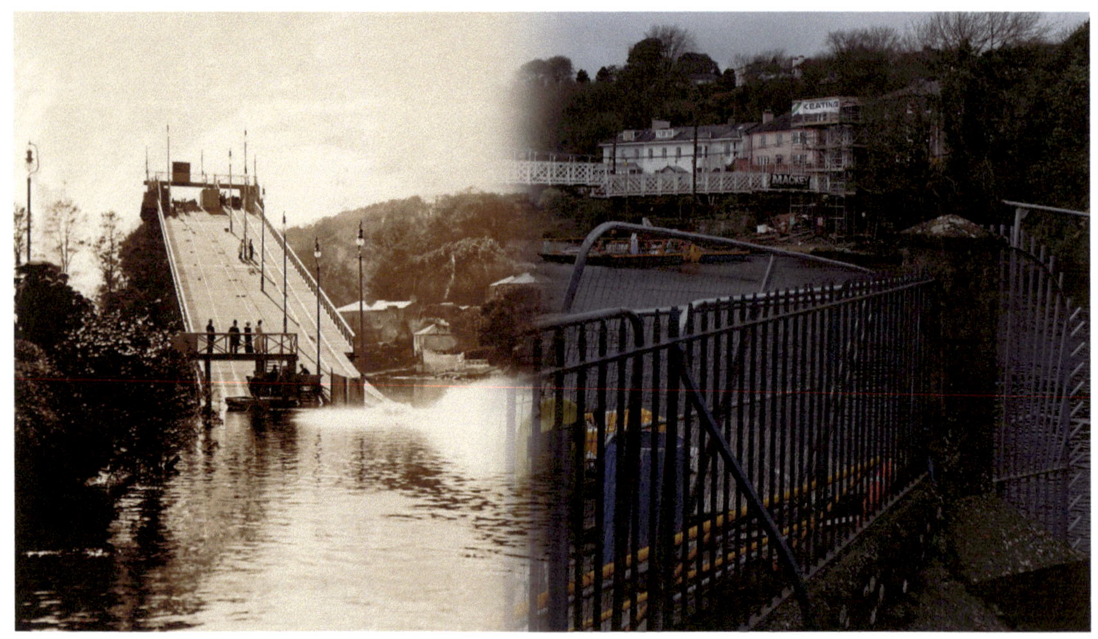

The Great Chute

This postcard is of the Cork International Exhibition's great chute or slide. It is now the site of Daly's Bridge. The bridge was built in 1927 and was overseen by the City Engineer, Stephen Farrington, and constructed by suspension bridge experts David and Rowell & Co., Liverpool. The bridge was financed by James Daly, a Cork Butter merchant. Public demands for the bridge appear in Corporation minute books in 1922, to serve the large numbers of people from Sunday's Well who wished to cross the river in order to attend rugby matches held in the Mardyke. In 2020, the bridge underwent cleaning and rehabilitation.

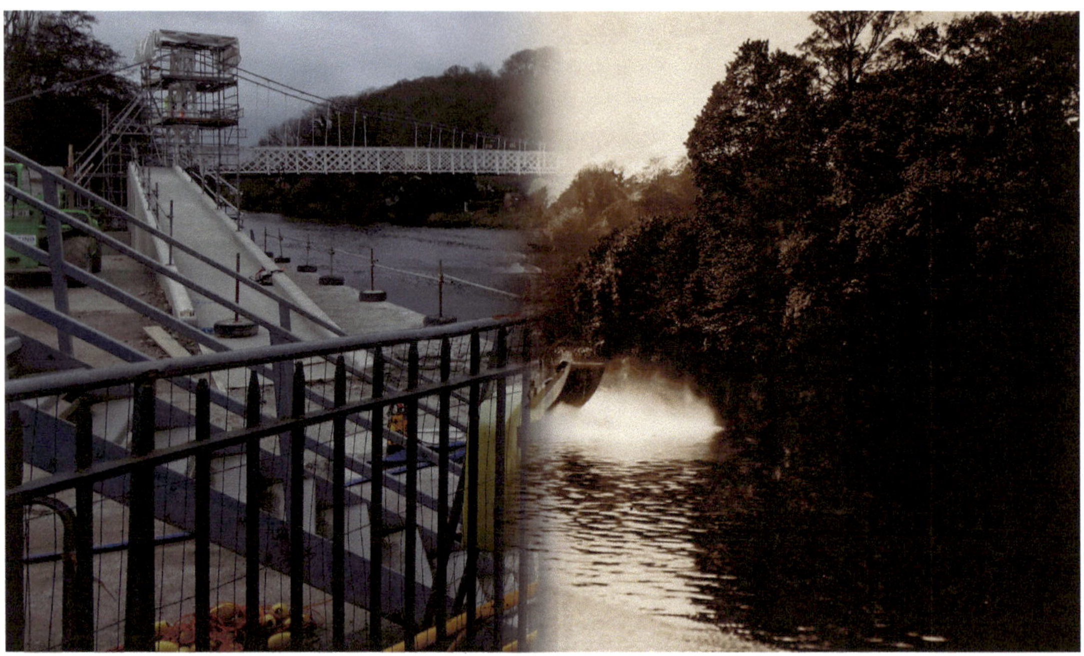

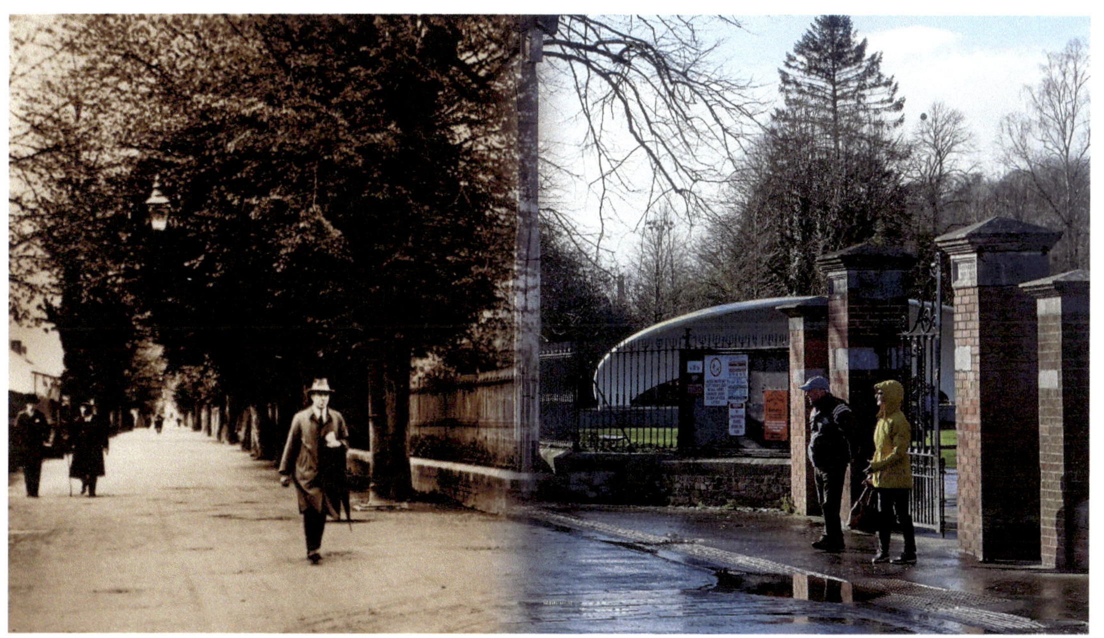

Fitzgerald Park

At the end of the Cork International Exhibition in 1903, the organisers felt that the grounds would make an ideal place of recreation for the people of Cork. A decision was taken to name the new park after Edward Fitzgerald, the organiser of the exhibition and Lord Mayor of Cork from 1901 to 1903. A general Park Committee was agreed upon and established by the exhibition committee. In March 1906, it was agreed to vest the Park and the Shrubberies House in Cork Corporation. A further provision provided that the Shrubberies House be turned into a municipal museum, which was eventually opened in 1945.

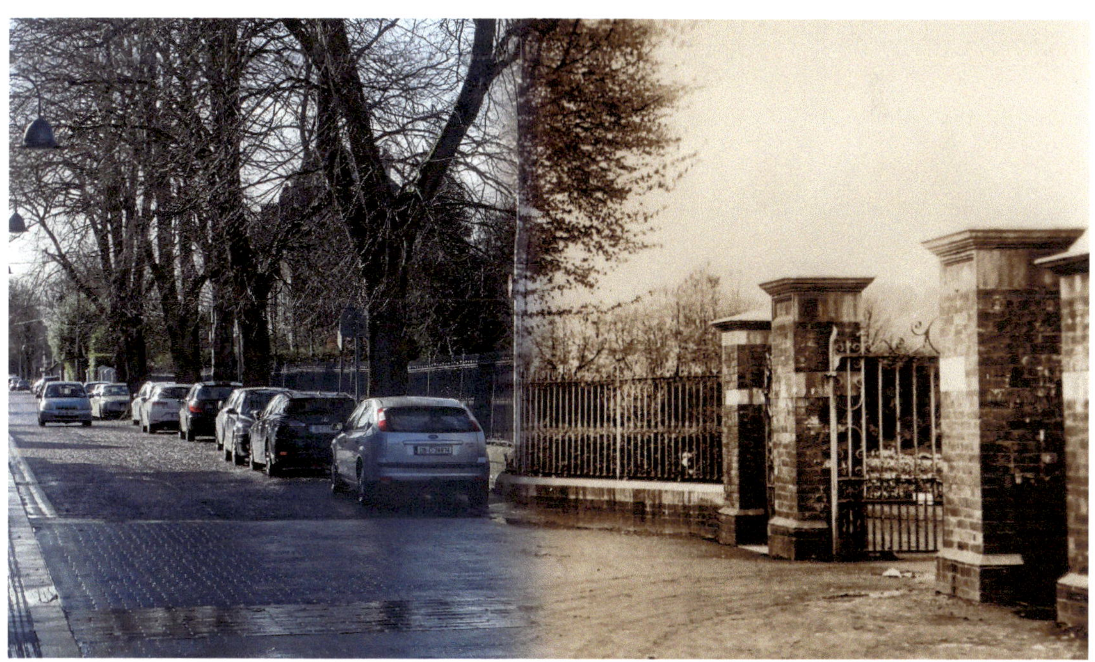

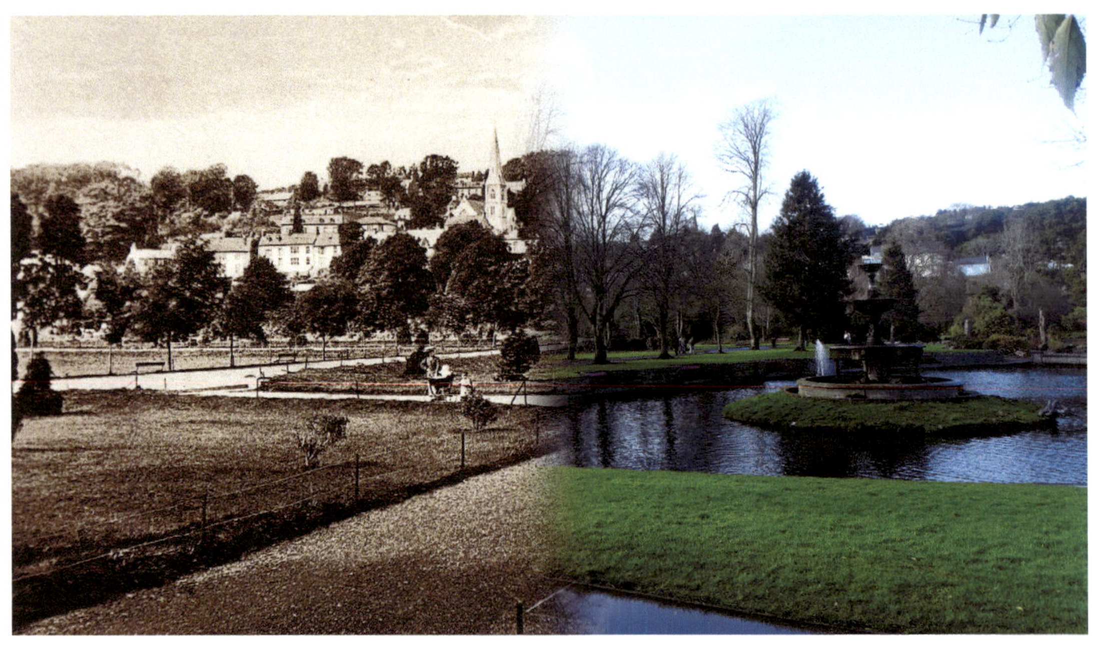

Father Mathew Memorial Fountain

The area immediately around Cork International Exhibition's Father Mathew Memorial Fountain, which was in front of the main exhibition pavilion, was filled in with a pond in 1913. The pond's first two swans were donated by Sir Edward Fitzgerald. The fountain was designed for the exhibition grounds by Henry Cutler and constructed by local builder J. Hegarty. It was constructed in a Celtic revival style. Elaborate Celtic revival detail can be seen on the bowls, including interlacing strapwork, stylised mask, knotwork, etc. The inscription in Gaelic font reads 'Father Mathew Memorial Fountain'. In recent years, the park has seen more and more outdoor activities, from food festivals to the successful World Street Performing Championships and the Cork Carnival of Science.

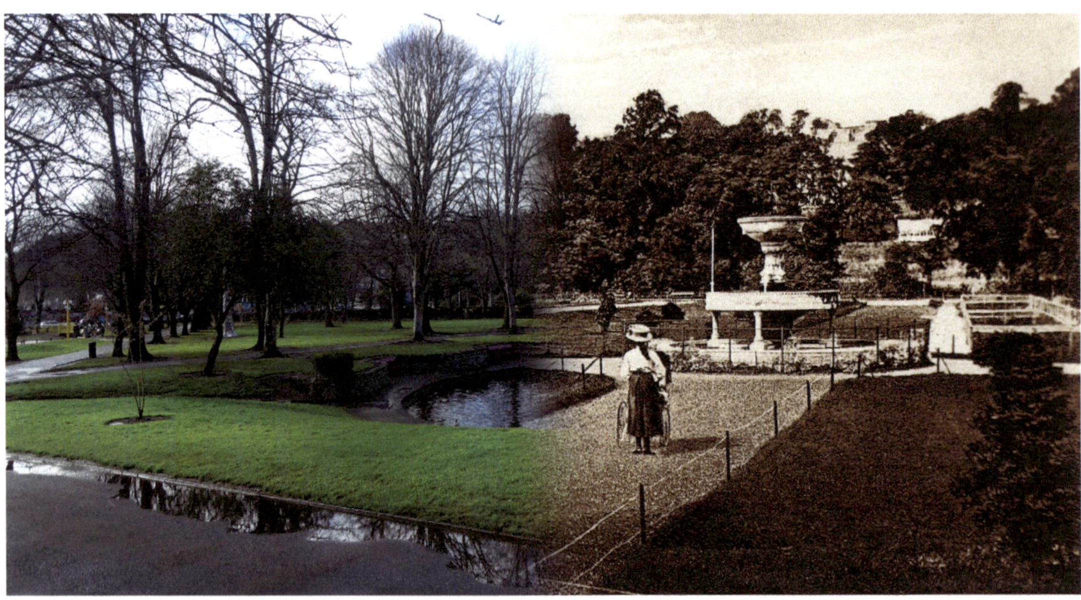

Public Buildings – The Façade of a City

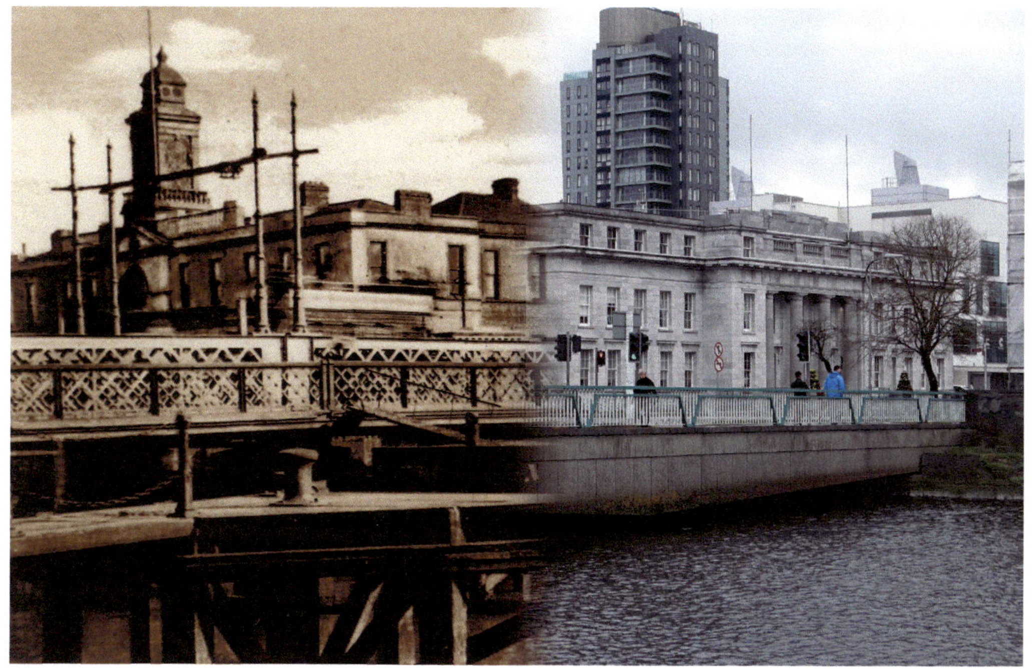

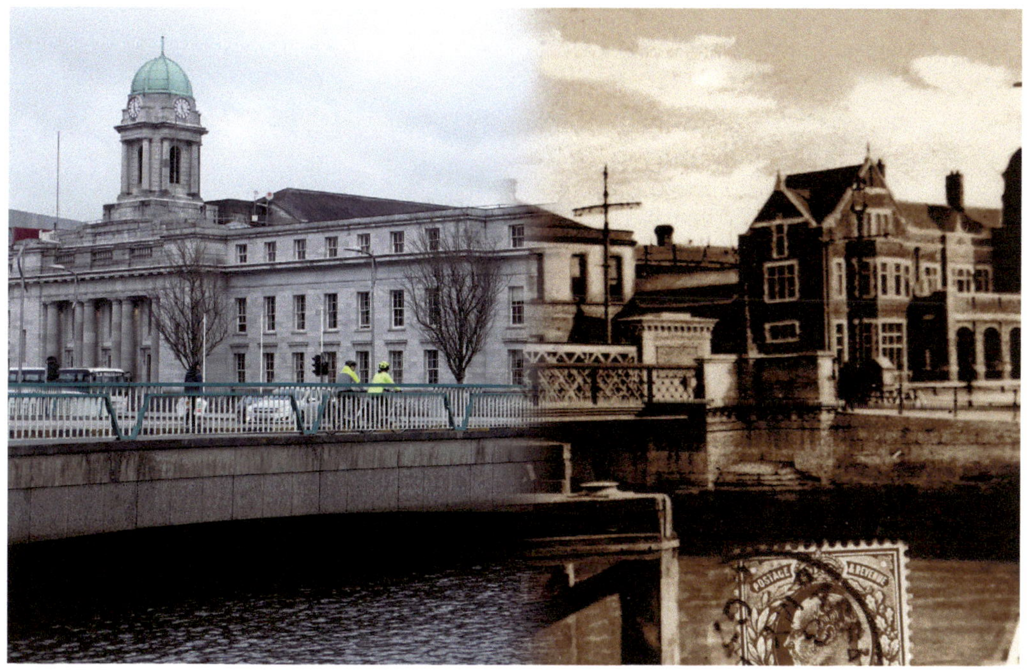

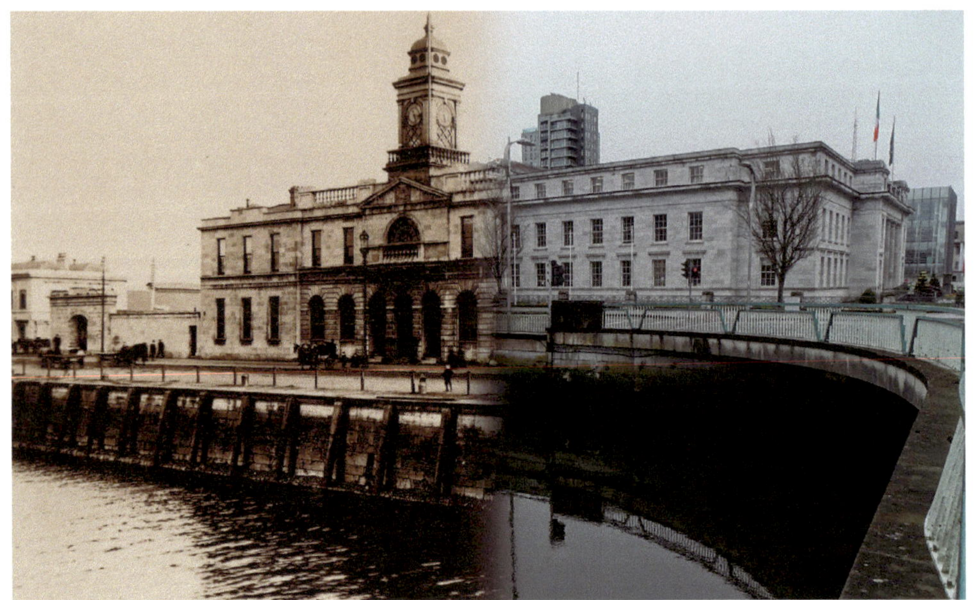

Cork City Hall

Cork has had a number of City Hall sites through the ages. In the age of the Anglo-Norman walled town and the eighteenth century, civic business was conducted in King's Castle. Business was also conducted in Cork City Courthouse for a time in the nineteenth century. In 1883, it was decided by a number of Cork businessmen that the Corn Exchange should be converted into an exhibition centre, a centre which in 1892 became Cork City Hall. Another significant change at the turn of the twentieth century was the changing of the title Mayor to Lord Mayor in 1900. In that year, the elected mayor was Daniel J. Hegarty. On 3 April 1900, Queen Victoria sailed into Kingstown (now Dún Laoghaire) on an Irish tour. The mayor and sheriff of Cork were invited to the celebrations in Dublin. To mark the occasion, on the eve of her return to London, Queen Victoria conferred the honour of baronetcy on the Lord Mayors of Cork, Dublin and Belfast.

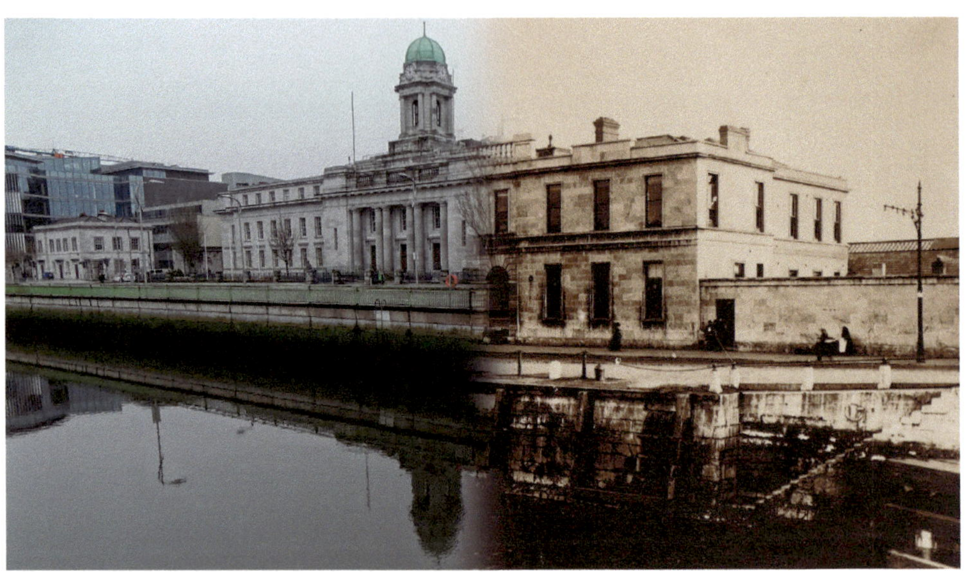

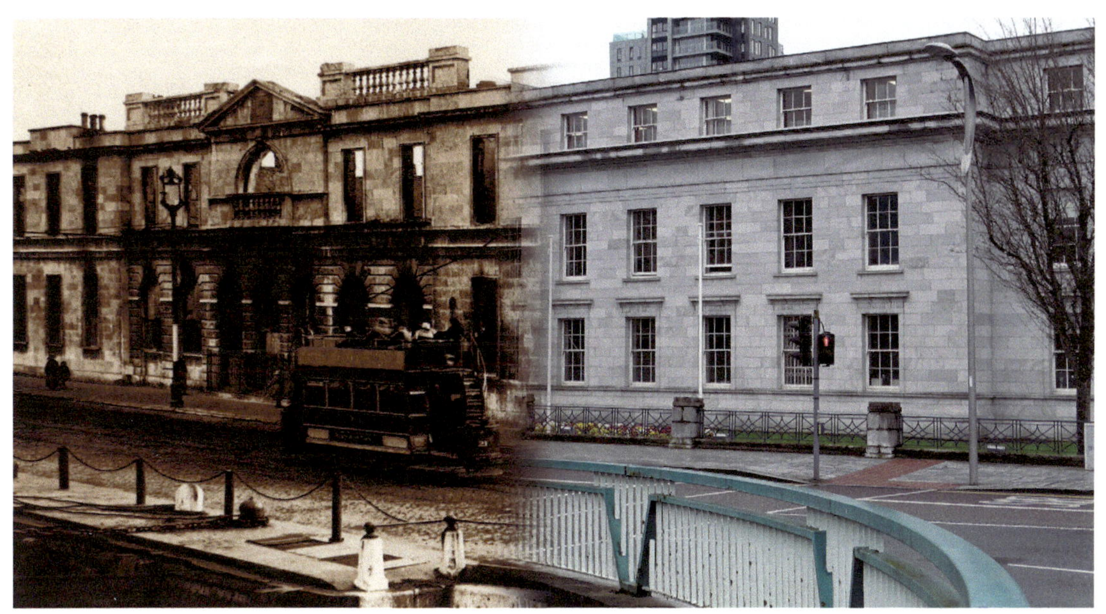

Cork City Hall

In the early hours of Sunday Morning on 12 December 1920, the late nineteenth-century City Hall was destroyed by fire by auxiliaries of the Royal Irish Constabulary. They formed the British side against the Irish Republican Army (IRA) in the Irish War of Independence. President of the Executive Council of the Irish Free State Eamon de Valera officially opened the new City Hall on 8 September 1936. The building is a fine structure, comprised of limestone from Little Island Quarries in County Cork. The building has an eighteenth-century style to it – neoclassical Doric. Today the building accommodates some of the principal departments of the Corporation, including the Lord Mayor's Office. A major extension was opened in 2007 just behind the old building.

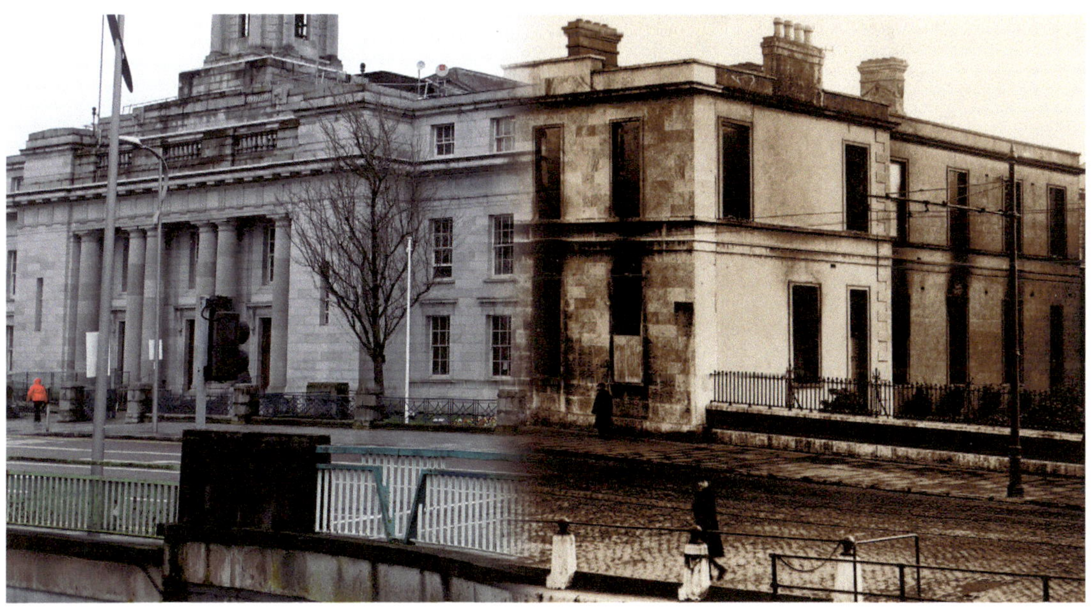

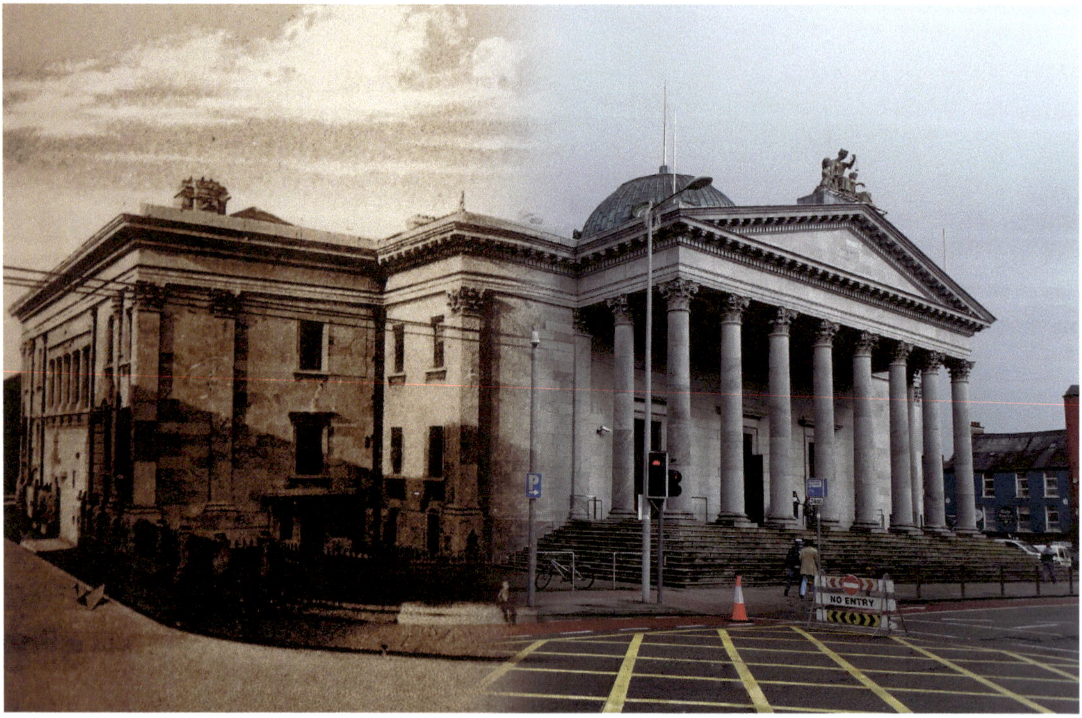

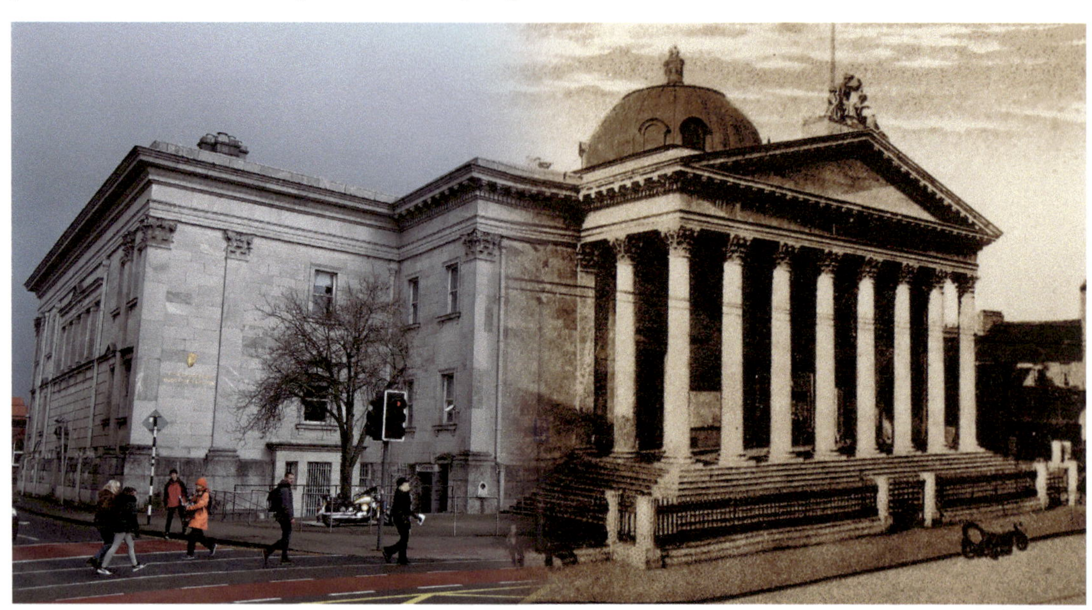

Cork City Courthouse

In 1829, it was decided by Cork Corporation that both the City and County Courthouses should be incorporated into one building, to be located on Great George's Street (now Washington Street). Designed by George Pain, the Courthouse was opened in 1835. Years later, on Good Friday 27 March 1891, the interior was destroyed by fire. William Henry Hill was chosen to oversee the reconstruction of the building. On 18 March 1895, the first rooms of the new and present Courthouse were opened for the Spring Assizes.

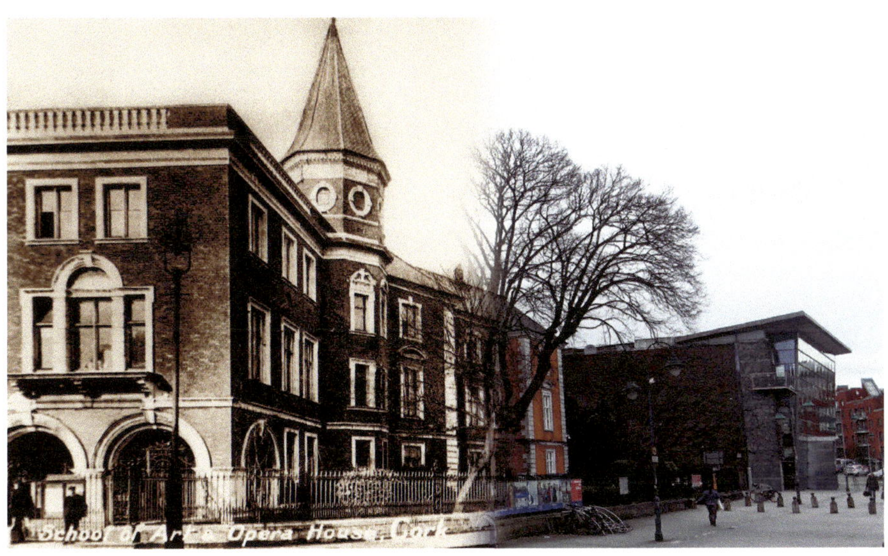

Crawford School of Art

In 1883 a deputation consisting of Mr James Brenan, RHA, schoolmaster of the Cork School of Art and the Honorary Secretary, was sent to London to request further finance from Mr Mundella, the then Vice-President of the Committee of Council for Education, for finance to construct a municipal art gallery. Several months later, through the efforts of the committee and headmaster, James Brenan, William Horatio Crawford, a prominent Cork City merchant, decided to donate the necessary finance to complete a renovation of and extension to the existing School of Art. The cost was £20,000, and Arthur Hill of the architect firm Hill & Co. designed the renovated the building and extension. In the preface of the School of Art's 1919 prospectus the objects of the institution were given as: 'to give a practical knowledge of drawing, design, modeling, painting, etc. and to furnish useful training to those whose vocation depends in any way on the application of art to the trades, crafts, or professions; so that the workman can become more skilled in his trade or craft and the designer possesses more knowledge in the application to the various processes of manufacture and handicraft'.

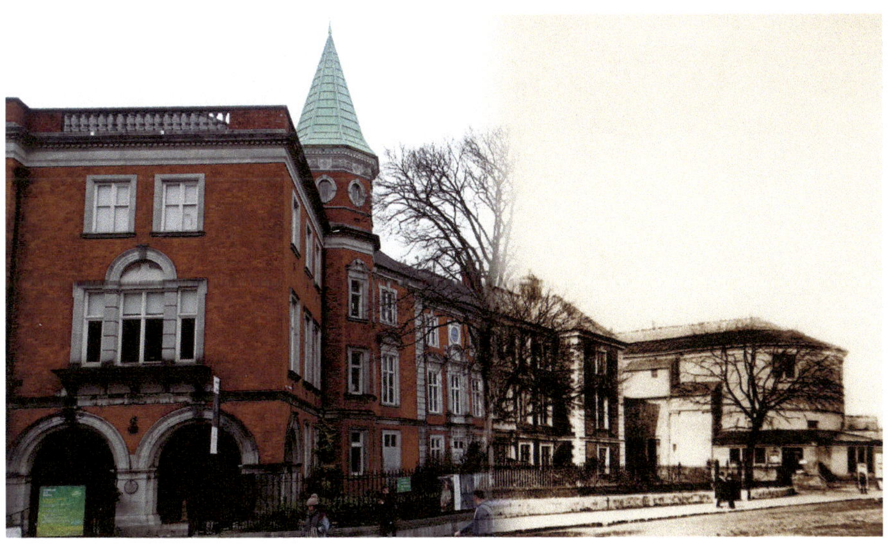

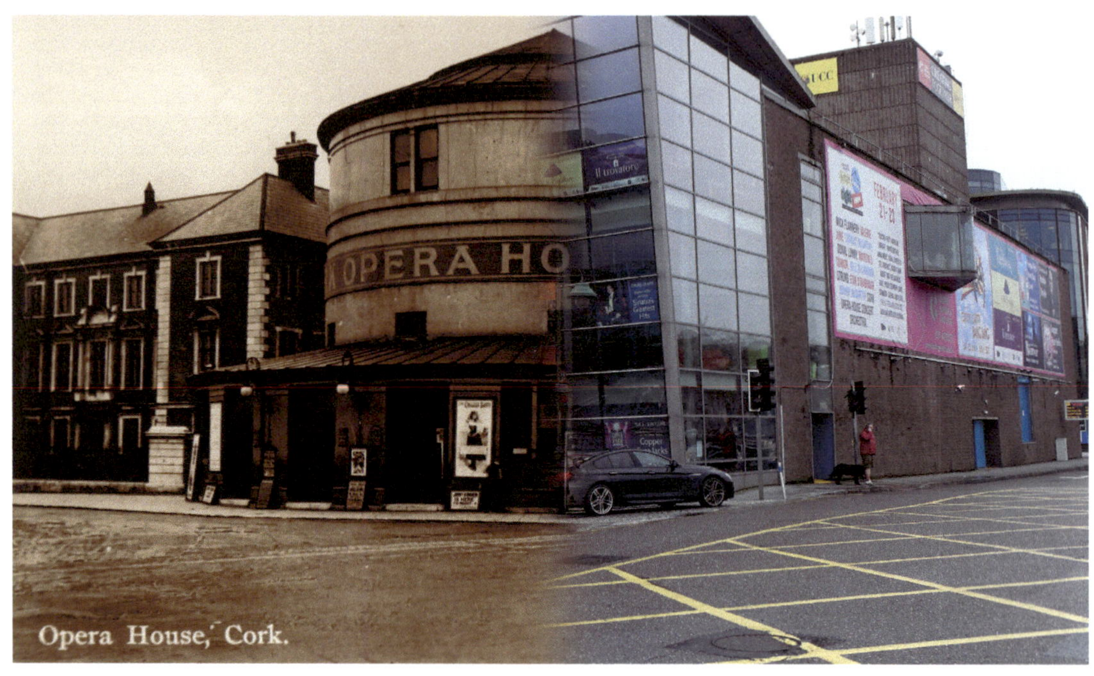

Opera House, Cork.

Cork Opera House

On 17 September 1877, Cork Opera House opened its doors to begin its long illustrious career as Cork's principal theatre. Mr C. J. Phipps of London was commissioned to design the Cork Opera House. It opened with a performance of H. J. Byron's comedy *Our Boys* by William Duck and his company. The first manager of Cork Opera House, James Scanlan, operated under a board of directors acting on behalf of a private limited company. The theatre burned down decades later in 1955 and reopened with a new look in October 1965. It was revamped again in recent years, plus now hosts a myriad of events every year, from music to drama and film.

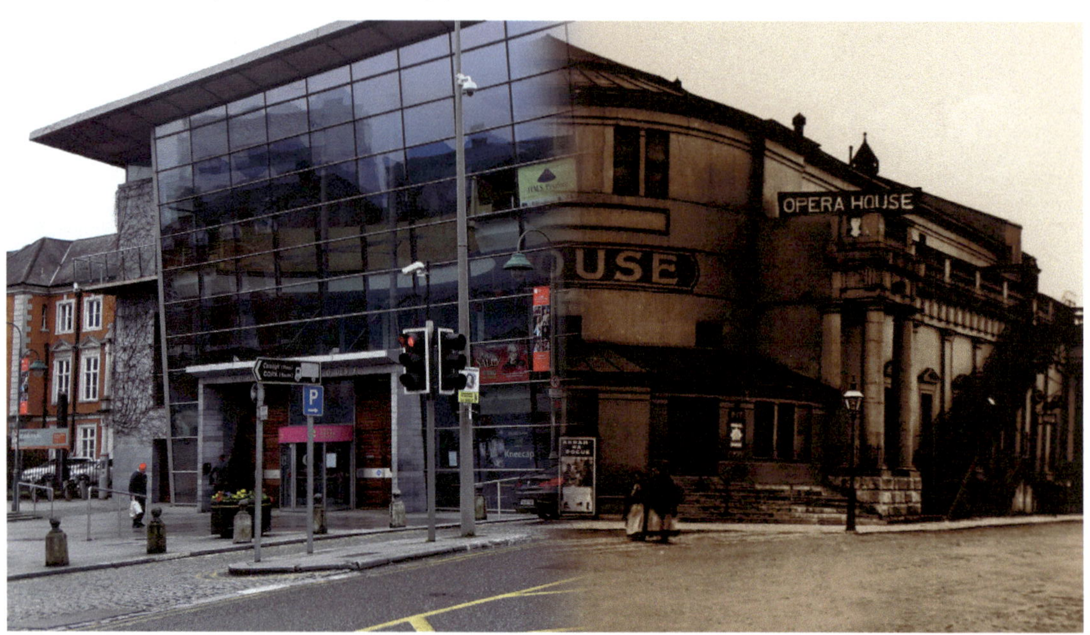

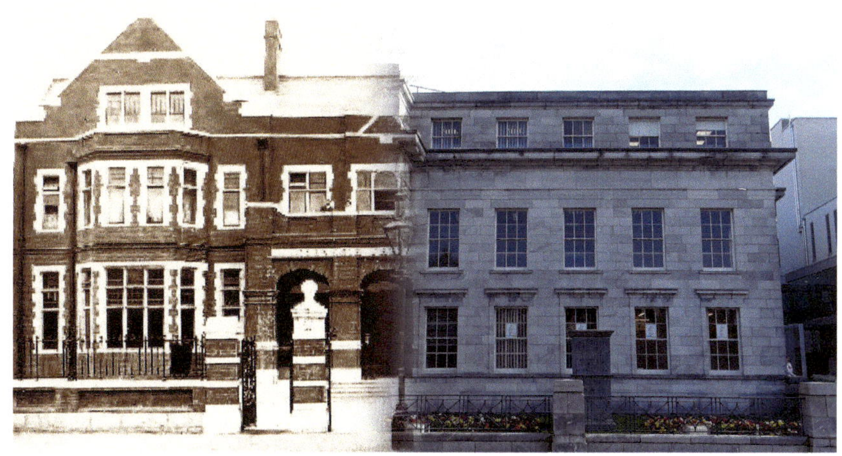

Cork Carnegie Library

Scottish-American philanthropist and industrialist Andrew Carnegie invested personally in the provision of 660 public libraries across Britain and Ireland alone at the turn of the twentieth century. On 21 October 1903 the foundation stone of the Cork Carnegie Library was laid by Andrew Carnegie and afterwards on the same day he received the Freedom of the City. Andrew's action in providing the citizens of Cork with a sum of £11,000 for the erection of the library at Anglesea Street, and a sum of £1,000 towards the furnishing of the building, was greatly appreciated. The new library was to replace a public library (est. 1892) within the School of Art on Nelson's Place. The new Carnegie Library was located on Anglesea Street next to Cork City Hall and had a lifespan of only fifteen years, until it was burnt down during the Burning of Cork in 1920. The Carnegie link was broken with Cork but a new Cork City public library was opened once more in 1930 on the Grand Parade, where it is still based. The campaign to rebuild it was headed up by the astute and active City Librarian, James Wilkinson.

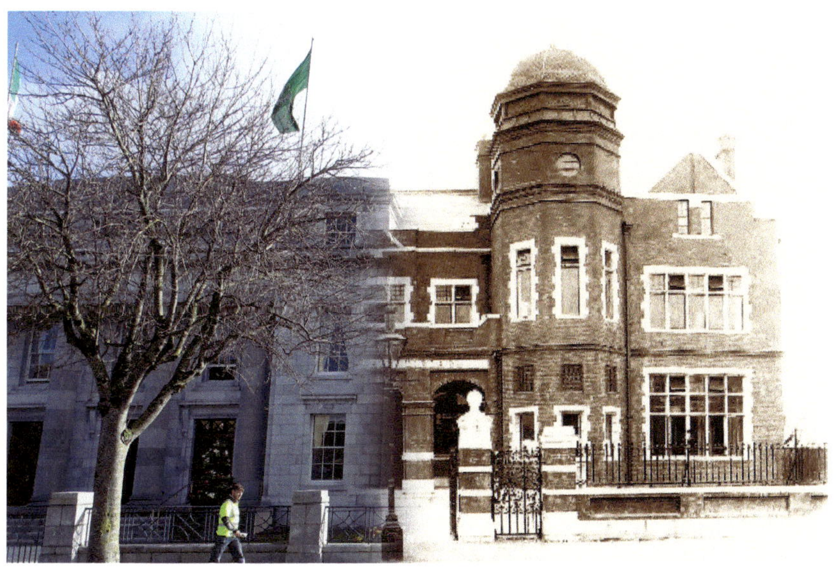

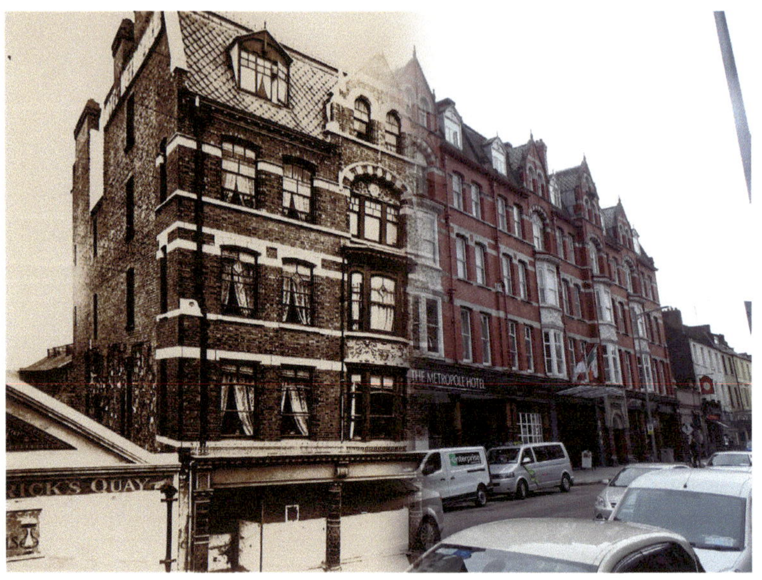

Metropole Hotel

In 1876, the brothers Stuart and Thomas Musgrave opened a grocery on North Main Street in Cork. They were aged twenty-five and eighteen respectively and had moved to Cork from County Leitrim. The business incorporated in 1894 as Musgrave Brothers Ltd, with a charter to retail and wholesale sugar, coffee, tea, spices, fruit, olive oil, and other foodstuffs. The company also ran a bakery and confectionary and was listed as a mineral water manufacturer, iron and hardware merchant, druggist, fish and ice merchant, stationer and haberdasher. At the same time, the Musgrave brothers built and ran Cork's iconic Metropole Hotel, as well as a sweet factory and a laundry. The prospectus for the hotel in 1897 sold its luxuriousness and taste which extended throughout the new building. These encompassed the 'necessary public rooms, including spacious dining room, ladies' writing and drawing rooms, private sitting rooms, commercial room, billiard room, smoking room, and numerous stock rooms, together with fifty well-appointed bedrooms'.

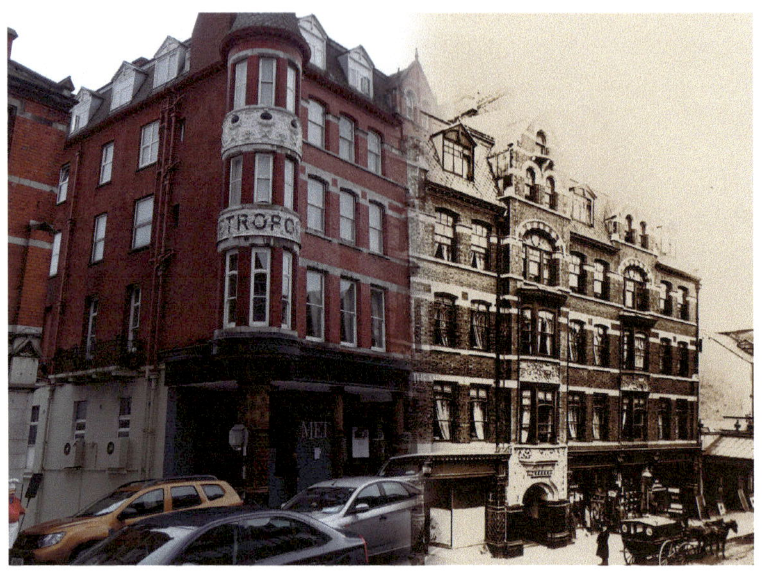

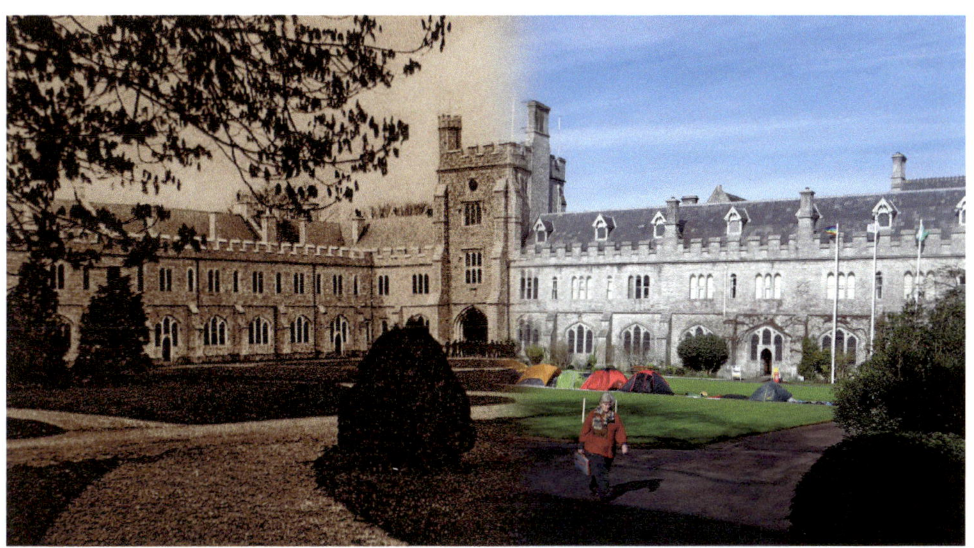

University College Cork

Affectionately known by Corkonians as 'The College', University College Cork was founded under the provisions made by Queen Victoria to endow new colleges in Ireland for the advancement of learning. Under the powers given by this Act the three colleges of Belfast, Cork and Galway were incorporated on 30 December 1845. Architects Benjamin Woodward and Sir Thomas Deane adopted a perpendicular Gothic style for the Cork college. It was opened on 7 November 1849. In 1908, the Queen's College, Cork, was established as a National University of Ireland under the 1908 constitution. During that era, medical buildings and the engineering school had been considerably improved, and new laboratories for physics and chemistry had been constructed. In 1917 there were thirty-three professors, twenty-three lecturers and ten demonstrators. A Faculty of Commerce had been founded (in association with the Incorporated Cork Chamber of Commerce and Shipping), as well as a Department of Dentistry. With the aid of a grant from the Cork Corporation, evening lectures for working men had been instituted in connection with the Workers' Education Association. Today, University College Cork has over 12,000 students and 1,700 staff.

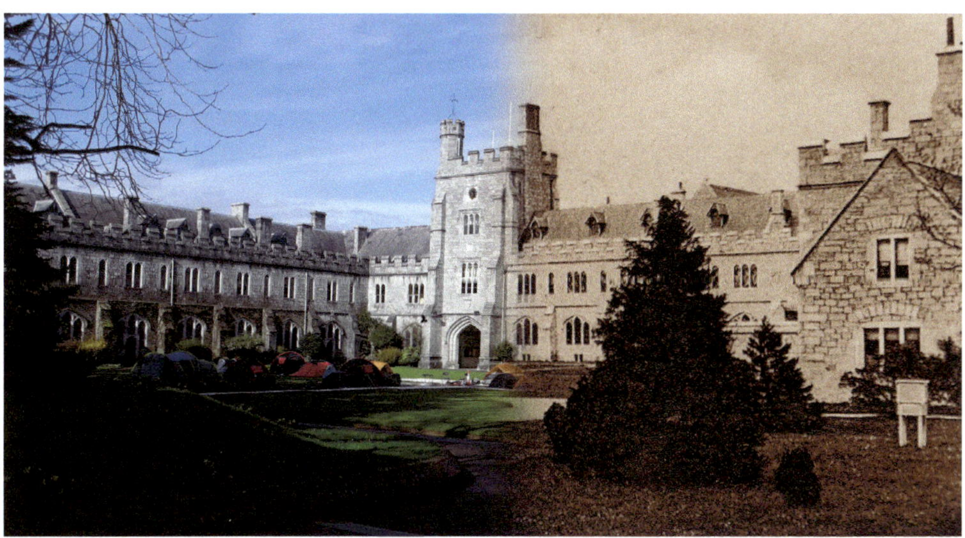

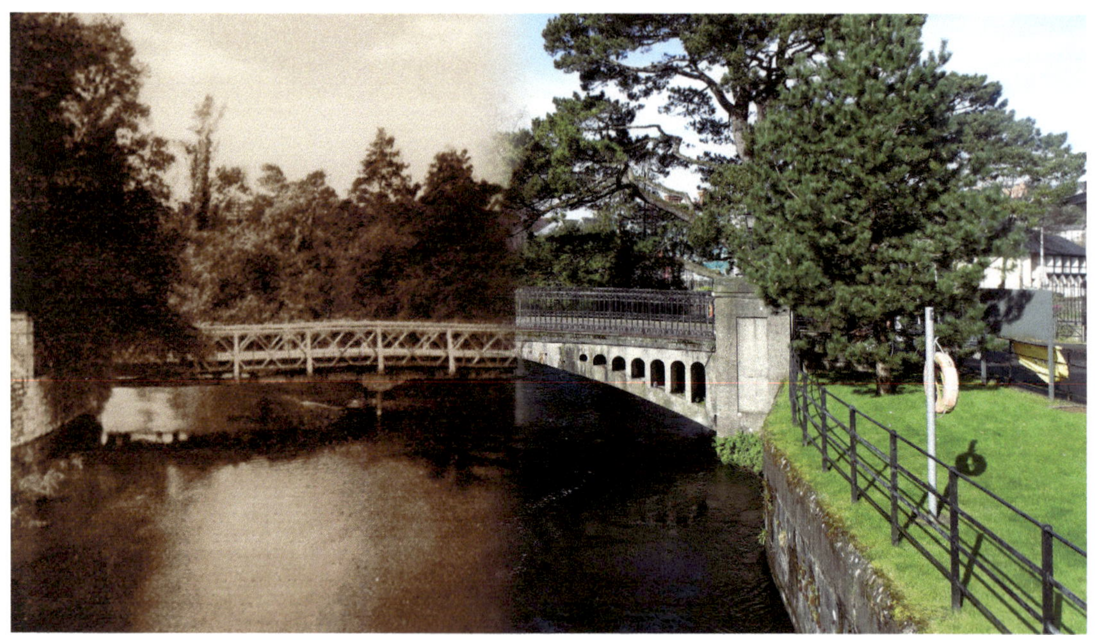

A Porter's Lodge

Opening in 1879, the entrance to the university provided an alternative to the existing entrance to the college. Its principal western entrance had been too close to the city's County Gaol in terms of convenience, prestige and security. The entrance comprised a head porter's lodge and bridge of Oregon pine, as seen below. In 1910 the bridge was replaced by a reinforced concrete structure. In November 1916, the bridge was struck by severe flooding, which caused it to collapse. Due to war and the shortage of finance and material, the new bridge was not opened until1929. In 2019, the bridge was renamed the 'Alumni Bridge'.

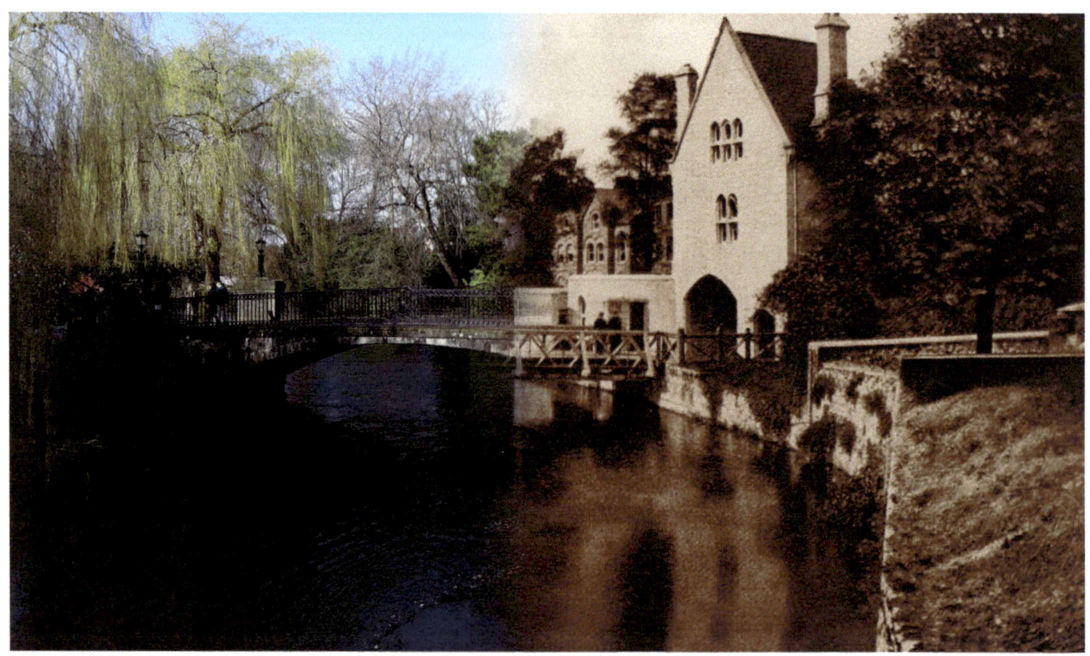

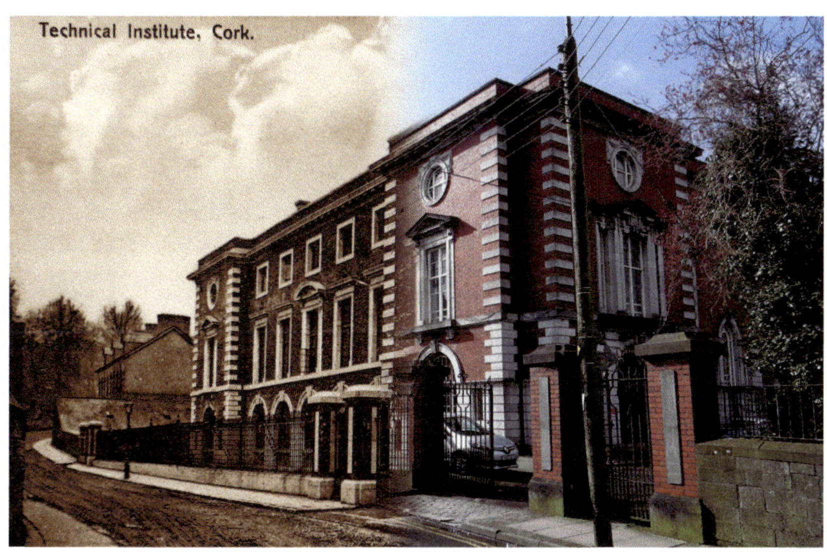

Crawford Municipal Technical Institute

On 16 January 1912, the official opening of Crawford Municipal Technical Institute took place with an official address by Thomas Wallace Russell, Vice-President of the Department of Agricultural and Technical Instruction. The architect of the building was Arthur Hill (1846–1921). On the ground floor on the east side (Sharman Crawford Street) were the administration offices, library and physics laboratory. On the south side of the building next to the physics laboratory was the preparation room, which served both the laboratory and the electrical engineering lecture room. Across the yard were two workshops for plumbing and carpentry of practically equal size. On the ground floor on the west side was the mechanical engineering department. On the east side of the first floor over the entrance hall and general office were the botanical laboratory and the two engineering drawing offices. The other rooms on this floor were the building construction room, tailors' cutting room, two introductory course classrooms, junior dress-making room, two painters' and decorators' shops, and printers' workshop. From the first floor, two separate staircases led to the chemistry department and domestic science section, respectively.

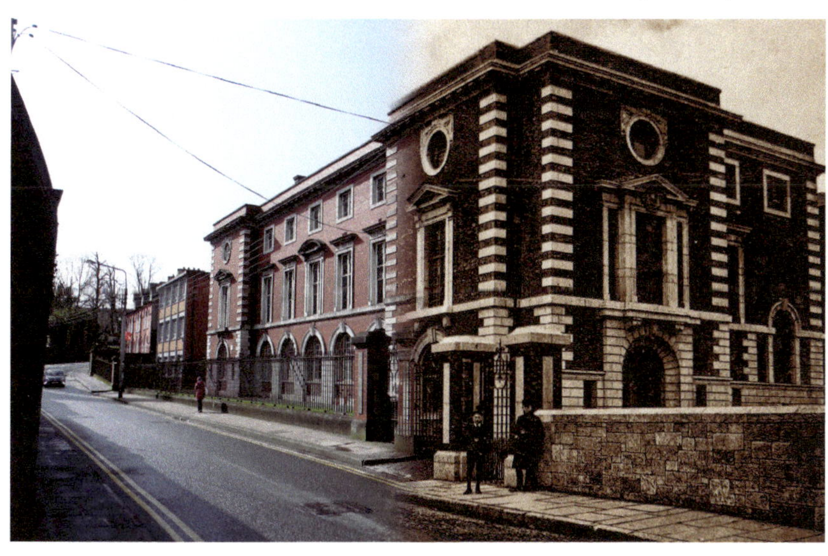

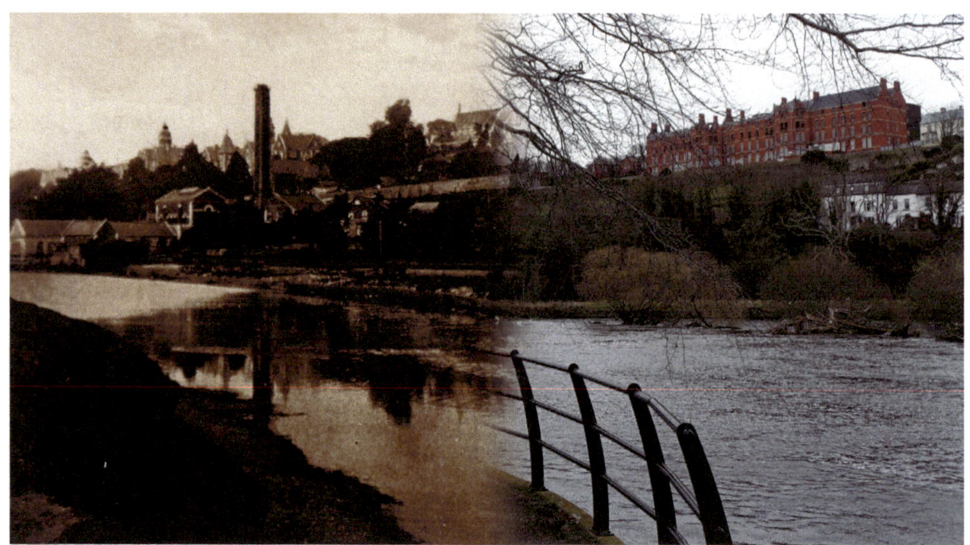

Cork City Waterworks

In 1919 the total population of the city supplied with water was 91,250 – over 90 per cent. The area supplied was divided into four districts, three of which – North, Centre and South districts – derived their supply from a Low-Level Reservoir. The fourth district, which was the high-level district, was supplied from the High-Level Reservoir. Around 4.3 million gallons per day were extracted from a culvert connected to the river complete with a filtration system of sand and gravel. By 1919, through leaks and wastage, the waterworks department estimated that almost 50 per cent of the supply was wasted and the waterworks reports record continuous attempts to inform the population of the need to conserve water for the proper running of the city's water supply. The buildings that stand on the Cork Waterworks site today date from the 1800s and 1900s but water has been supplied to the city of Cork from the site since 1768. The majority of the buildings date to February 1857, when they formed part of architect John Benson's plan for a new waterworks, which he gave to several eminent engineers in London for consultation before they were built. Today the Old Cork Waterworks host an interactive tourist programme and daily science workshops for Cork children.

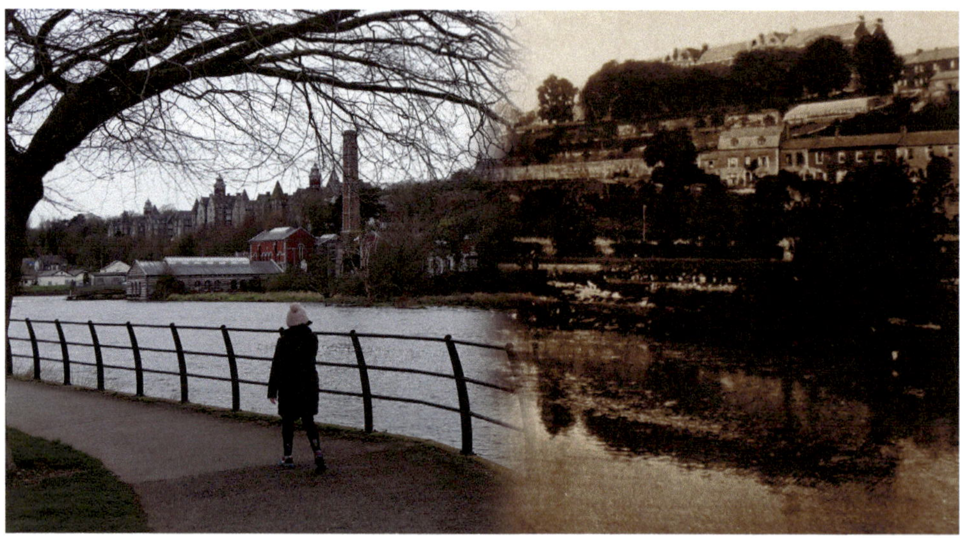

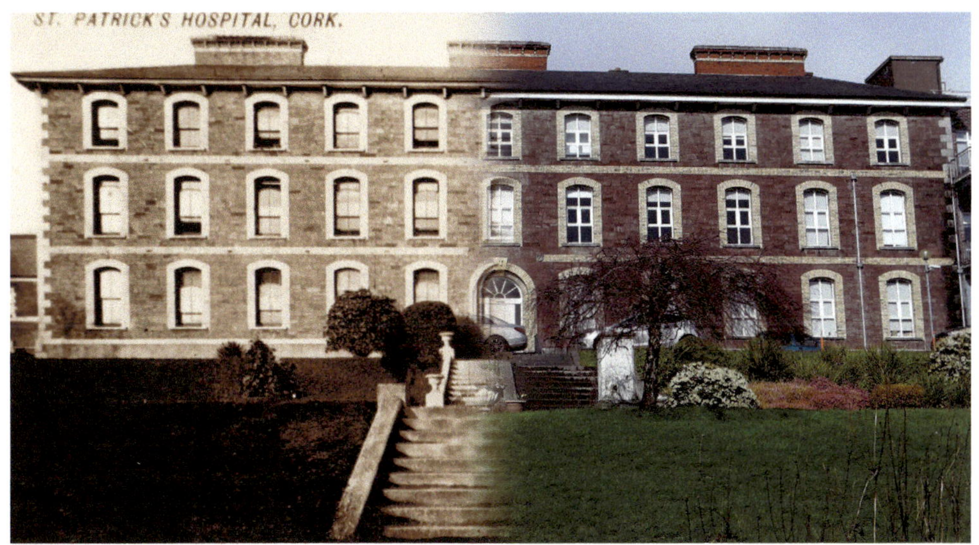

St Patrick's Hospital

Opened in 1870, St Patrick's Hospital quickly became an important addition to the healthcare of Cork. The hospital report of 1903 details that there were seven wards in the hospital for Roman Catholic patients. Of these, two were set apart for cancer patients (one male ward and one female ward). The remaining wards were for the reception of patients suffering from diseases pronounced incurable. The hospital report shows that several of the other patients who, though they were received as seemingly incurable cases, lived several years in the hospital owing to the 'care received and the rest enjoyed'. More patients suffered from consumption than from any other diseases. Several of these improved so much during their stay that they were able to return to their families and seek employment. Some were permanently cured, while others, a few years after they left the hospital, returned again to pass their last days within its precincts. In 2011, the hospital with Marymount Hospice removed from the building to a purpose-built campus in Cork's Curraheen. This important Cork health facility is now named **Marymount University Hospital & Hospice.**

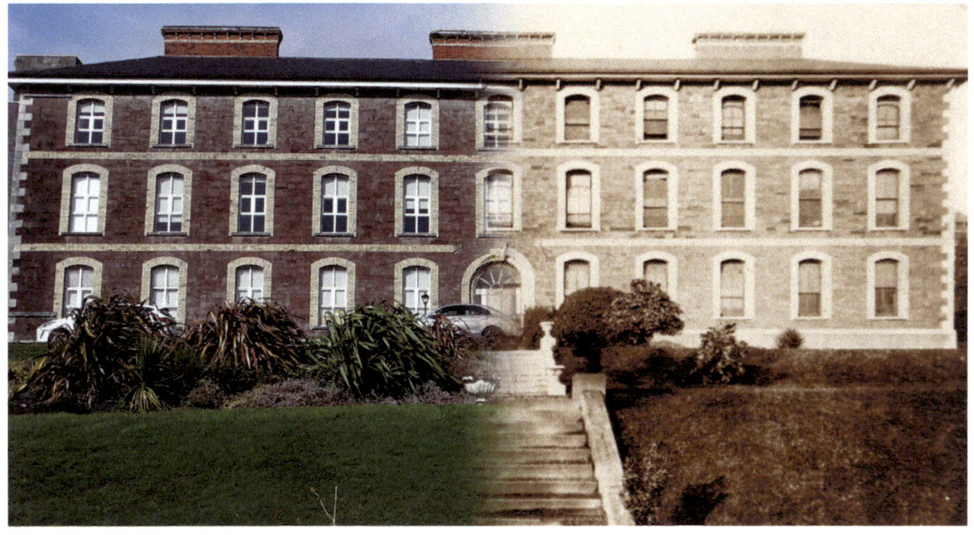

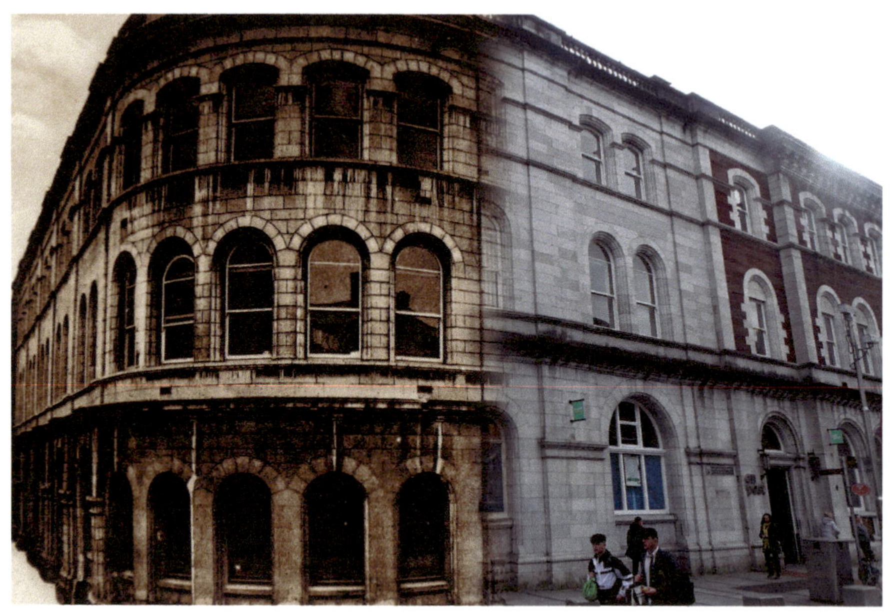

General Post Office

In 1875, owner James Scanlan sold the Cork Theatre Royal on Oliver Plunkett Street to the postal authorities as part of an elaborate building project for the city's post and telegraph authorities. Four years later in early May 1879, a new building opened. Costing £8,000, the building, which still stands today, comprises limestone, sandstone and cement. It is the design of Mr James Higgins Owens, architect of the Board of Works, and his assistant Enoch Trevor Owens, and the contract was carried out by Mr Richard Evans, Cork. The division walls, steps of stairs, arches and floors are made of concrete. It was one of the first buildings in Cork to have concrete as a building material. The building still stands as the General Post Office or GPO for the city.

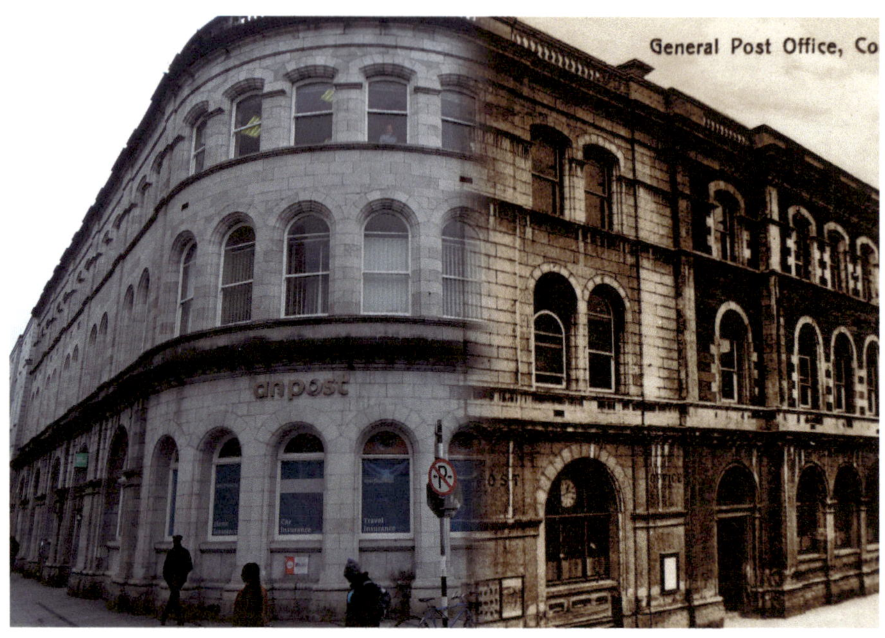

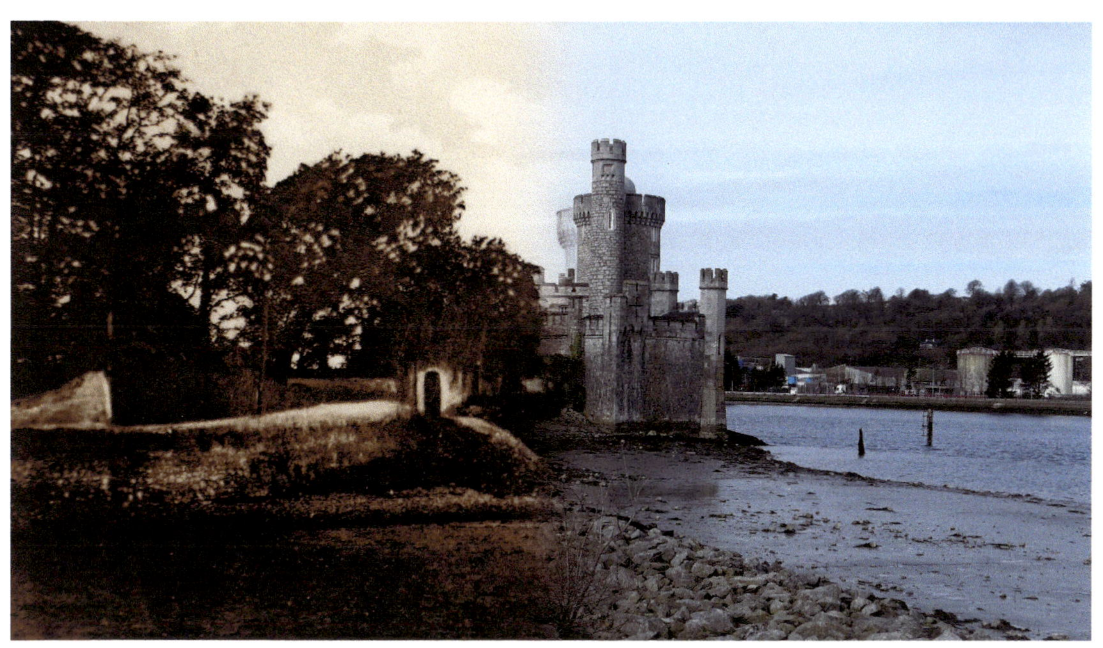

Blackrock Castle

The citizens of Cork built Blackrock Castle in 1582 to safeguard ships against pirates who would come into the harbour and steal their vessels. The fort, which was then a basic circular tower, was used as a beacon light from a turf fire to guide shipping. The building has been destroyed by fire twice (in 1722 and 1827) and rebuilt with more elaborate additions. In the eighteenth century Admiralty Courts were held at Blackrock Castle to oversee fishery rights in the River Lee estuary. It was the court's job to also organise an important ceremony called Throwing the Dart. This was a rite by which the Mayor of Cork threw a metre-long dart into the water of Cork Harbour in order to show his authority over the port and harbour. This is a function still carried out by the Lord Mayor of Cork today. The castle now hosts an interactive astronomy science centre.

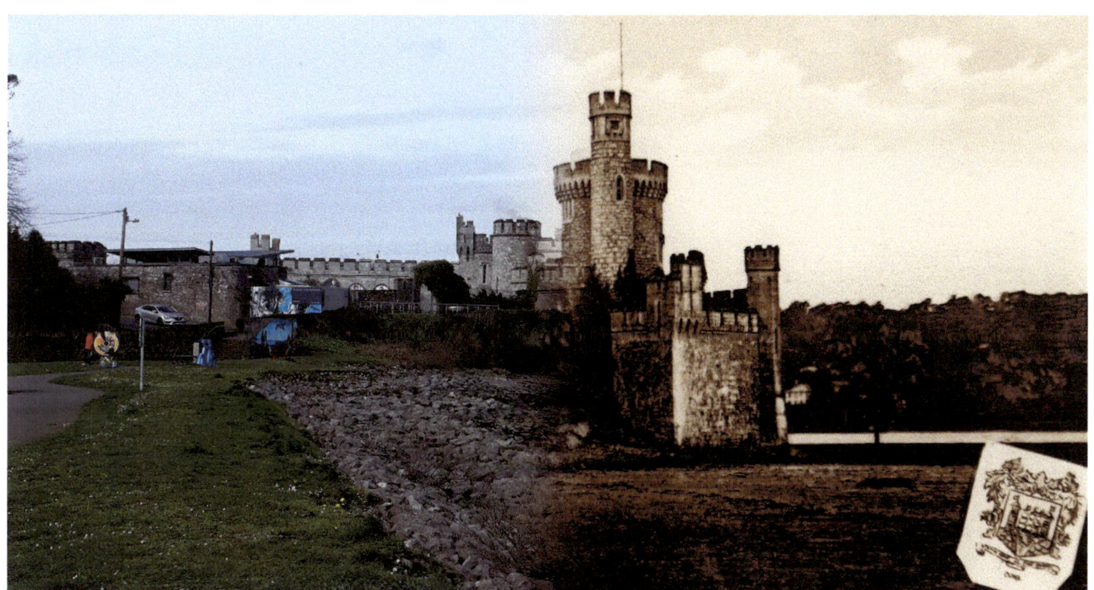

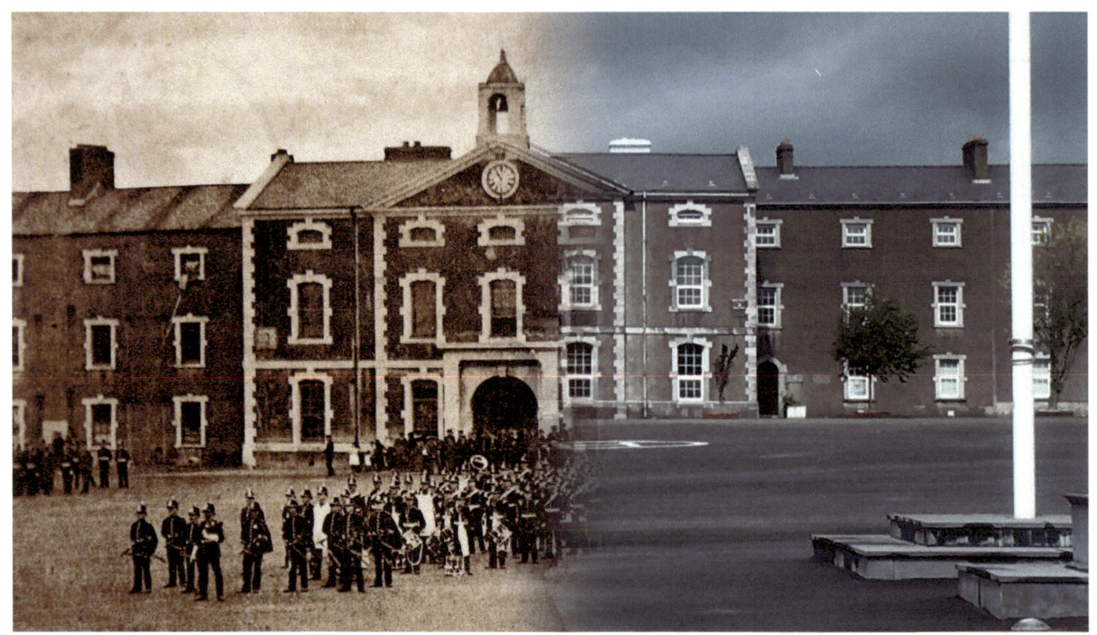

Victoria Barracks

Originally erected between 1801 and 1806, the works were completed by Abraham Hargrave to designs by John Gibson in a prominent position on the hills overlooking the city and the River Lee. Initially known simply as *The Barracks*, the complex was extended in 1849 and renamed *Victoria Barracks*, to celebrate a visit by Queen Victoria. After housing British forces in the city for more than 100 years, the barracks were handed over by the British government under the terms of the Anglo-Irish Treaty in 1922 (which marked the end of the Irish War of Independence). The barracks were soon renamed following the assassination of Michael Collins, the first commander-in-chief of the Free State, and a native of West Cork.

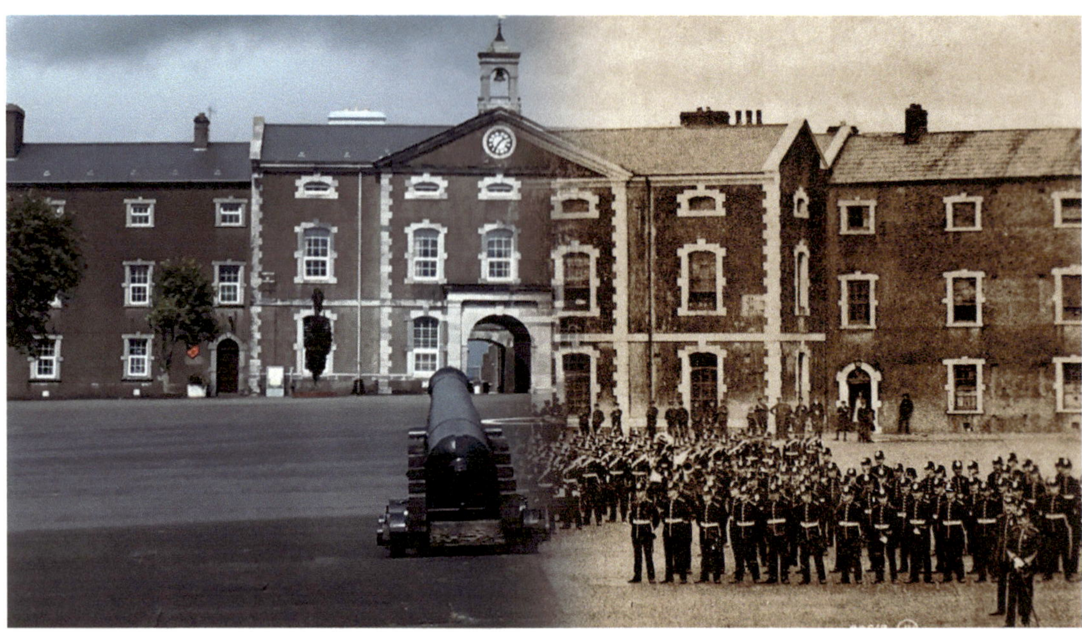

Wandering City Streets

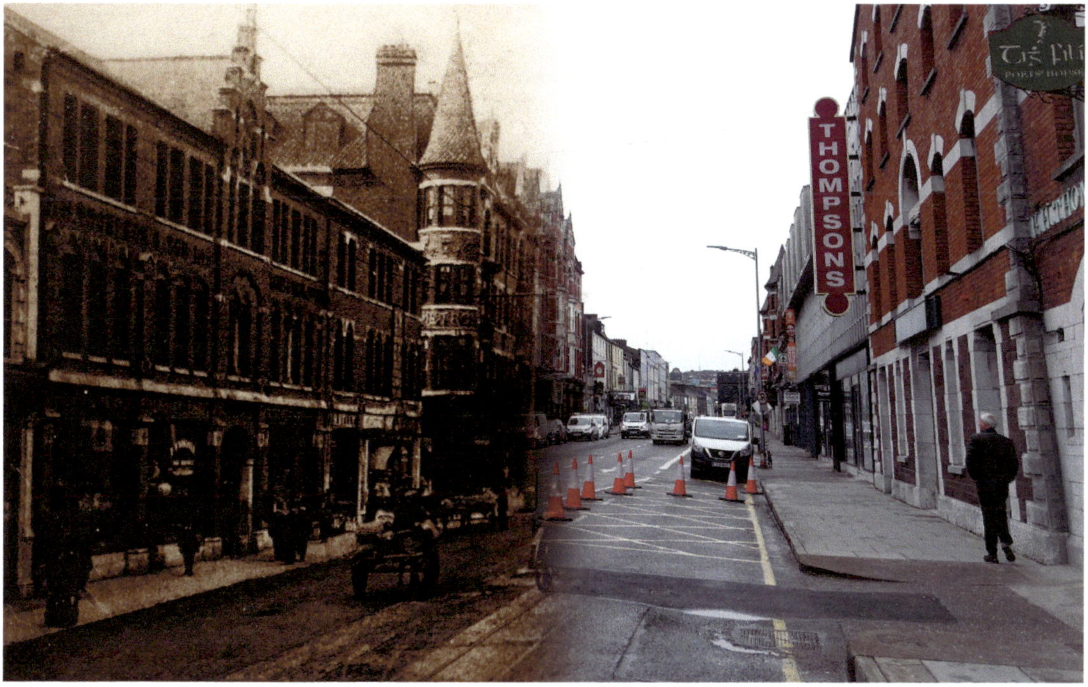

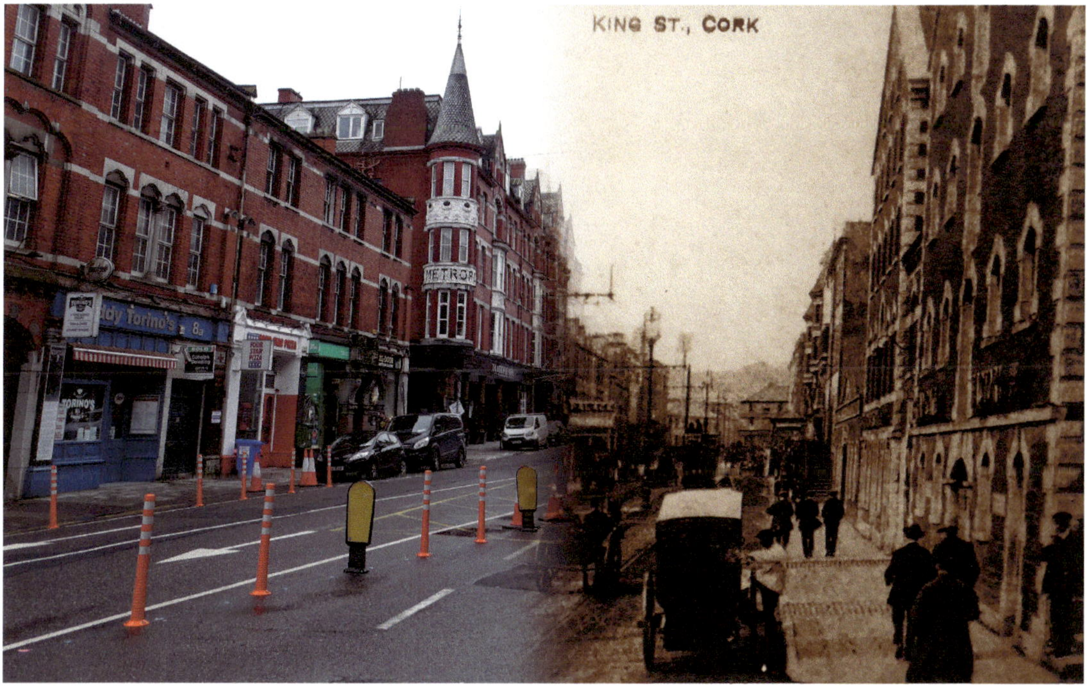

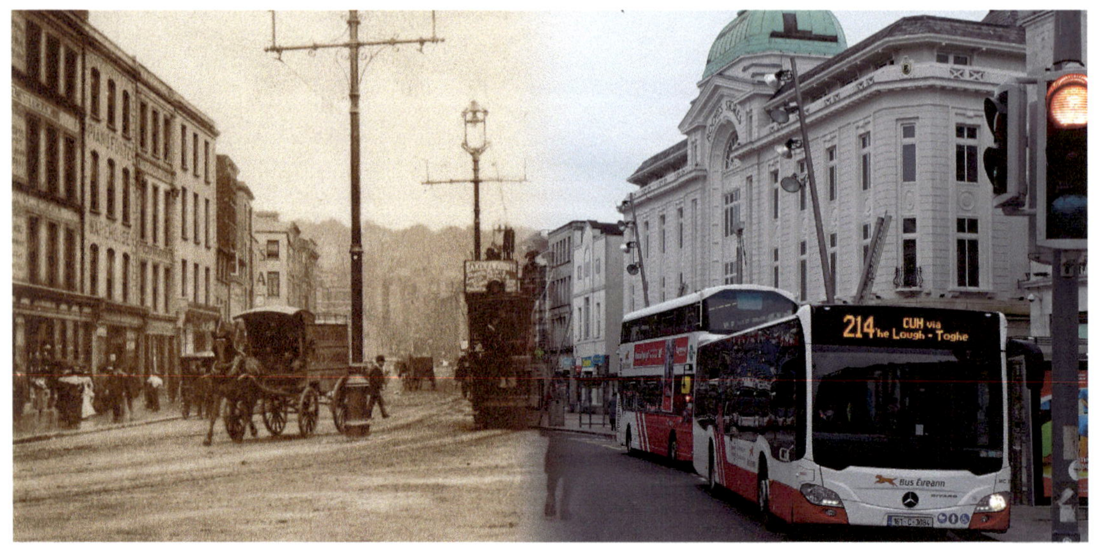

St Patrick's Street

The area of land surrounding St Patrick's Street, locally known as 'Pana', was the brainchild of Huguenot and Quaker city merchants in the early eighteenth century. Prior to the 1700s, the area was just marshland, which was reclaimed as the eighteenth century progressed. Indeed, St Patrick's Street was formerly a curving channel of the River Lee – the curve within the present-day street is clearly seen. Between 1700 and 1725, the river channel was turned into a canal with quays, shops and warehouses on both sides of it. Around 1780, the canal was filled, which created a wide and elegant thoroughfare. During the late 1990s, the Catalan architect Beth Gali was chosen by Cork Corporation to recover the public space of the street for citizens. The entire street was repaved in high-quality materials, granite and limestone, and the pavements widened to create plaza areas.

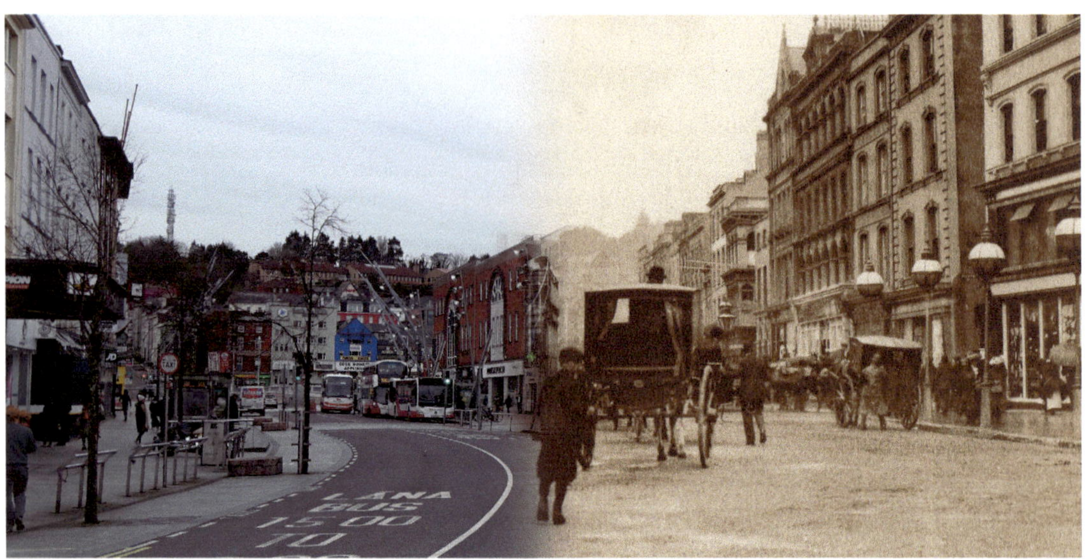

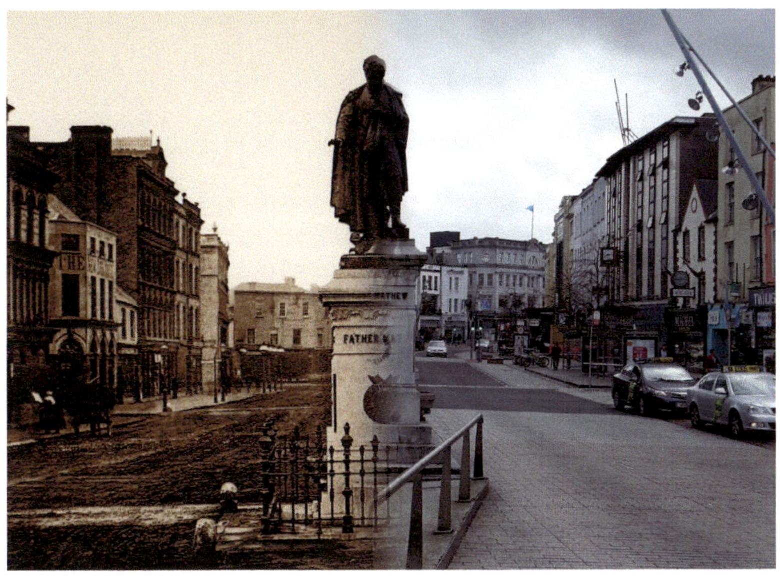

Father Theobald Mathew

In the period 1830 to 1850, one of Cork's most famous historical characters Father Theobald Mathew came to prominence to aid the impoverished of the city. He was a Tipperary man and was ordained a priest in the Capuchin order in 1814. Subsequently, he was assigned by the Provincial of the Order to the South Friary in Blackamoor Lane, near Sullivan's Quay. Father Mathew established a boys' school near Blackamoor Lane, following the example of the local Christian Brothers who were providing education for poor boys in the northern part of the city. Perhaps his most known work of charity in the city was his involvement in the creation of an effective temperance movement. He died in 1856 and was buried in St Joseph's Cemetery. In 1864, a statue was erected to Father Mathew at the eastern end of St Patrick's Street with support from Cork Corporation and the citizens of the city. The statue appears in several postcards from the early twentieth century of St Patrick's Street.

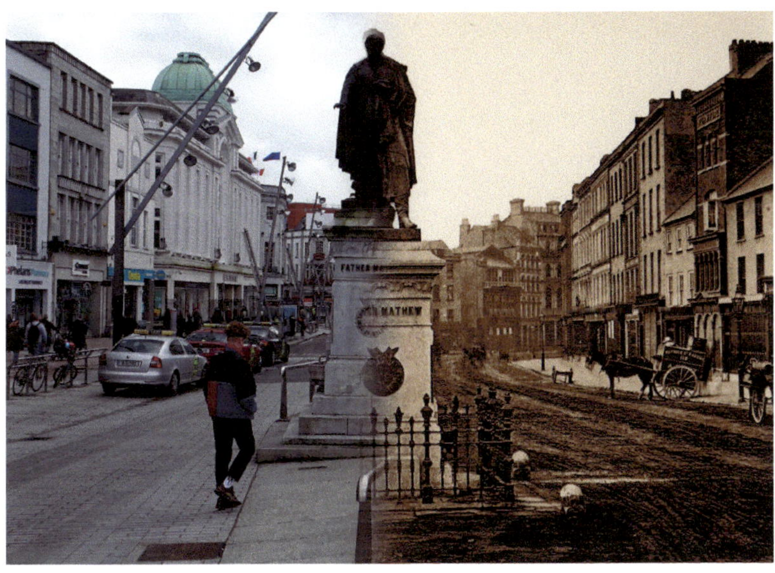

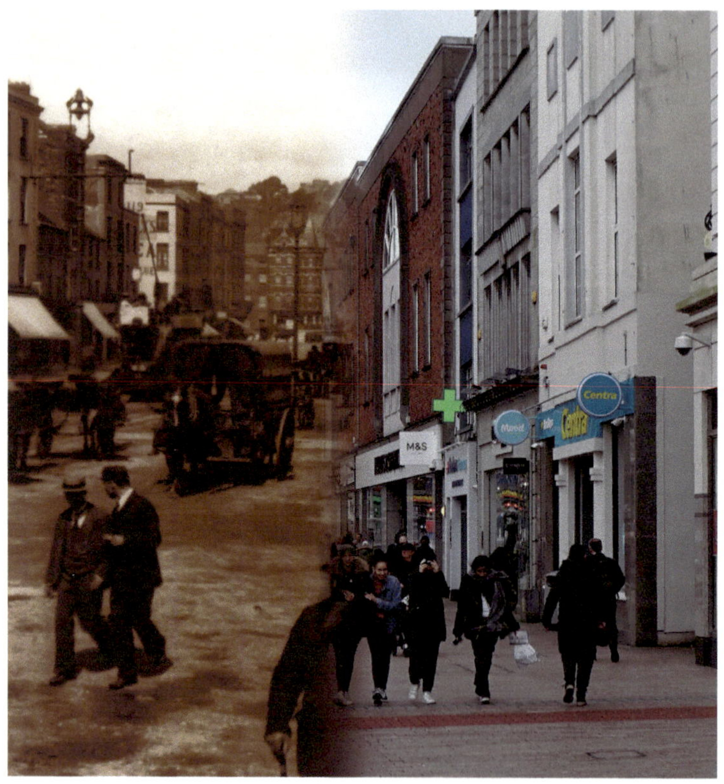

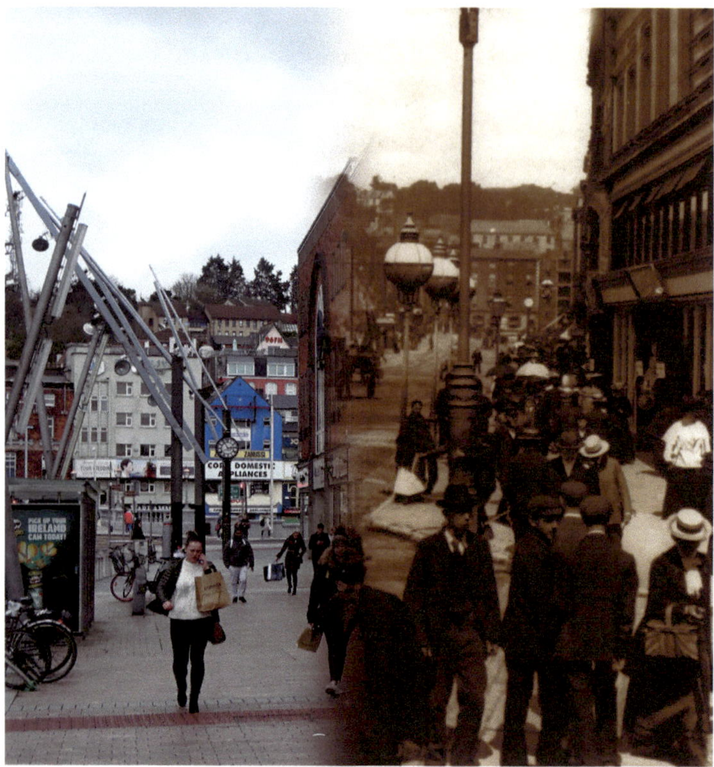

Businesses of a Main Street

In 1911, the street directories for St Patrick's Street record a busy street of varied businesses. On the Mangan's Clock quarter of the street, the businesses listed included Barry's wine and spirits; Russell's provision warehouse; Mangan's watchmakers; silversmiths and opticians; Henry O'Shea's Tivoli Restaurant; Clarke & Son's tobacco manufacturers; John Blair & Son's pharmaceutical chemists; Andrew & Co.'s newsagents and stationers; O'Grady's tobacconist; Lamkin Brothers, tobacco manufacturers; James Simcox's grocers; the Hill's dress warerooms; Andrew's teeth specialist; Evan's booksellers; O'Sullivan's tobacconists; Criger's dentistry; Wolfe's ladies' outfitters; London House warehousemen; James Archer's engravers; John Belas's commercial agency; Harte's dress warerooms; Lee Boot Manufacturing Co.; Scully, Connell & Co.'s children's outfitters; and Cash and Co.'s drapers and general warehousemen.

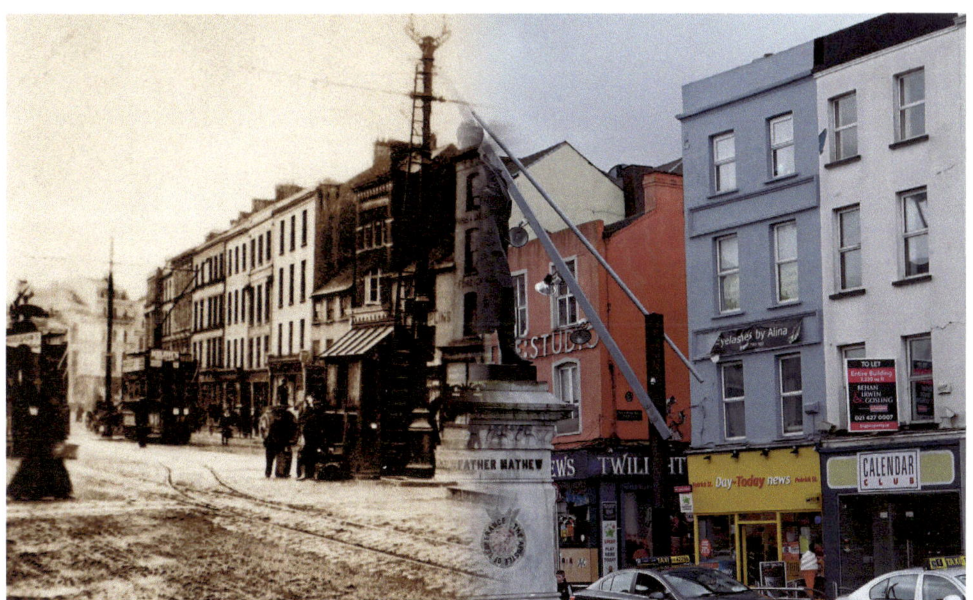

Fireman's Hut

Adjacent to the Father Mathew statue was the fireman's hut, which had rescue equipment and one man on duty at it during night-time hours. In 1910 there were three brigade stations: a central one on Sullivan's Quay and two auxillary stations – one at the rear of the Courthouse on Grattan Street and one at the top of Shandon Street The engines at this time were two Merryweather steam pumps, which were drawn by teams of horses and these were purchased in 1892. The brigade at that time consisted of six regular men and two turncocks living in the station with six auxiliary firemen, all Corporation employees, and with local volunteers a total force of thirty men could be mustered in a few minutes. A report from the chief at the time suggested that a night response took around 2.5 minutes with men fully dressed and horses out.

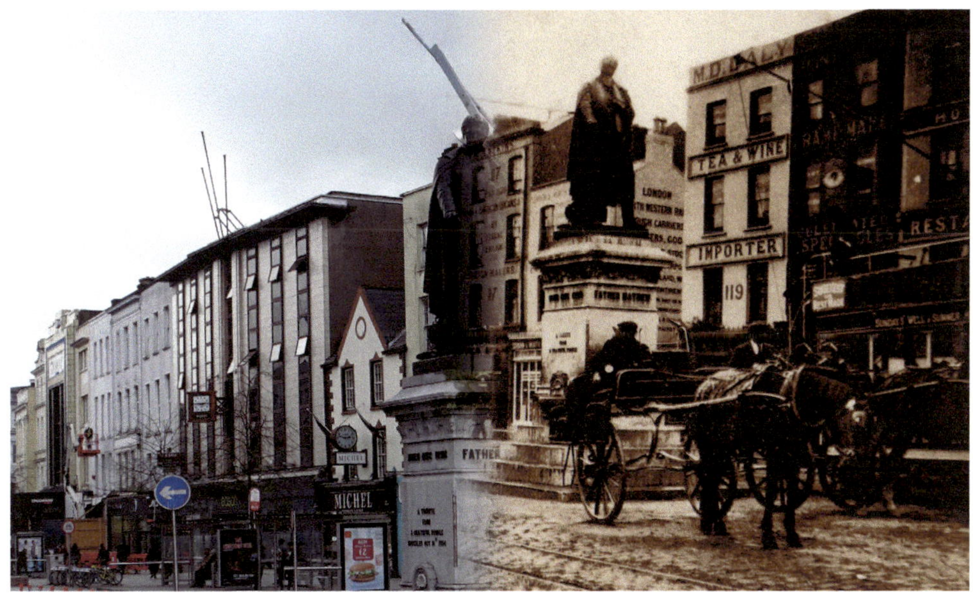

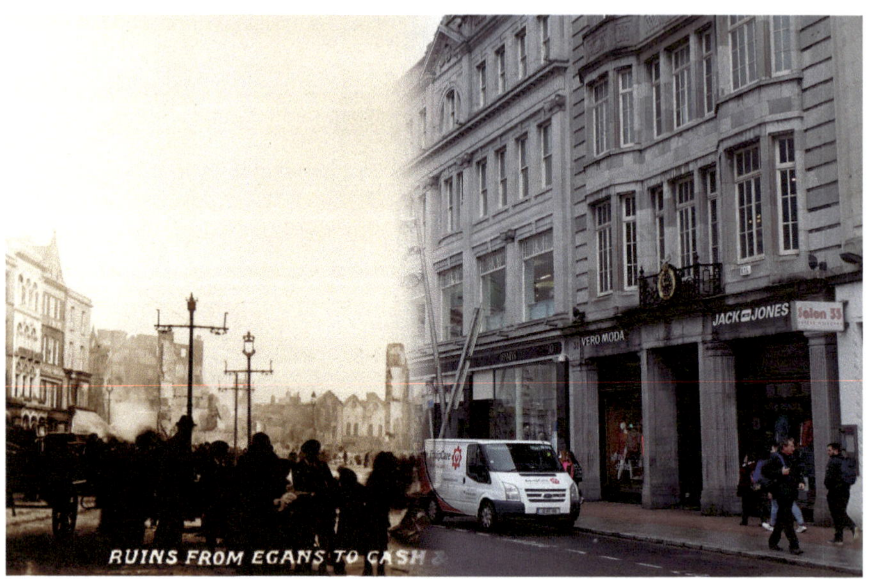

Burning of Cork, 1920

During Ireland's War of Independence (1919–21) violence escalated on both sides between Ireland and Britain. In response to Irish Republican Army activities in Cork and in the country as a whole, from January 1920 the British government increased the number of men serving in the Royal Irish Constabulary, recruiting the infamous Black and Tans to swell the ranks. In December 1920, six unknown IRA men ambushed a troupe of auxiliaries within a hundred metres of the central military barracks near Dillion's Cross on the north side of Cork City. At least one auxiliary was killed and twelve others wounded. In retaliation, indiscriminate shooting commenced by the auxiliaries and Black and Tans in the main city centre streets shortly after eight o'clock. Soon, petrol was brought into the city centre and various premises were set alight at random. The fires spread rapidly and soon most of the southern side of St Patrick's Street was ablaze. In time this side was rebuilt with many of the buildings being opened in the late 1920s, such as that of the present-day Penneys (below).

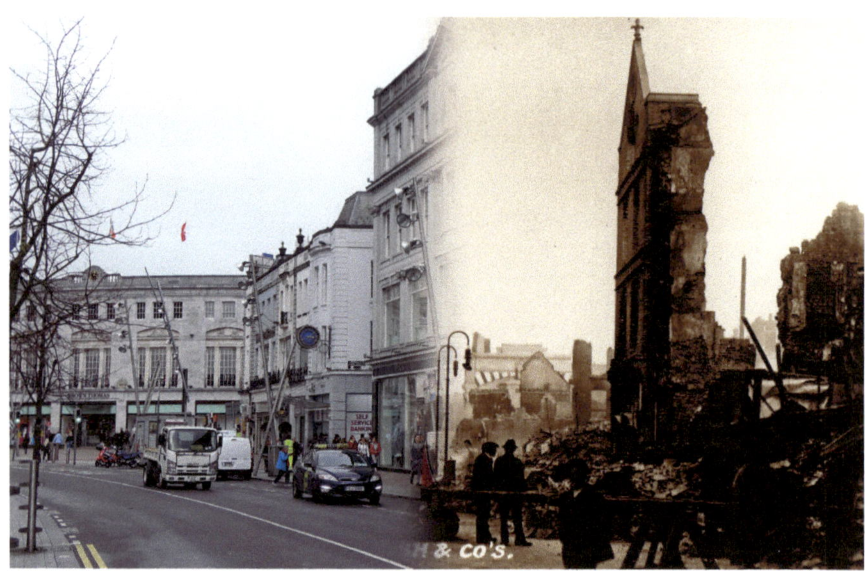

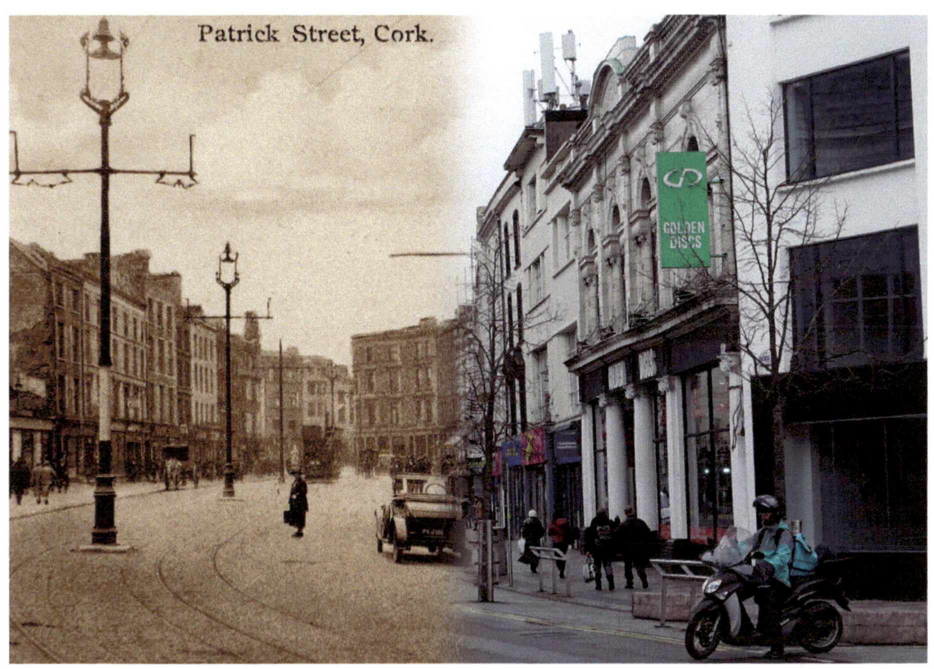

Central St Patrick's Street

In 1916, the street directories for the city reveal the businesses on the right-hand side of this old postcard (centre right upwards). These included Francis Brennan, jeweller; Denis Buckley, tobacconist; Cork Chemical & Drug Co. Ltd; Mathew Bolster, grocer; Elvery & Co.; Elephant House, waterproofers; Barry Gerald, ladies' outfitter; Miss Cashman, dress and mantle warehouses; J. English, grocer; Bernard Alcock, grocer; Liptons Market; and F. H. Thompson, confectioners.

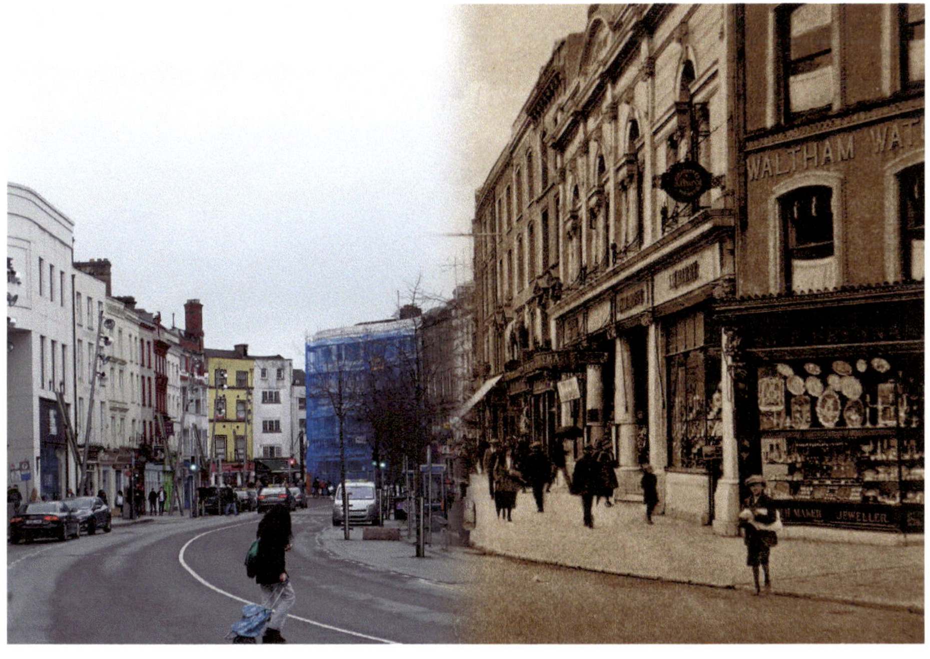

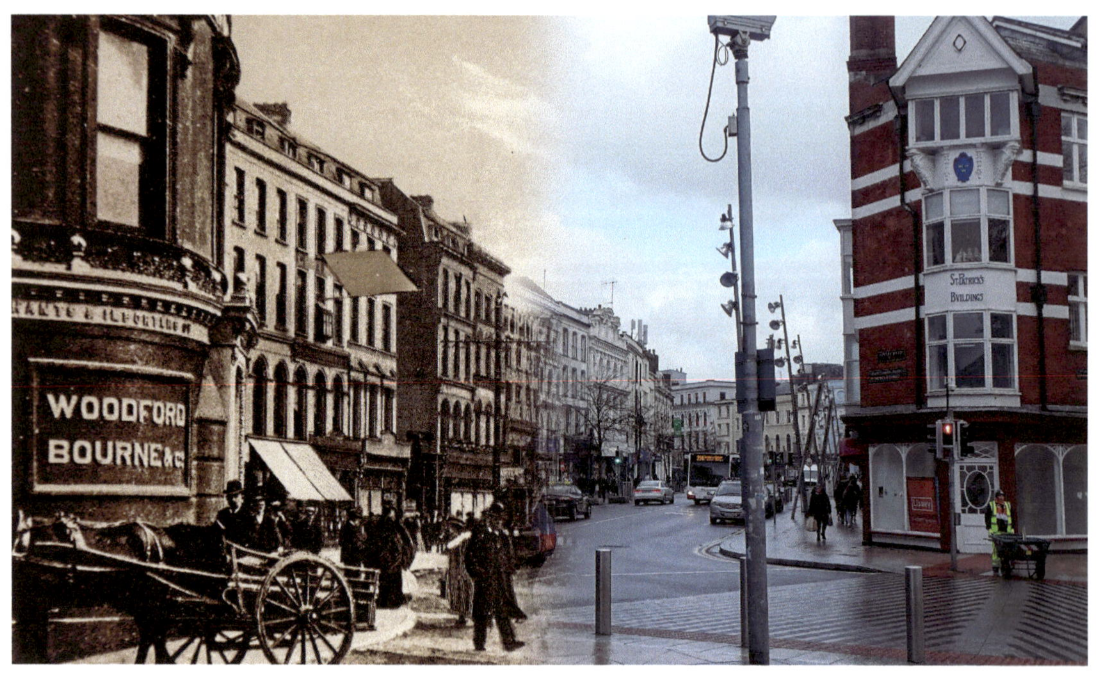

Western St Patrick's Street

The elegant St Patrick's buildings in 1911 hosted a number of prominent businesses including the Paris Photographic Studio, *Irish Times* offices and Teape's Jewellers. As in the above image Woodford Bourne and Co., grocers and wine merchants; Miss Dale's Music School; Fielding's chemists and opticians; Provincial Bank of Ireland; Guy & Co.'s wholesale paper merchants; Domestic Bazaar Company; Cole's Income Tax Office; Allen's clothier; Guy and Co.'s stationers with their associated photographic studio; and Thompson and Son's bakers and confectioners.

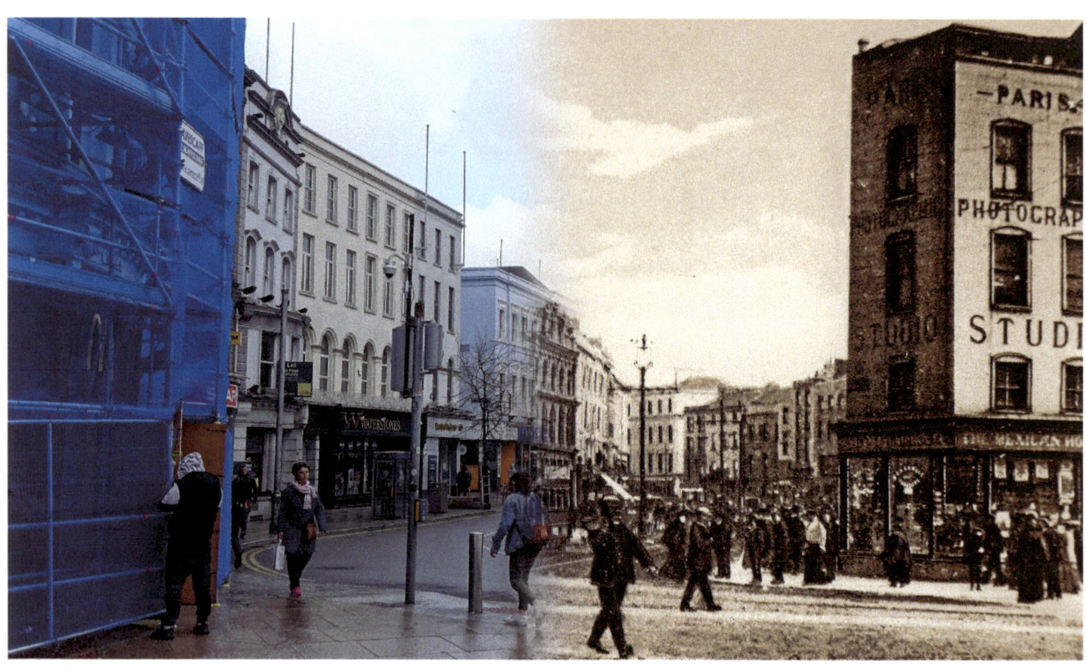

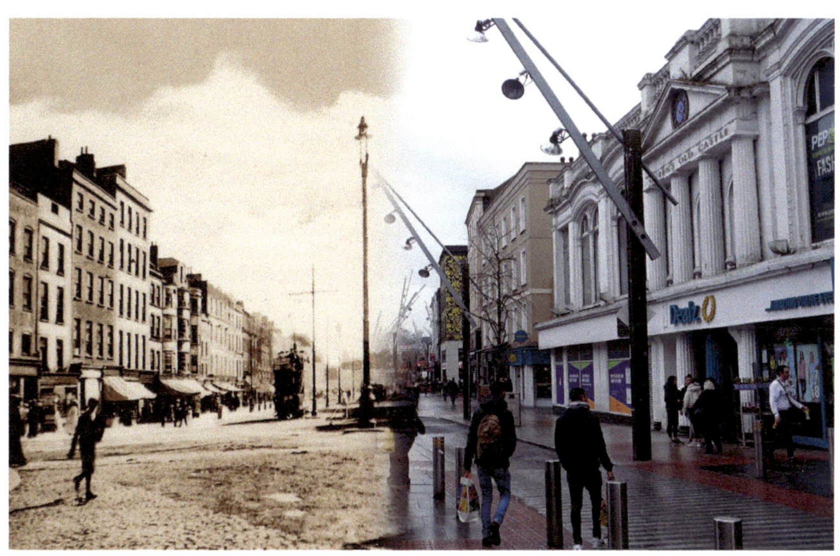

Queen's Old Castle, Daunt's Square

On the right of the below postcard. Mr William Fitzgibbon established the Queen's Old Castle company in the 1840s (following the site being used as the city's courthouse before the one on Washington Street was constructed in the 1830s). Nearby was Messrs Alexander & Co., of St Patrick Street, which was inaugurated in the 1850s under the auspices of Sir John Arnott. Mr Arnott was the pioneer in Ireland of what is designated the 'Monster Warehouse' system of trading. After some years Sir John Arnott was joined by Mr Alexander Grant, the title being then altered to Arnott & Co., with Sir John as the managing director. In 1873 Mr Victor Beare Fitzgibbon of Queen's Old Castle and Messrs. Alexander Grant and T. Lyons merged the three business into a limited liability company under the title of T. Lyons and Co. Ltd. The three businesses formed the principal members of the directorate. They established a trade, which in point of magnitude and volume, had never before been equalled in the annals of commercial enterprise in the south of Ireland. All three firms, though, continued their respective operations.

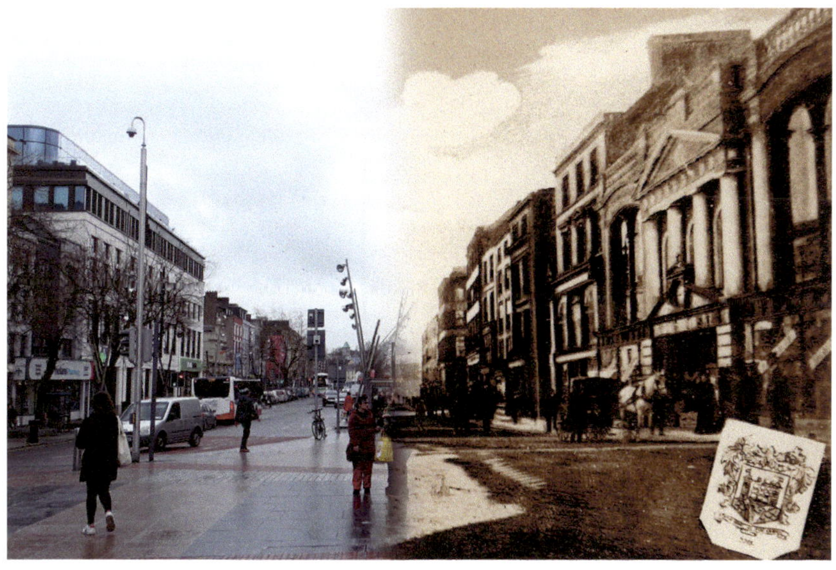

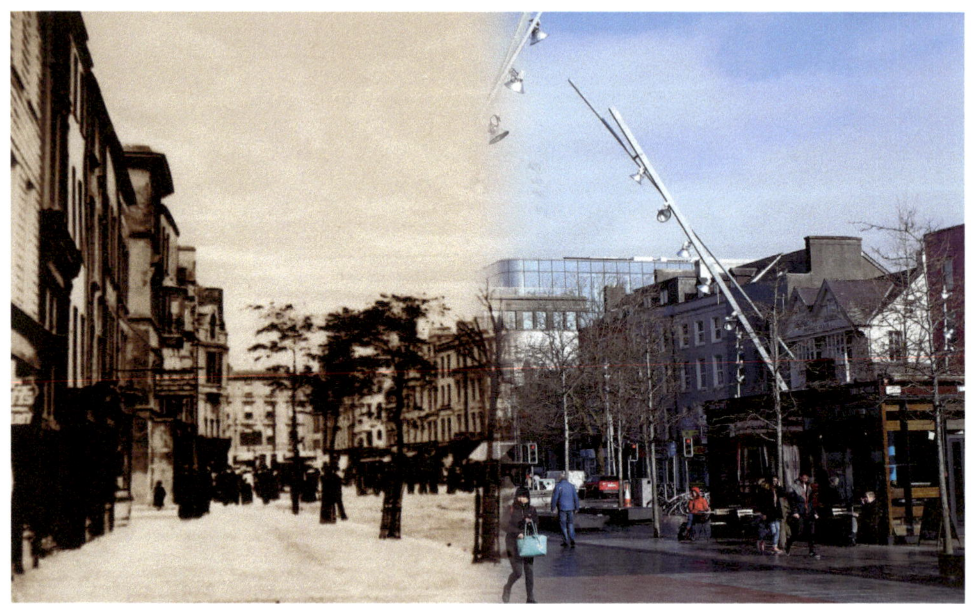

The Grand Parade

The Grand Parade was also a canal at one stage in its history, which was arched over *c.* 1780. In 1911, the businesses that extended from the corner of St Patrick's Street to the buildings on the right of the postcard included The Mexican Tobacconist, Murray's Stationers, The Central Dairy, Butterfield's Dentistry, Gabriel's Hosiery, Foley's Confectioners, Post Office, Music Supply Stores, Smith's Hosiery, Elliott's Dress Warehouse Rooms, Bollar's Baby Linen Warehouse, Munster Boot Company, Cudmore's Fruiterer, Greig's tailor and clothier, Murphy's shirt maker and hosiery, Grant's Furnishing Warehouse Rooms, Wolfe's Outfitters, Lebin's Millinery warehouse rooms, and Central Boot Stores.

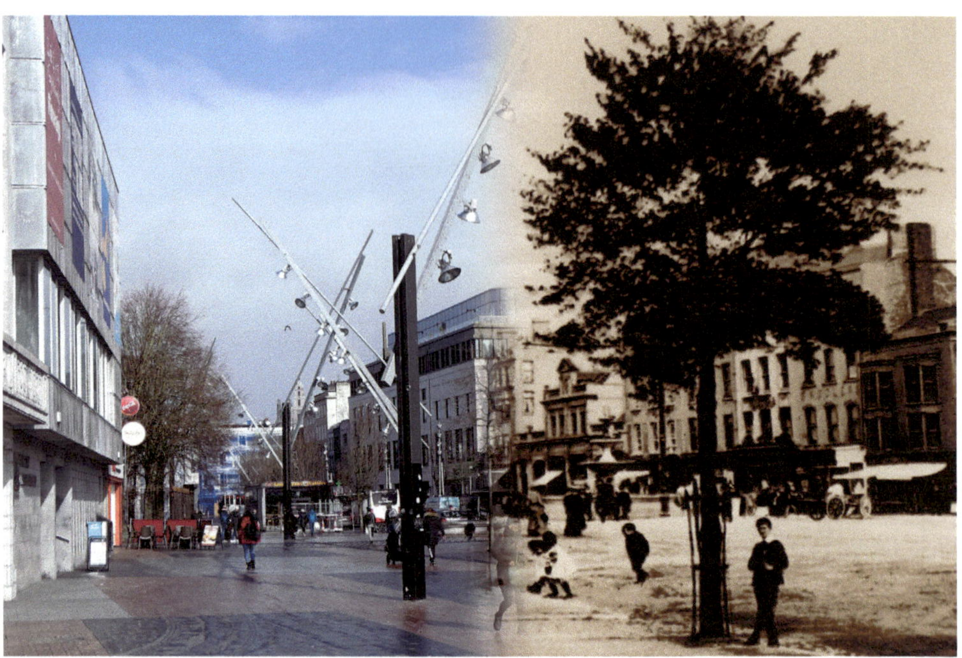

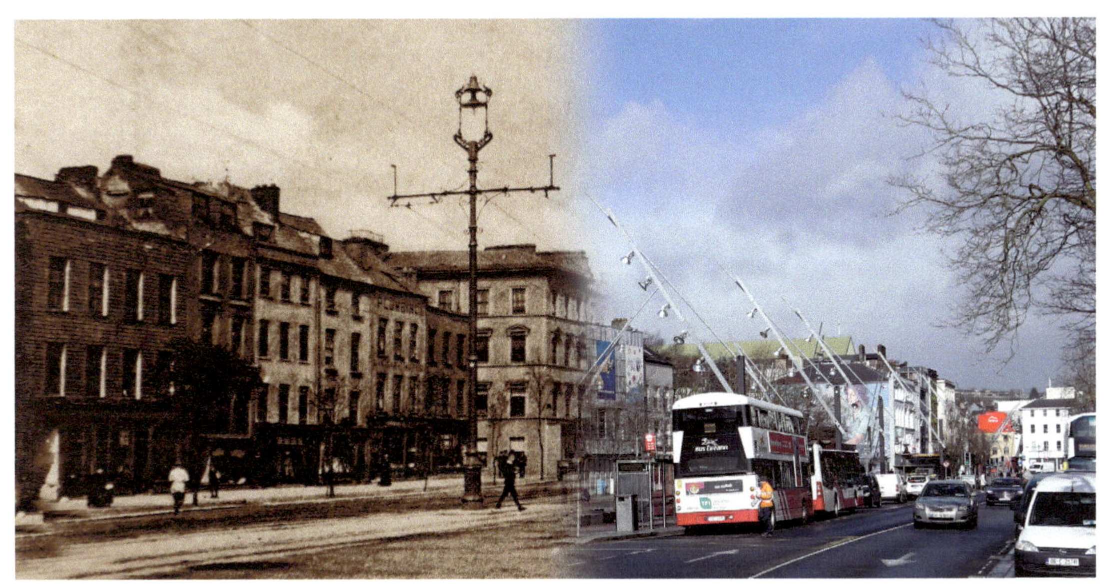

Businesses of the Grand Parade

In 1916, the street directories for the city revealed that on the left of the postcard, a variety of trades and professions were open for business. These included The Cork City Club; Dominic O'Connor, architect; Maurice Healy, solicitor; D. J. O'Leary, tuner; piano and gramophone warehouse; Public Telephone Call Office; Graham Gould, solicitor; Grand Parade Carriage Works; Mrs O'Regan, Hotel; Corker & Levis, solicitors; H. C. Charde, portrait painter; D. Flynn and Co., discount office; J. C. Flynn, insurance agent; Miss Adams, Professor of Music; D. Nunan, piano warerooms; Sealy & Co. Ltd, loan and discount offices; William Ryder Crawford, Civil Engineer; H. S. Gibbons, dental surgery; B. O'Flynn, engineer and architect; Miss Browne, costumier; Harris & Beale, oil and colour merchants; W. G. Beale, agent; The Irish United Assurance Society; F. Boylan, millinery warehouse; Cork Central Friendly Society; P. Curtis and Co., decorators; Joseph Curtis, Professor of Singing; J. Buchanan, decorator; Richard Hennessy, plumber and gas fitter; and P. J. O'Flynn & Sons, merchant tailors.

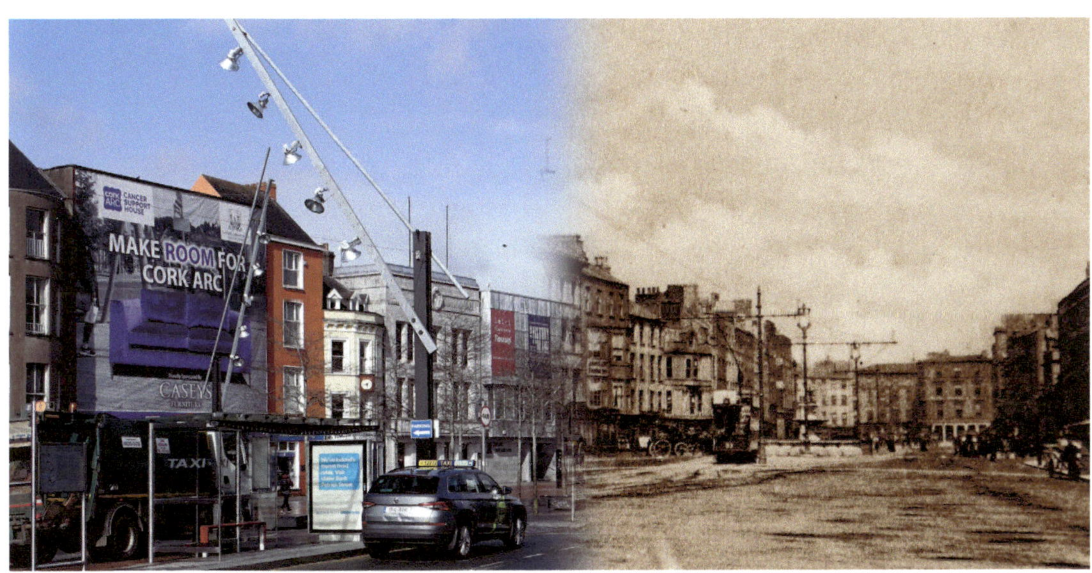

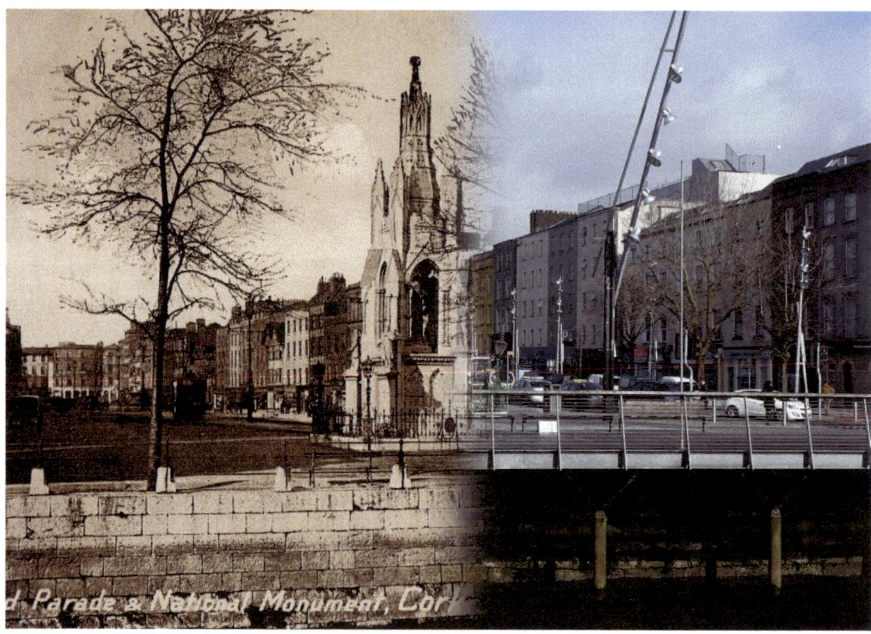

National Monument, Grand Parade

The National Monument on the Grand Parade in Cork was unveiled on St Patrick's Day 1906. The monument commemorates the rebellions of 1798, 1803, 1848 and 1867. D. J. Coakley, a well-known architect, designed the monument. John Francis Davis, a Kilkenny man, sculpted the figures of Wolfe Tone, Michael Dwyer, Thomas Davis, Peter O'Neill Crowley and 'Mother Erin'. D. J. Coakley had designed the façade of the Holy Trinity Church, and the design of the National Monument resembles the design of the church façade. The nearby Nano Nagle Bridge also remembers the leader of the Presentation Sisters who established schools for the education of the poor in late eighteenth-century Cork.

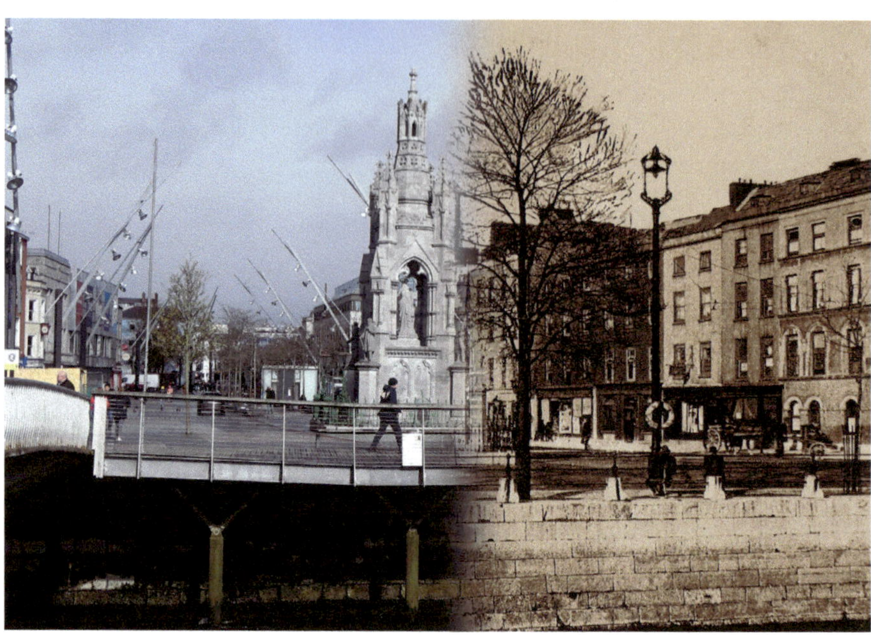

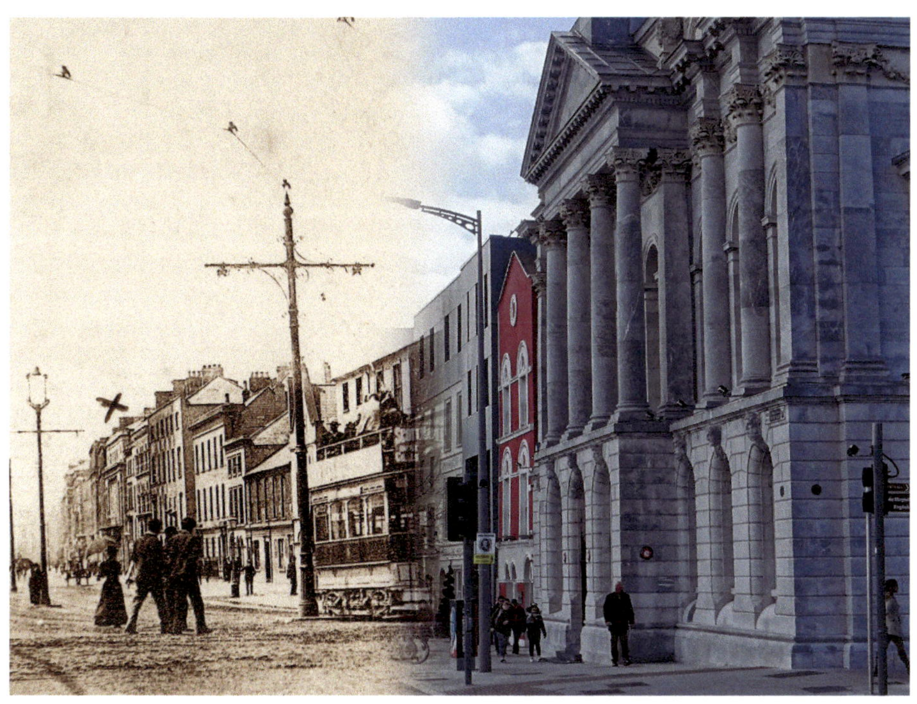

Provincial Bank, South Mall

Located on the corner of the South Mall and Parnell Place, overlooking Parnell Bridge, the Cork Provincial Bank was built between 1863 and 1865 and was acclaimed by many Corkonians on its opening in 1865 as the 'handsomest' public building in Cork. Its white limestone composition was designed by Alexander Deane, an uncle of eminent Cork architect Sir Thomas Deane, with William J. Murray the architect.

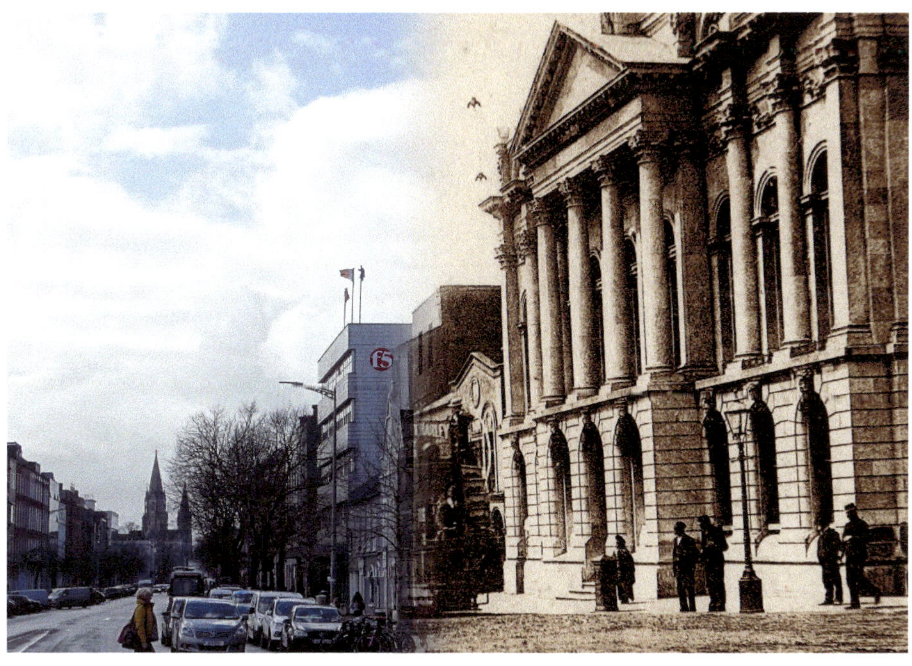

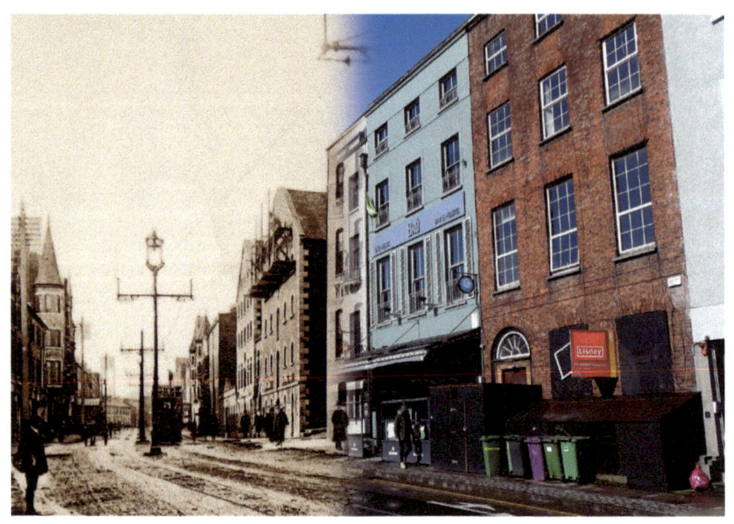

King Street/MacCurtain Street

Formerly known as King Street, the street was a small routeway out of the city in the eighteenth century but was substantially widened and realigned by 1840. The King family was a key on the street. The street was renamed MacCurtain Street in April 1920. During the Irish War of Independence the city's uncompromising stance was epitomized by two men: Tomás MacCurtain and Terence MacSwiney. MacCurtain was born in Ballyknockane, Mallow, County Cork. His passion for Irish culture led him to join the Cork-Blackpool branch of the Gaelic League in 1901. In 1907, MacCurtain contributed to the national council of Sinn Féin and in the same year he became a member of the Irish Republican Brotherhood. He enlisted as an Irish Volunteer in late 1913 and was periodically imprisoned in various English jails, such as Reading, Wakefield and Frongoch. In January 1920 he was elected Sinn Féin Councillor for the electoral area of Cork North West, and on 30 January 1920, he became Lord Mayor of Cork. He was made commander of the Irish Republican Army (IRA) Cork Brigade. Early on the morning of 20 March 1920, Lord Mayor Tomás MacCurtain was murdered at his home as a reprisal for his involvement in IRA activity.

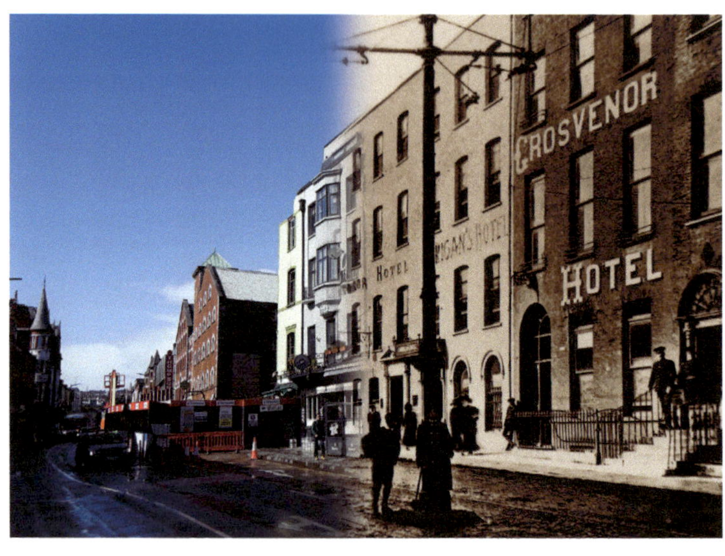

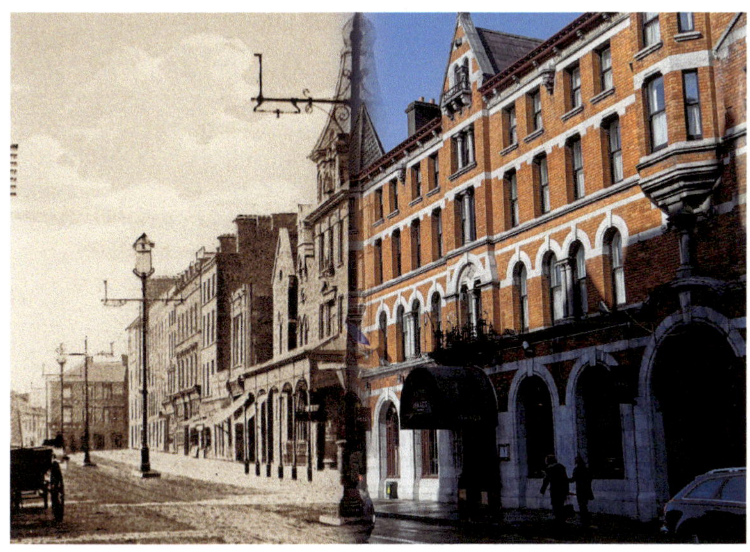

Dobbin, Ogilvie and Company

The business Messrs Dobbin, Ogilvie and Company, which was established in the year 1855, was a successful enterprise on the South Mall and on Princes Street. In 1877, newly erected buildings, known as the Hibernia Buildings (on the right), on King street were occupied, and trade was further developed. The main or centre structure contained the counting-house and the general warehouse, in which all kinds of merchandise was stored. Brandies, whiskeys, oils, chandlery and other inflammable materials were among the goods that filled this large section. At the right stood the building in which the confectionery was manufactured. The building at the left side was the one in which the important work of tobacco spinning was carried out. The tobacco factory was deemed to be fitted with 'machinery of a very expensive and elaborate character'. Following a fire in 1883, some of the building was remodelled by Henry Arthur Hill and was known for its cupola atop it. One hundred years ago, the company, in addition to its general business and tobacco manufacture, was engaged in the army canteen trade on a very considerable scale. The firm went into voluntary liquidation in April 1926. The site now hosts Isaac's Restaurant and Hotel.

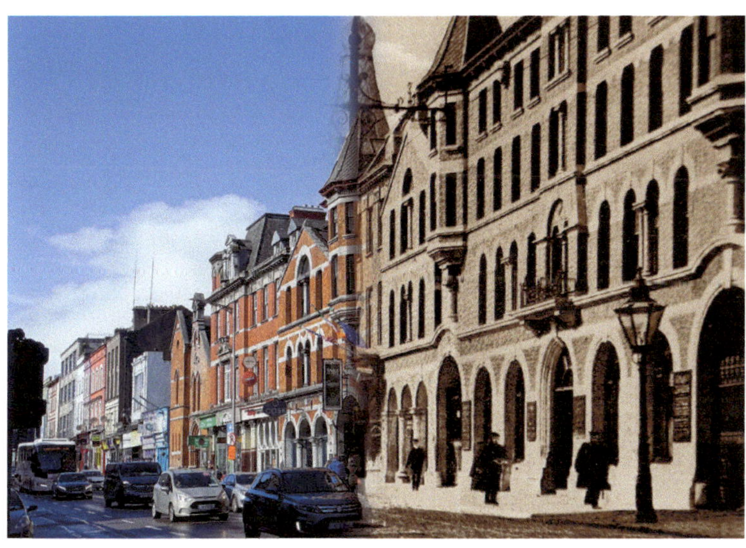

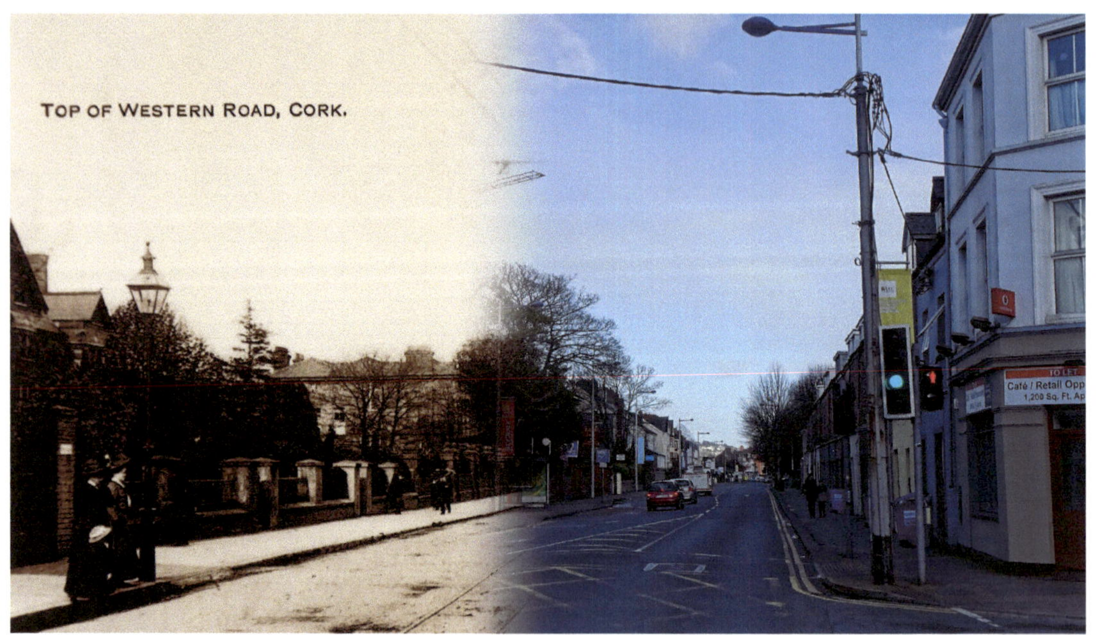

Western Road

Work on a new road, known as the Western Road, commenced in 1821 and it was completed by 1831. It joined Great George's Street and a new bridge named Brunswick Bridge (now O'Neill Crowley Bridge), which spanned the southern channel of the River Lee. The bridge, designed by brothers James and George Richard Pain, has three segmental arches. In 1825, the Western Road was extended across part of the Mardyke to the north channel of the River Lee. Another arched stone bridge was built there in 1826, designed by Richard Griffith and the Pain Brothers. It was known as Wellington Bridge, later renamed Thomas Davis Bridge. Mallow-born Thomas Davis (1814–45) was a Cork poet, journalist and promoter of Irish culture.

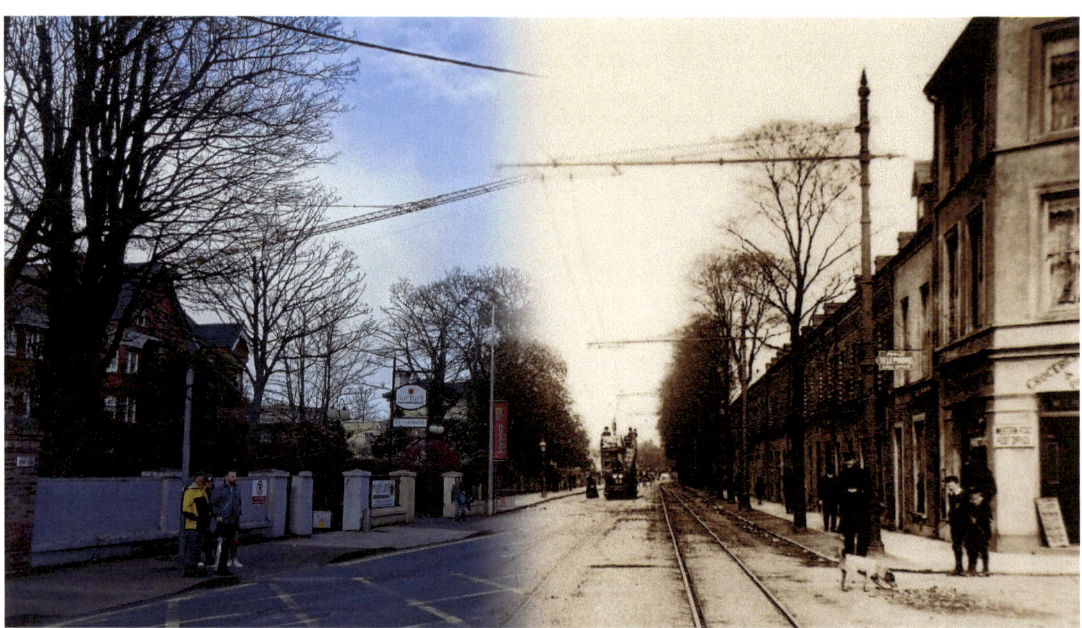

Religious Spaces – A City of Religion

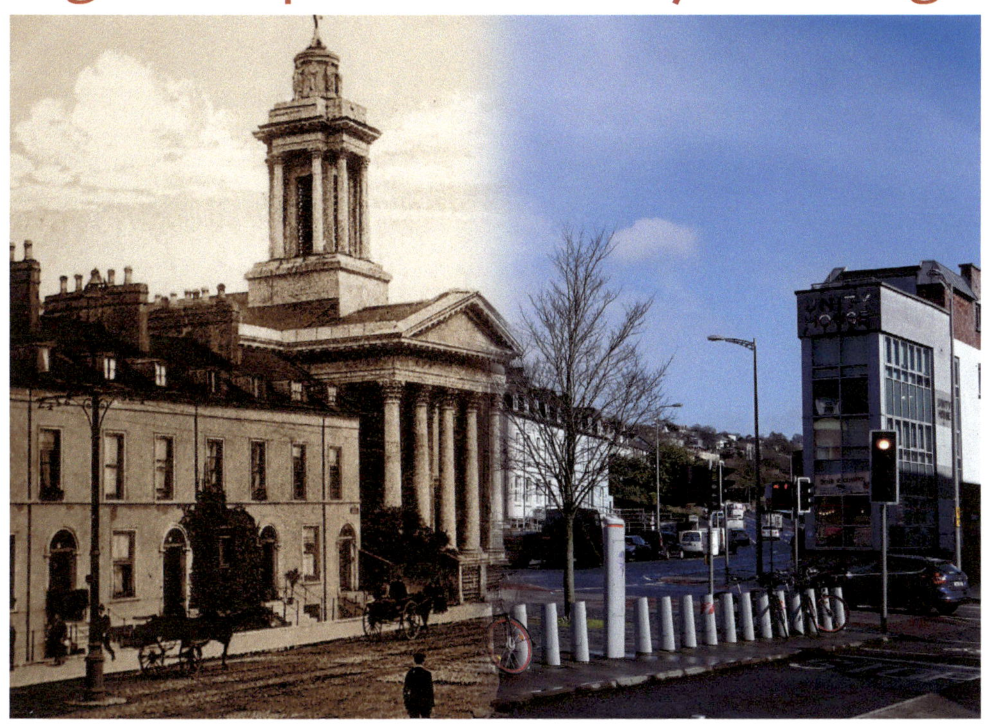

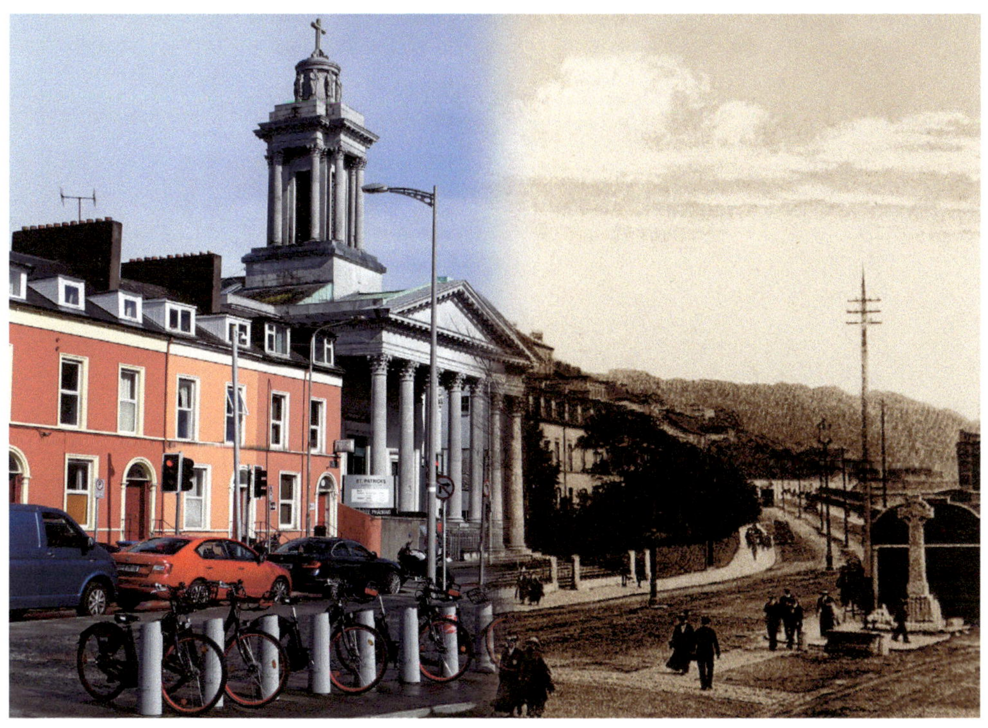

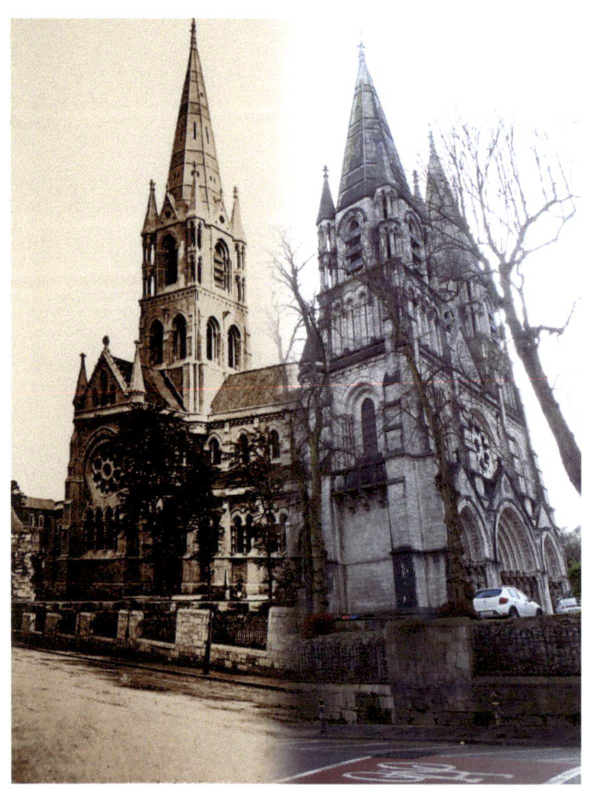

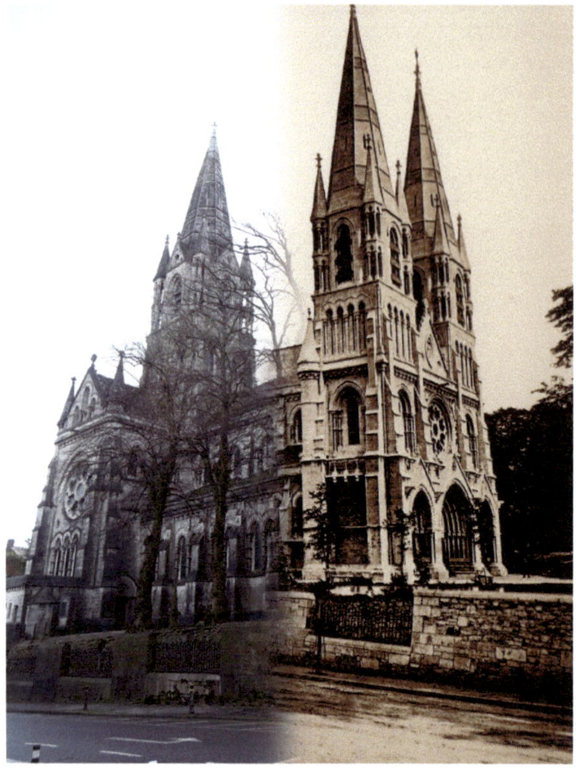

St Fin Barre's Cathedral

The cathedral's foundation stone was laid in 1865 to make way for, in the words of the bishop of Cork at the time, 'a structure more worthy of the name, Cork Cathedral'. The unanimous choice out of sixty-eight entrants from Ireland, Britain and the Continent was Londoner William Burges for the design inscribed 'Non Mortuus Sed Virescrit', which means 'He is not dead but flourishing'. The large rose-type stained-glass windows provide a colourful array of light inside the church. The great piers, which support the roof, are of grey-brown Stourton stone. The reddish columns are of Cork red marble. The Golden Angel on the exterior was Burges' gift to the cathedral.

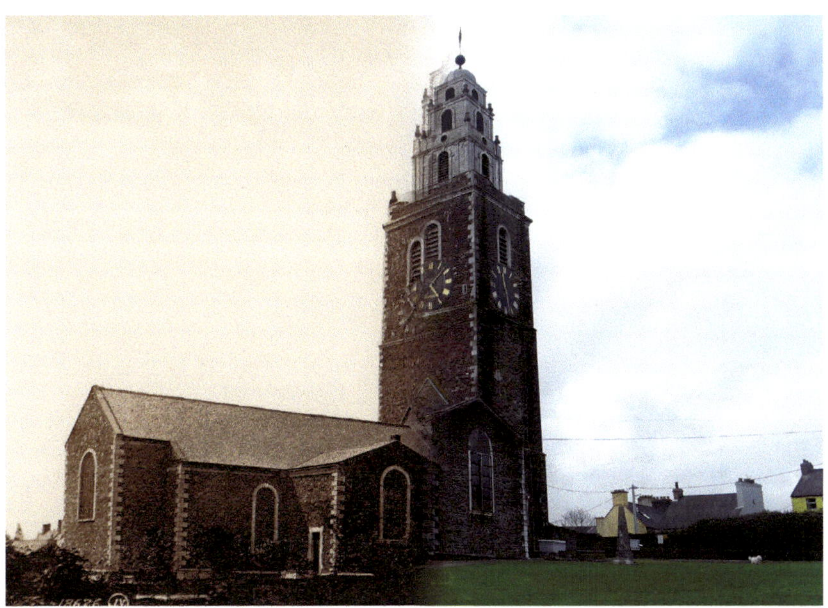

St Anne's Church, Shandon

The name Shandon comes from the Irish word '*Sean Dún*', which means 'old fort', and is said to mark the ringfort of the Irish family MacCarthaigh who lived in the area around AD 1,000. St Anne's Church, Shandon, was built in 1722. In 1750, the firm of Abel Rudhall in Gloucester cast the famous bells of Shandon. Inscriptions can be found on the bells, which contain messages of joy and death. The peculiar feature of the tall church tower approximately 40 metres in height is that the north and east sides are comprised of red sandstone while the south and west sides are composed of grey-hewn limestone. The giant gilded fish sculpture/weathervane, 4 to 5 metres in length, symbolises salmon fishing. The clock of Shandon with its four white faces was installed by Cork Corporation in 1847. It was made by James Mangan, a successful Cork clockmaker.

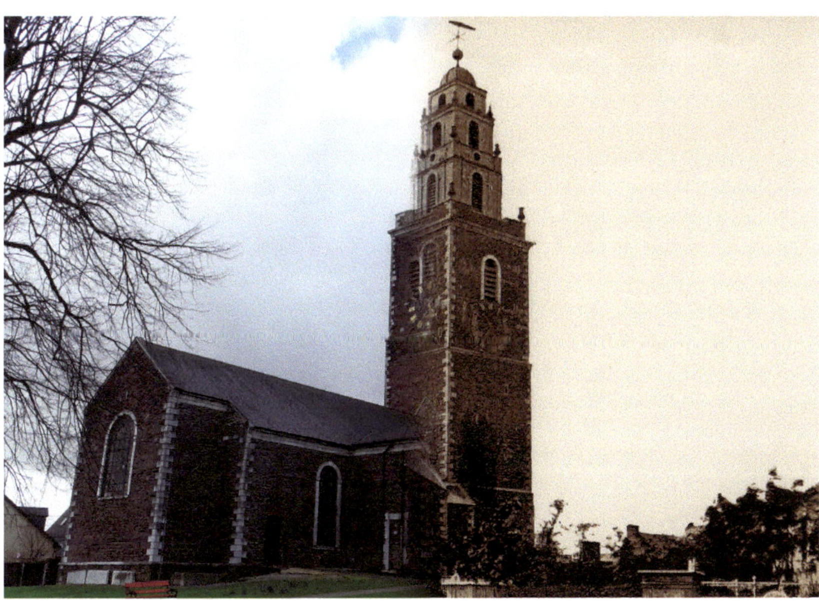

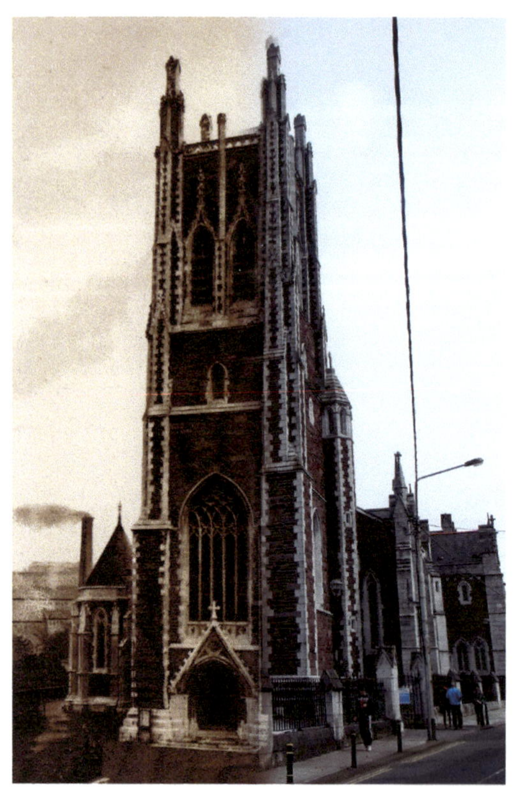

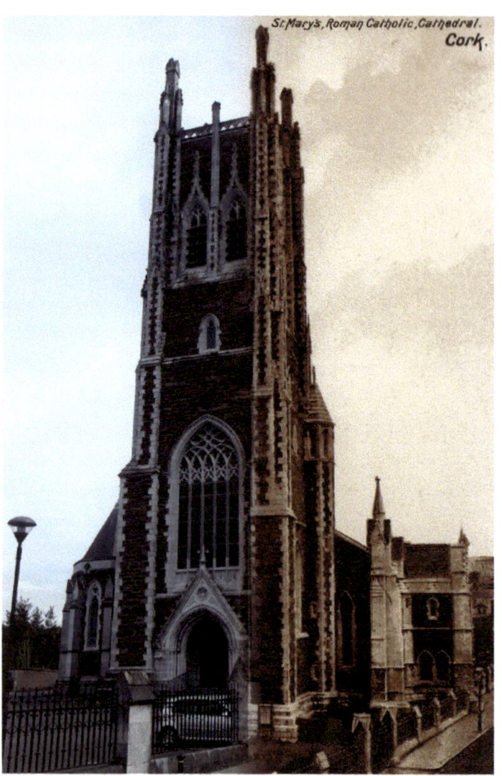

St Mary's and Anne's Cathedral

The present Catholic Cathedral of St Mary and Anne is the fifth church on the site since the early 1600s (1624, 1700, 1730, and 1808). In 1820, an immense fire greatly damaged the fourth cathedral so much so that it was really the skeleton structure of the burned cathedral that survived. However, all were not lost and shortly after, the Roman Catholic bishop of that time, John Murphy, delegated to architect George Pain the rebuilding of the then twelve-year-old cathedral, inside and outside. George Pain was also responsible for the design of Cork buildings such as Holy Trinity Church, St Patrick's Church and Blackrock Castle.

St Mary's Dominican Church, Pope's Quay

In 1697, penal laws restricted open Catholic worship. The Dominicans, who were based at Crosses Green, moved to a laneway (unknown today) off Shandon Street and established a smaller religious building for their community of over fifty priests. It was here in the early 1800s that a Dominican named Father Bartholomew Thomas Russell first came up with the idea of building St Mary's Church on Pope's Quay, an open site available for redevelopment. Architect Kearns Deane adopted a neoclassical design in compliance with the Grecian Ionic style of architecture. The foundation stone was laid in November 1832. One of the most impressive features overshadowing the sanctuary area is the *baldacchino* or canopy, which was erected in 1872.

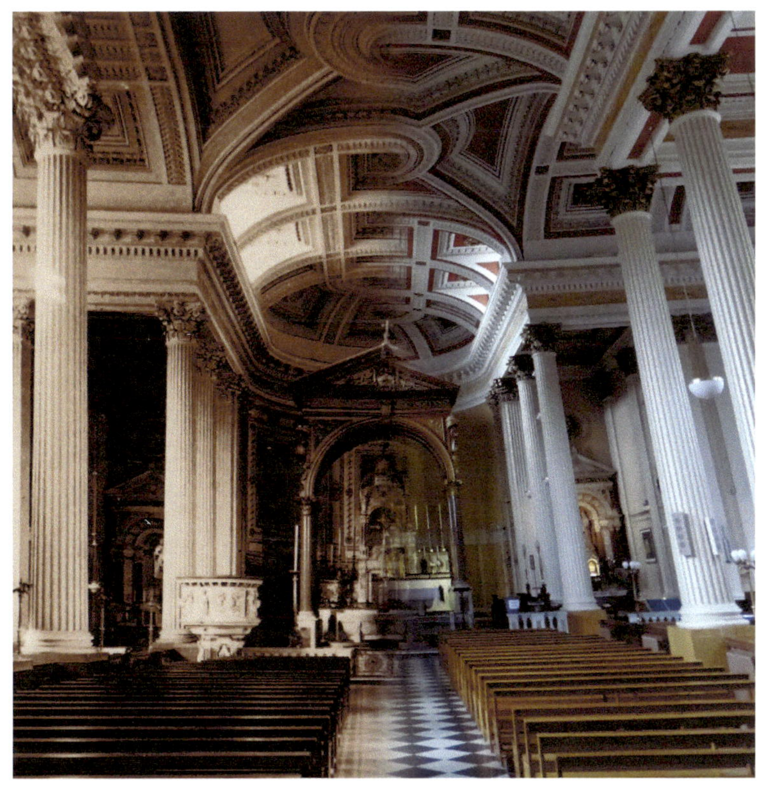

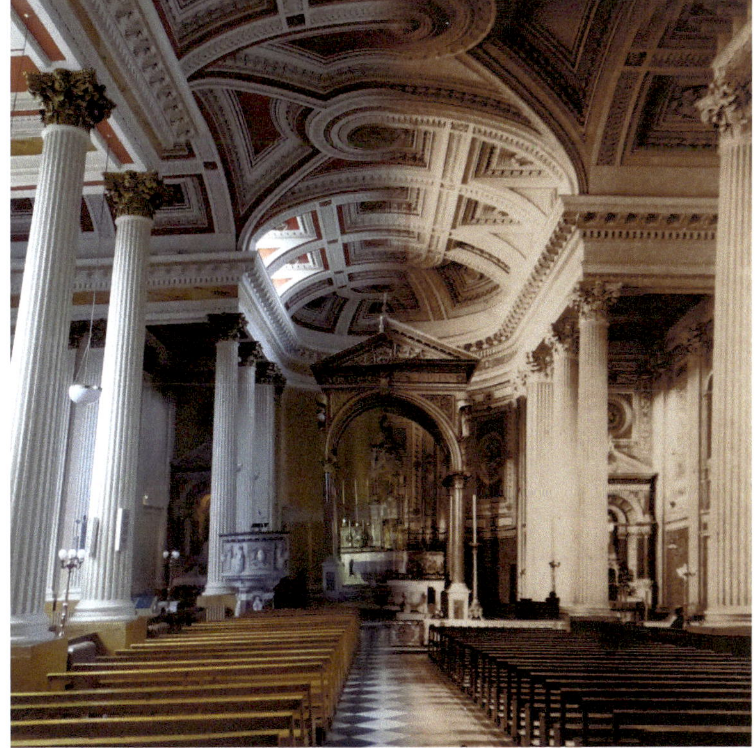

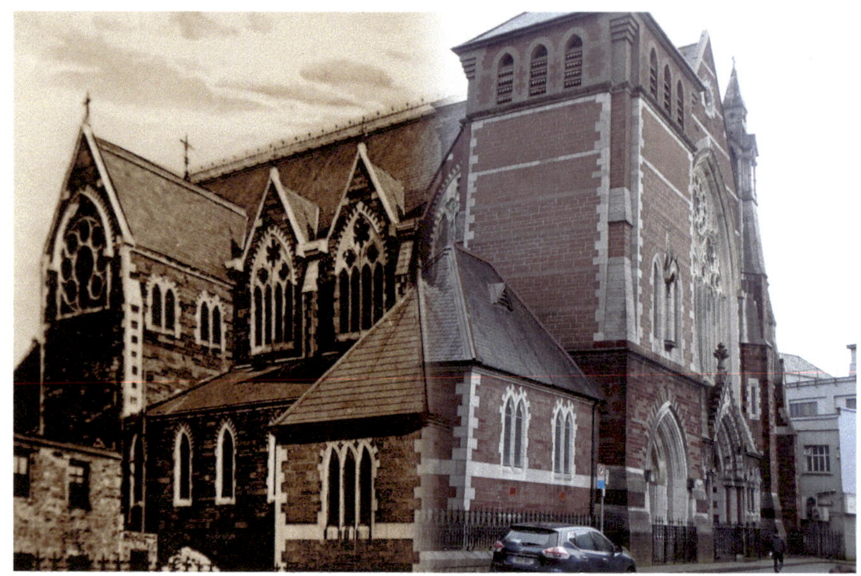

St Peter's and Paul's Church

In the late 1850s, a project began to replace the Catholic Mass House in the parish of St Peter and Paul's. The older church was known as Carey's Lane Chapel and was erected in 1786. Some of the old church structure was used in the building of the present sacristy. Edward Welby Pugin was selected as the outright architect in an architectural competition. At the age of twenty-seven, this was a major commission to receive. However, it should be said that the spire and a small tower of Pugin's design were taken out due to the proposed cost of constructing such features. The idea of a spire was replaced by a small turret. Work on the cathedral got underway straight away under the watchful eye of parish priest Father John Murphy and on 15 August 1859, the foundation stone was laid and was dedicated on 29 June 1866. The bases of all the interior columns are formed of black marble, obtained at the mouth of the Shannon at Foynes. Over these the plinths and columns rise, is polished red marble, which was obtained in County Cork from the locality of Churchtown.

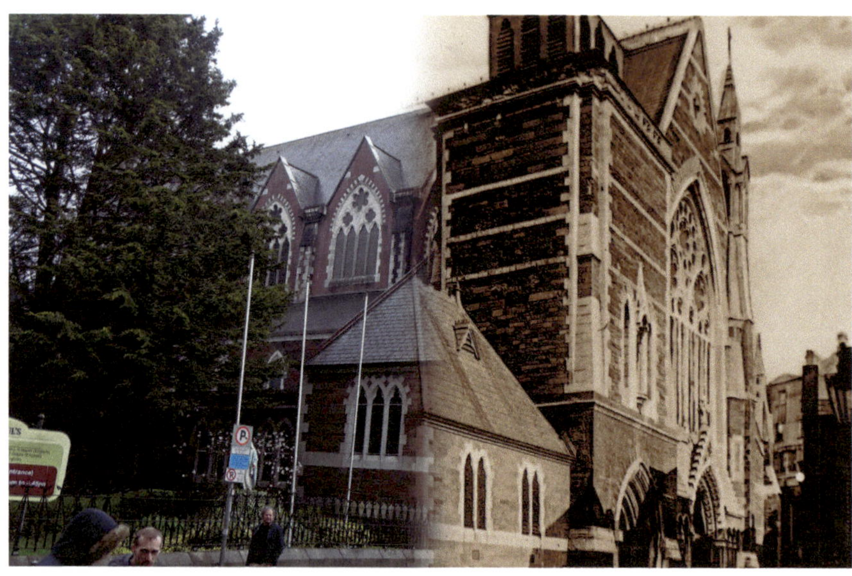

Honan Chapel

On 5 November 1916, the amazing architectural structure of St Finbarr's Chapel (or the Honan Chapel) at University College Cork had its official opening. It was funded through the trust fund of Isabella Honan and the architect was James F. McMullen. The chapel is based on the most famous Irish church of Hiberno Romanesque style – that of Cormac's Chapel on the Rock of Cashel. The series of stained-glass windows of the Munster Saints from the eminent studios of Harry Clarke and Sarah Purser begin on the north wall of the nave near the chancel with the window in honour of the patron saint of the diocese: St Finbarr. Then it runs to St Albert, the patron saint of Cashel, St Declan of Ardmore, St Ailbe of Emly, St Fachtna of Ross and St Munchin of Limerick. The first window on the south side is devoted to St Ita of Killeedy followed by St Colman of Cloyne, St Brendan the Navigator, St Gobnait of Ballyvourney, St Carthage of Lismore and St Flannan of Killaloe. The east window over the altar shows the Redeemer, while the three lights over the west entrance bear the three great Irish saints Patrick, Brigid and Colmcille.

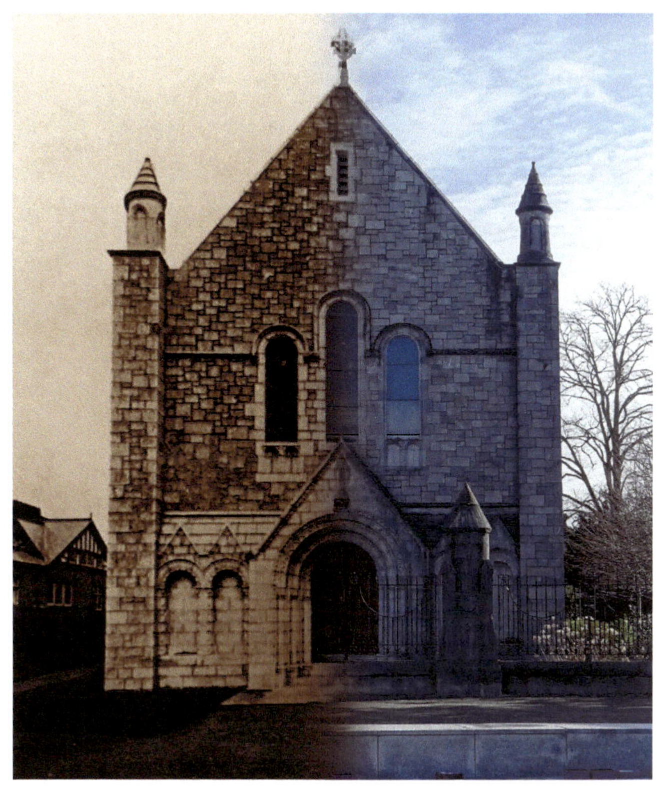

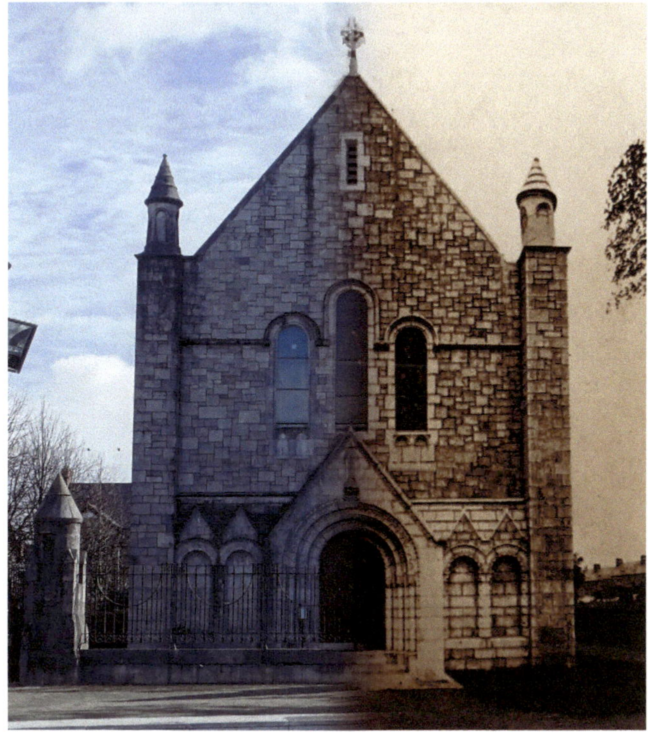

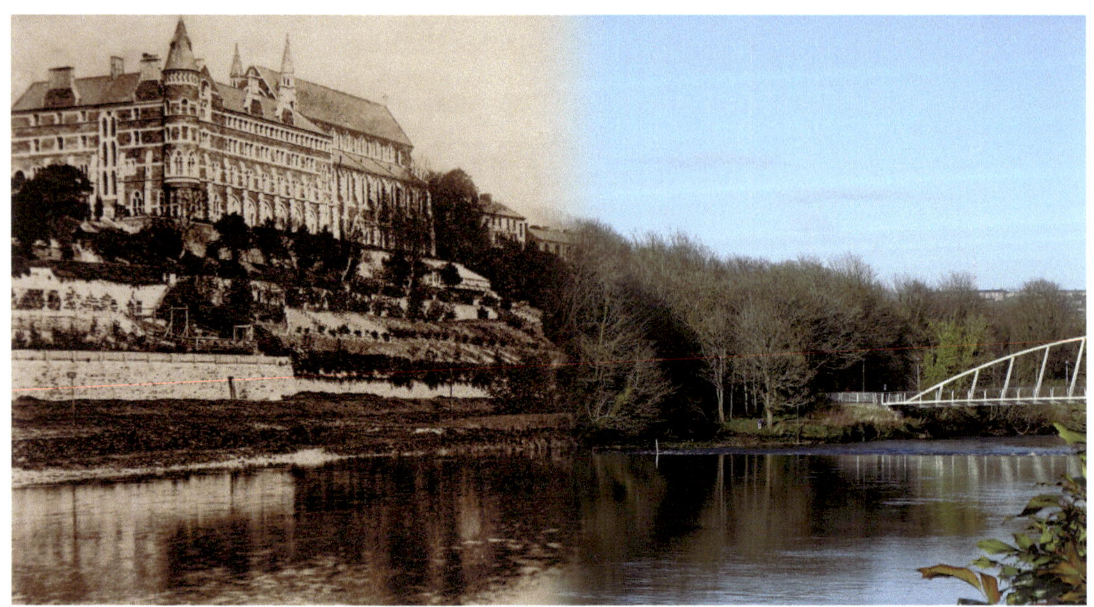

St Vincent's Church

The beautiful St Vincent's Church was designed by Sir John Benson. Its style is early Gothic and it is built mainly of red sandstone. It is built on a rocky outcrop of Sunday's Well. The site on which it is built was donated by Miss Mary MacSwiney, who was a resident of the area. The foundation stone was laid on 24 October 1851 by the Bishop of Cork, William Delaney. After much of the stonework had been completed and the church was partially roofed, disaster struck on 4 November 1853 when a severe storm destroyed the roof and blew down much of the stonework. The event created widespread sympathy, and donations for rebuilding the church were made from many Irish dioceses and private individuals. On 20 July 1856 the solemn dedication of the completed church took place. St Vincent's Church was consecrated on 14 October 1906.

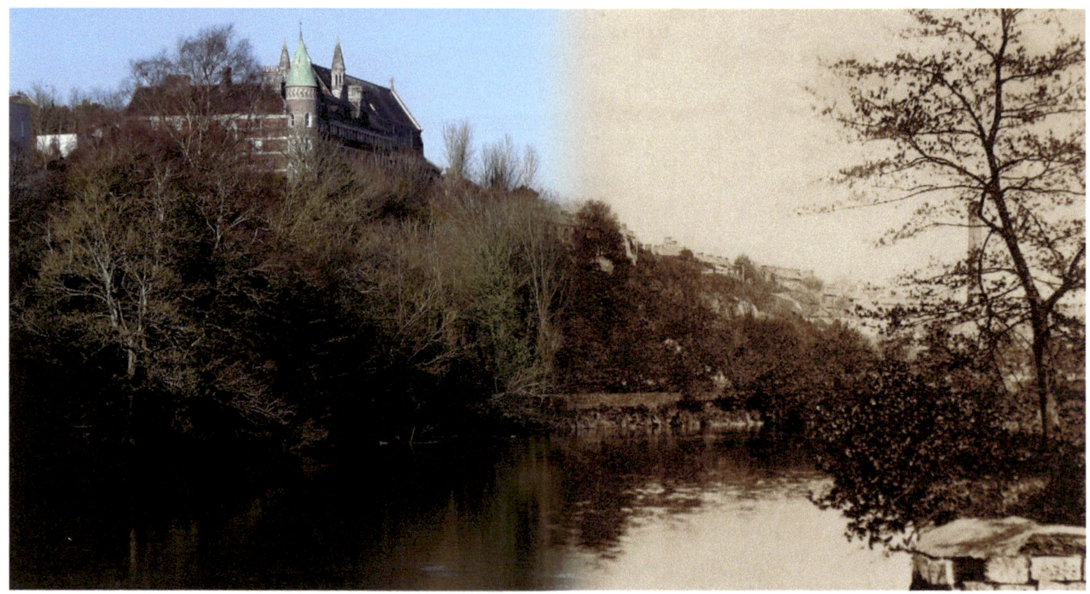

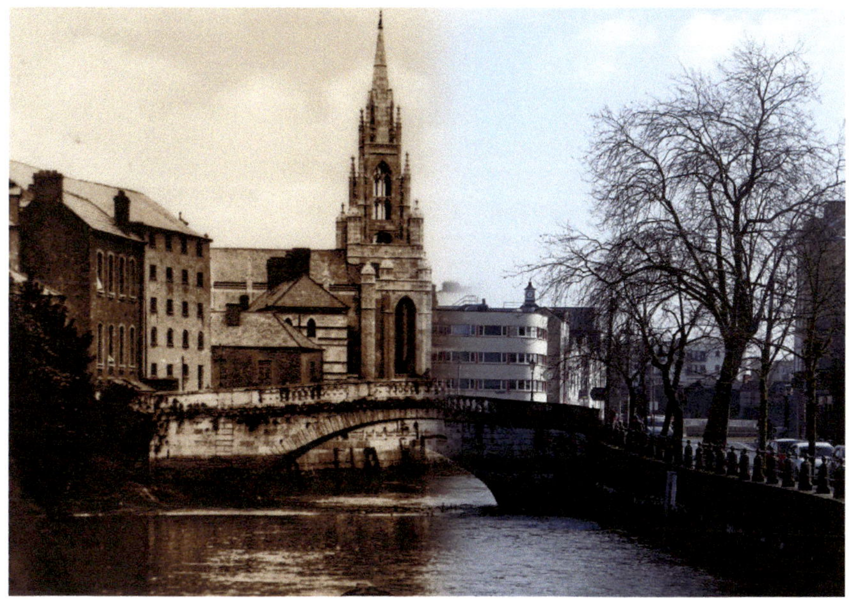

Holy Trinity Church

Although the Capuchins arrived in Cork as early as 1637, it was many years before they settled in the foundation which we now know as Holy Trinity Church and Friary. Their earliest recorded appearance is in the southern side of the city, just outside the 'South Gate'. Near the busy shipping centre of the southern channel Father Theobald Mathew selected a site for his church. The foundation stone was laid on 10 October 1832, but the church was not opened for public service until eighteen years later (10 October 1850). Shortly after the Great Famine, Cork Corporation decided to pledge an ample sum of money to a memorial for Irish MP Daniel O'Connell. The memorial in question is the absorbing stained-glass window behind the altar in the present-day church. The spire was added in 1891 to mark the centenary celebration of the birth of Father Mathew.

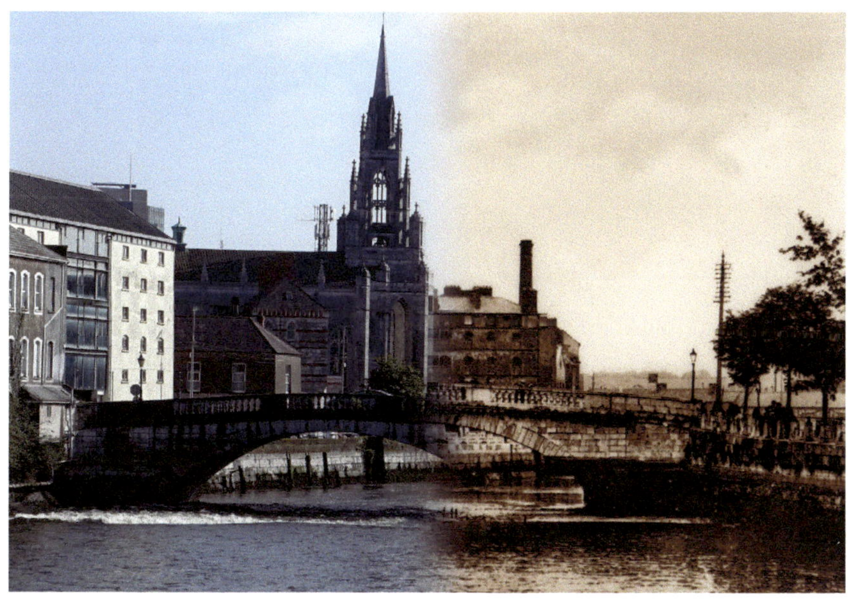

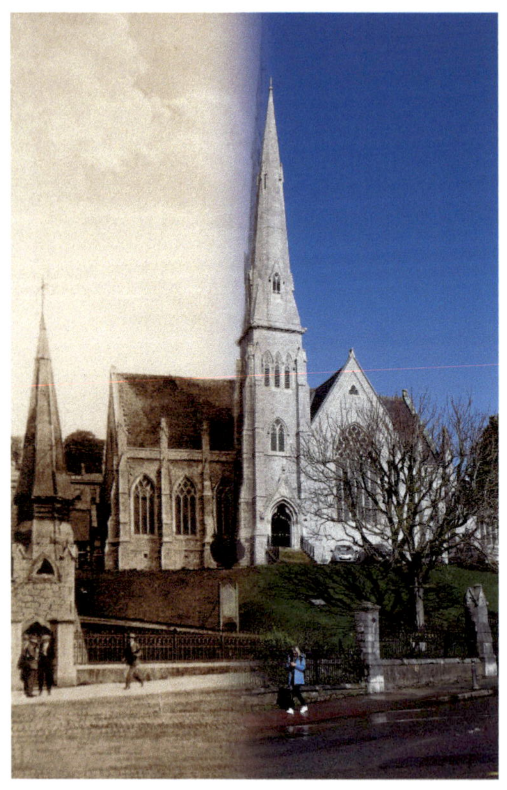

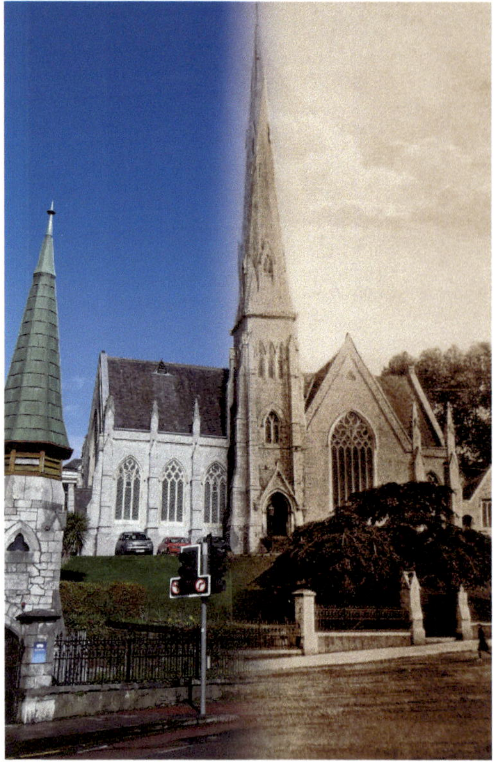

Trinity Presbyterian Church

In 1831, it is recorded in the minute book of Trinity Presbyterian Church that a number of Cork Presbyterians of Scottish ancestry wished that a new church be built, to hold their congregation and which would obey the doctrine and government of the Church of Scotland. In 1832, this congregation first met in a house in Tuckey Street. This set-up was to be short-lived as in 1841 a new church was built on Queen Street – present-day Father Mathew Street (adjacent to Holy Trinity Church). This building was known as the 'Scot's Church'. An increase in the population in the mid-nineteenth century in the city led to further interest in this religion, the result being that because of an increase in the congregation, a vote was taken that another new Presbyterian church would have to be built. On 28 July 1861, Trinity Presbyterian Church was opened at the foot of Summerhill. The architect was Englishman Mr Colin Tarring, who was responsible for many nonconformist church buildings in England. He was complimented at the time for his fine decision to combine the native limestone with his own native stone, Portland stone and Bath stone.

Transport – The Connecting City

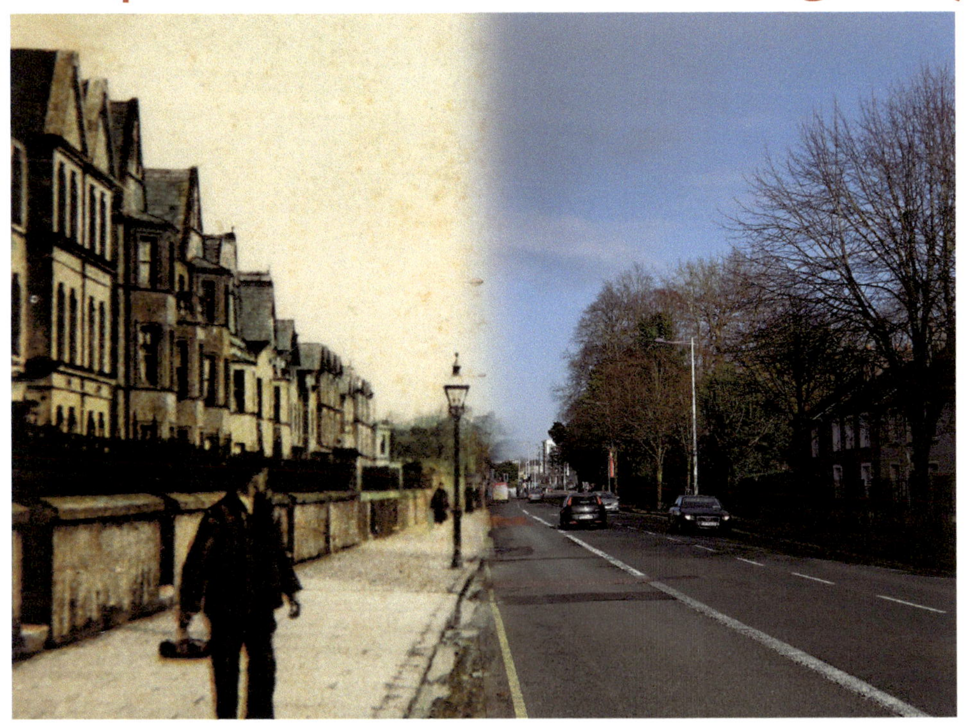

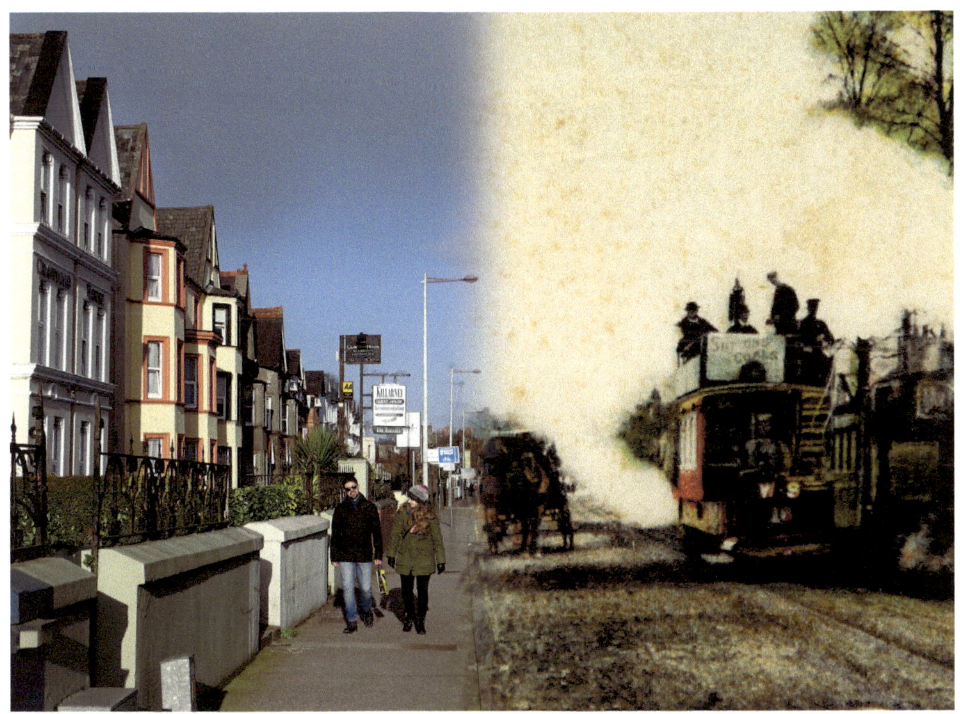

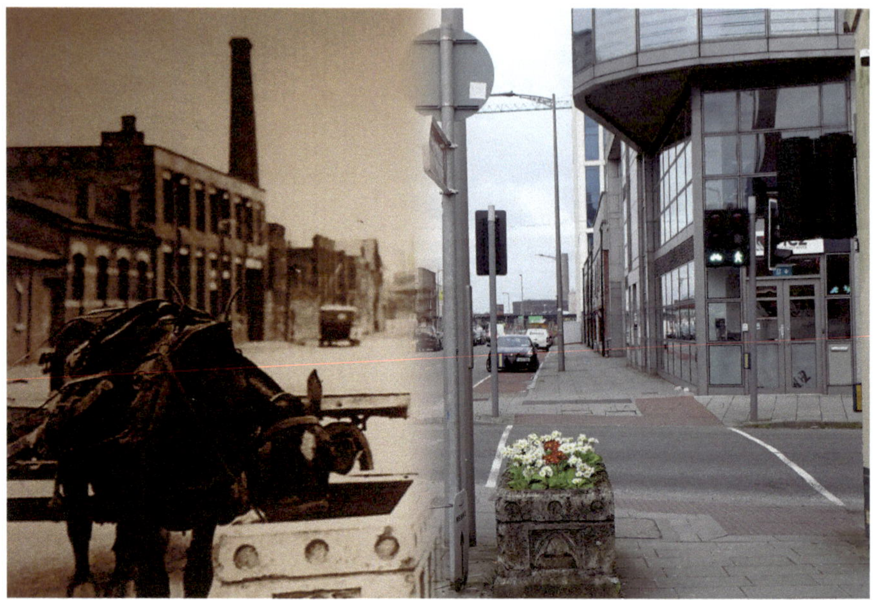

Horses and Troughs

Scattered across the centre of Cork City today are the remains of horse troughs. Many of them have become flower beds for Cork City Council, as seen in the image above, which is located on MacCurtain Street. Horses were an important aspect of city life. Farmers and market gardeners who traded their produce in the city used their horse and carts. In addition, according to the 1911 street directory of Cork City, there was an efficient service of hackney carriages plying for hire. All these vehicles were licensed and their fares set by the Hackney Carriages Committee of Cork Corporation, which controlled all matters relating to public traffic. In addition to the Outside Car (jaunting car), there was the Inside Car (jingle), the latter being a 'peculiar' vehicle to Cork.

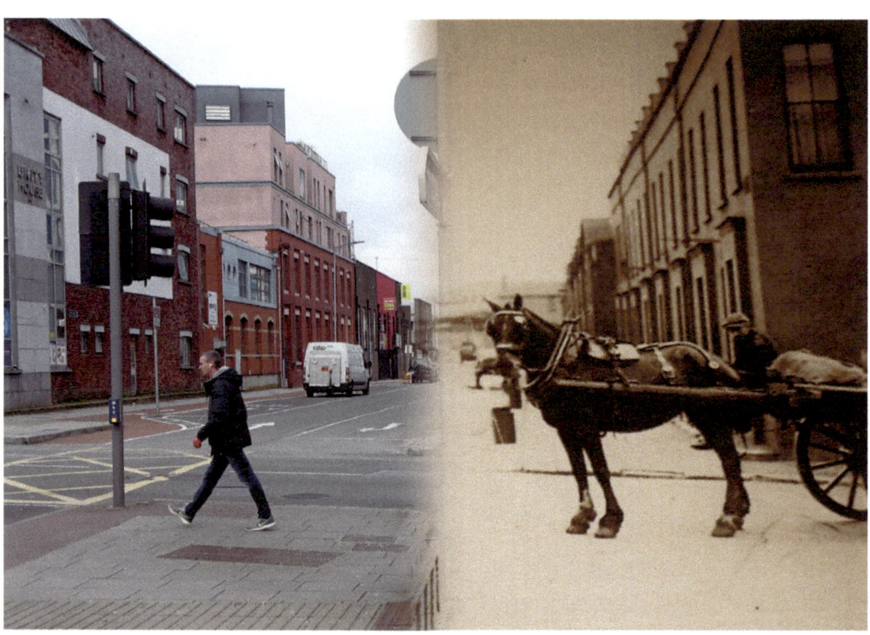

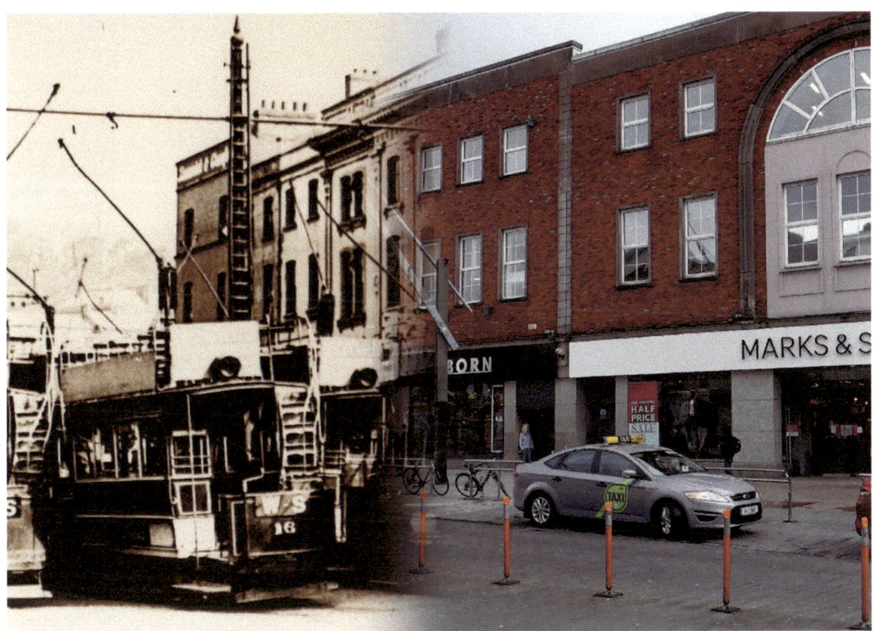

Trams, St Patrick's Street

In the closing years of the nineteenth century, Cork Corporation planned to establish a large electricity generating plant. The plant would provide public lighting and operate an electric tramcar service extending from Mangan's Clock, St Patrick's Street, to all of the popular suburbs. Eighteen tramcars arrived in 1898 for the opening, which occurred on 22 December. Cork was to become the eleventh city in Britain and Ireland to have operating electric trams. Four of the six suburban routes were complete for the line's commencement. Time on the street was given by James Mangan's Clock, which still operates (established in 1891).

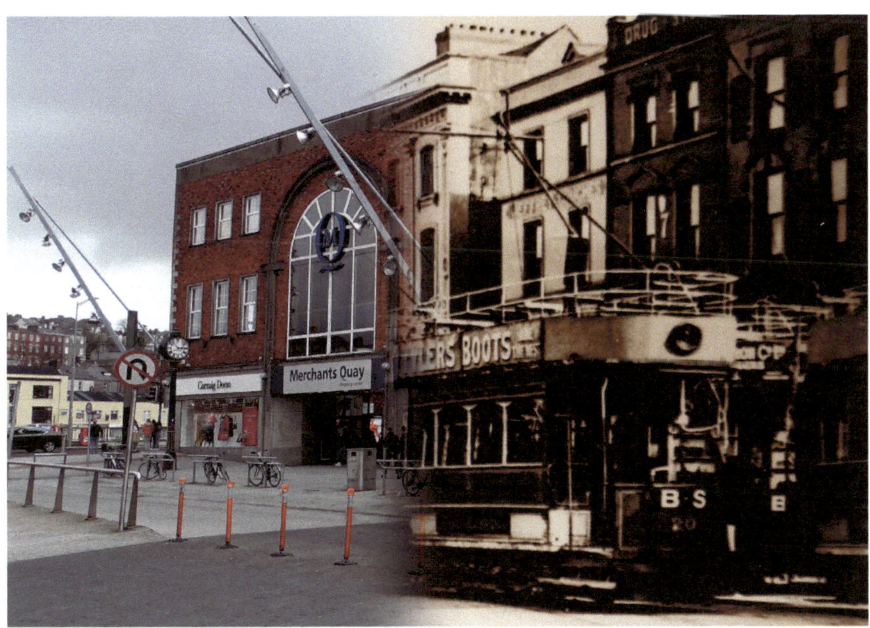

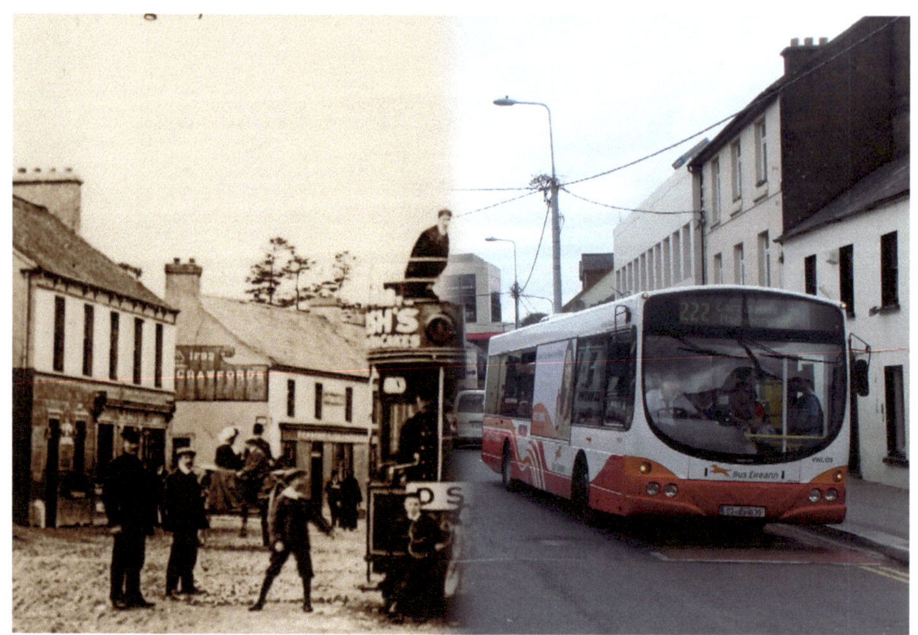

Suburban Trams

The termini included Sunday's Well, Blackpool, St Luke's Cross, Tivoli, Blackrock and Douglas. The supply of electricity to the city was in the hands of the Cork Electric Tramways and Lighting Co. Ltd, which started operations in 1898. The Power House was situated at Albert Road, and also housed the trams at night. The connections to the company's mains for lighting purposes at the end of 1916 were equivalent to 102,000 eight-candle power lamps. The electricity supply was 'direct' in nature and generated 500 volts to operate the trams that ran through the city's streets. The power station is now the National Sculpture Factory.

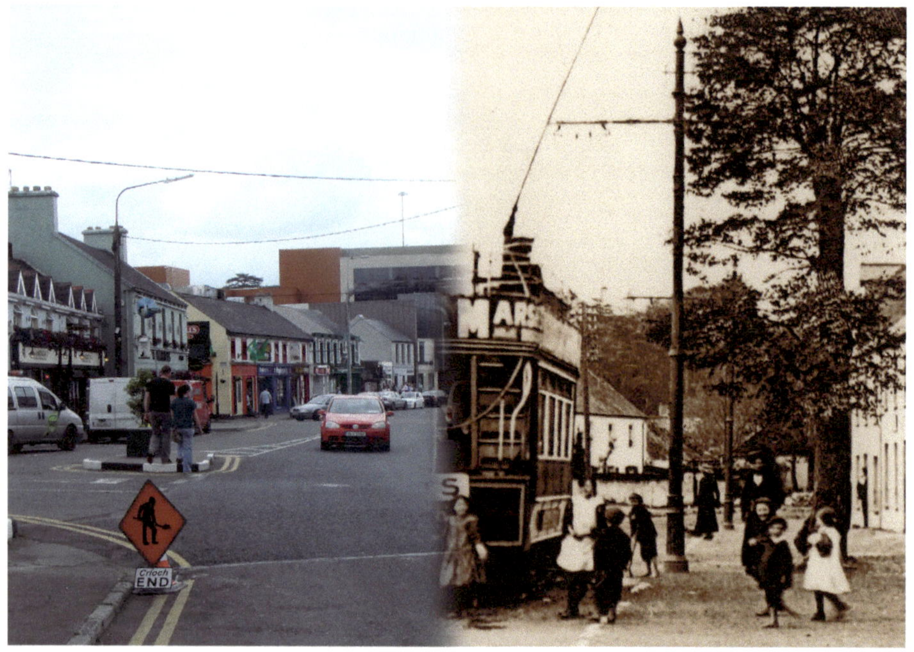

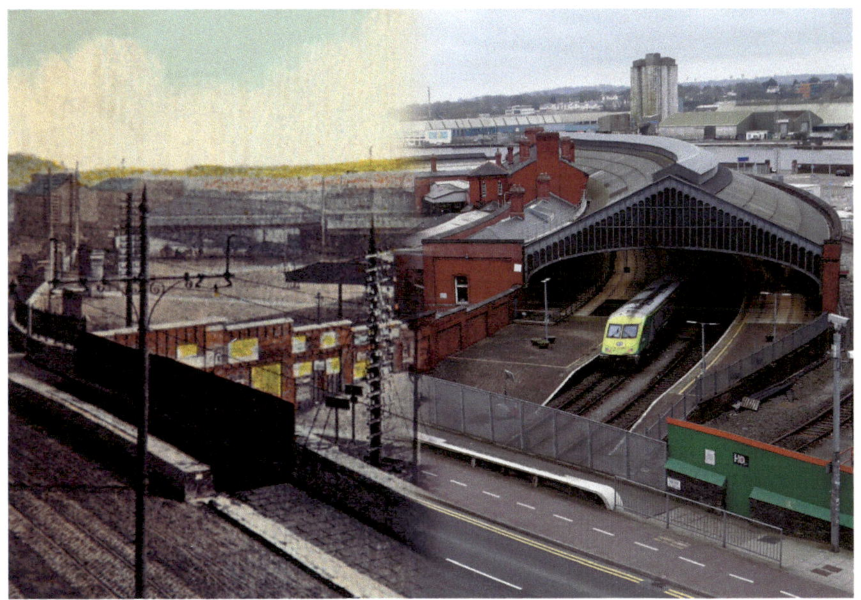

Kent Station

Kent station was originally built to replace the Dublin and Cobh termini, which were situated at Penrose Quay and Summerhill respectively. By 1890, the marshy land at the back of the houses on the Lower Glanmire Road overlooking the River Lee was filled in. Construction work began in the spring of 1891. The contractor was a Mr Samuel Hill, who was a native of Cork City. The architecture chosen for the station was basic and plain, primarily comprising Ruabon brick faced with limestone. The station was opened in February 1893. Kent station is dedicated to the memory of Volunteer Thomas Kent who was executed by the British government on 9 May 1916 on the charge of armed rebellion. He was initially buried at the then Victoria detention barracks but was exhumed in 2015 and reburied in the graveyard of St Nicholas' Church.

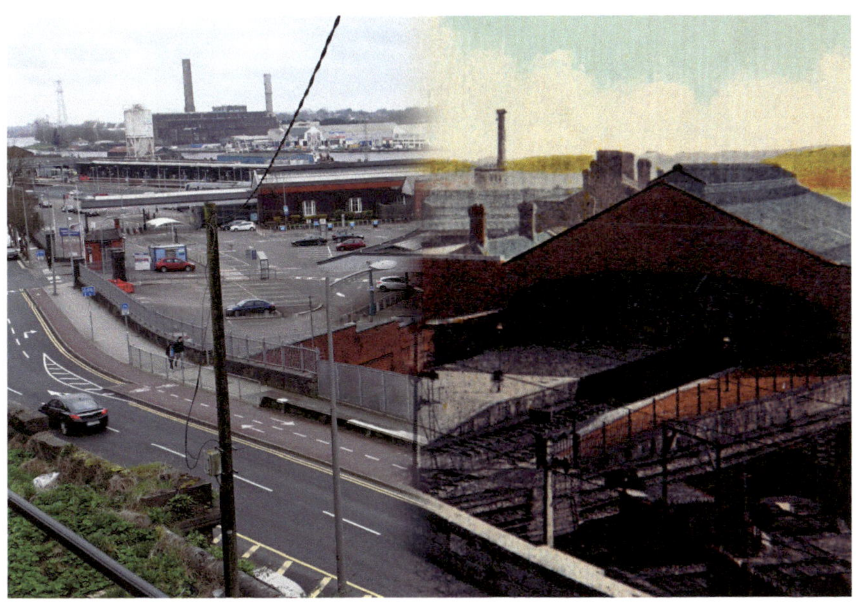

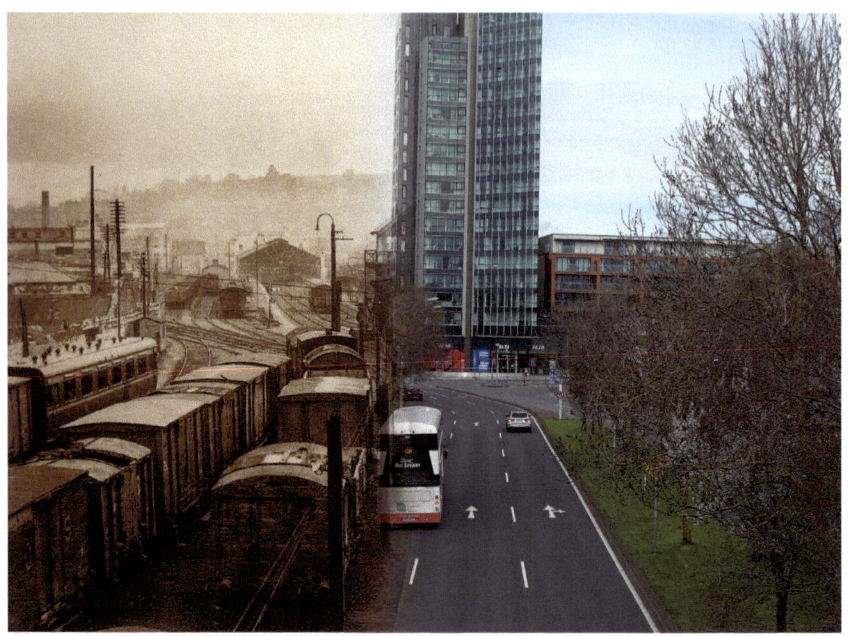

Cork, Bandon & South Coast Railway Terminus

The Cork, Bandon & South Coast Railway, 95 miles long, opened for traffic in 1851. It ran from Cork City to Bantry with extensions to Kinsale, Courtmacsherry, Clonakilty and Skibbereen. The line served the important agricultural districts of the south and west Cork and the well-known fishing ground on the south coast. In connection with the train service, a motor or bus service from Bantry to Killarney gave a direct route to the tourist town. A large number of men were employed at the Cork terminus in the extensive repairing shops and in the construction of rolling stock. The company also maintained a regular steamer service between Bantry and Glengarriff. The last passenger service to West Cork ceased in 1961.

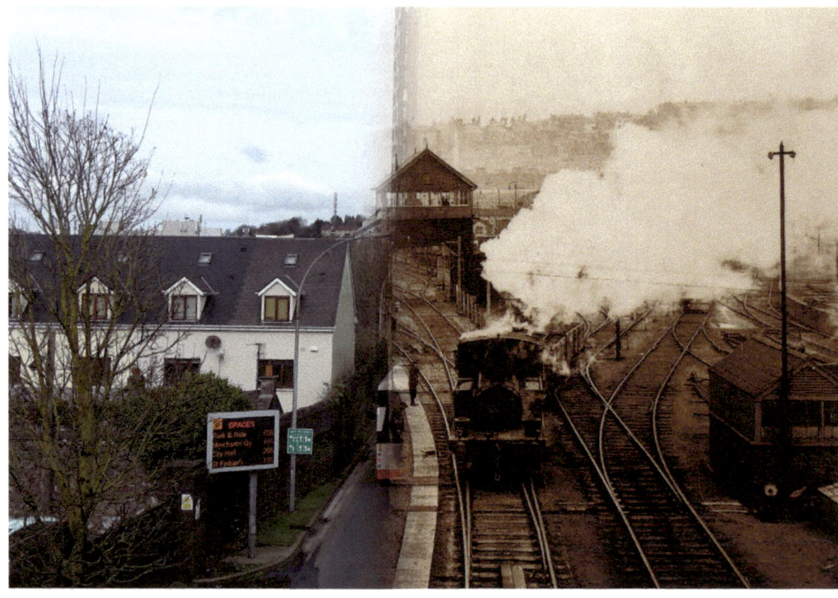

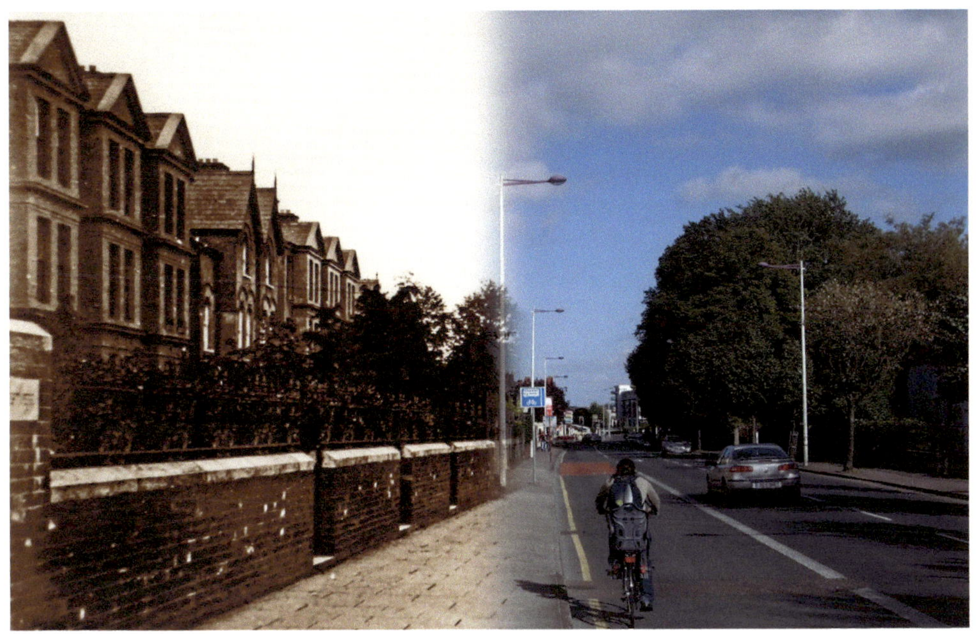

Cork & Muskerry Light Railway, Western Road

The Cork & Muskerry Railway was one the city's first narrow-gauge lines. It was established with the help of the Tramways and Public Expenses (Ireland) Act of 1883, which enabled companies to obtain part or all of the finance to construct a line. Primarily, the line was built for tourist reasons to link Cork to the tourist town of Blarney with its historic castle. Beginning on Bishop's Marsh (now the River Lee Hotel), the Cork terminus was a single-storey building covered by a corrugated iron roof with a long platform. The iron engine and carriage shed spanned three tracks. The first 4 miles of the line going west were very like that of a tramway.

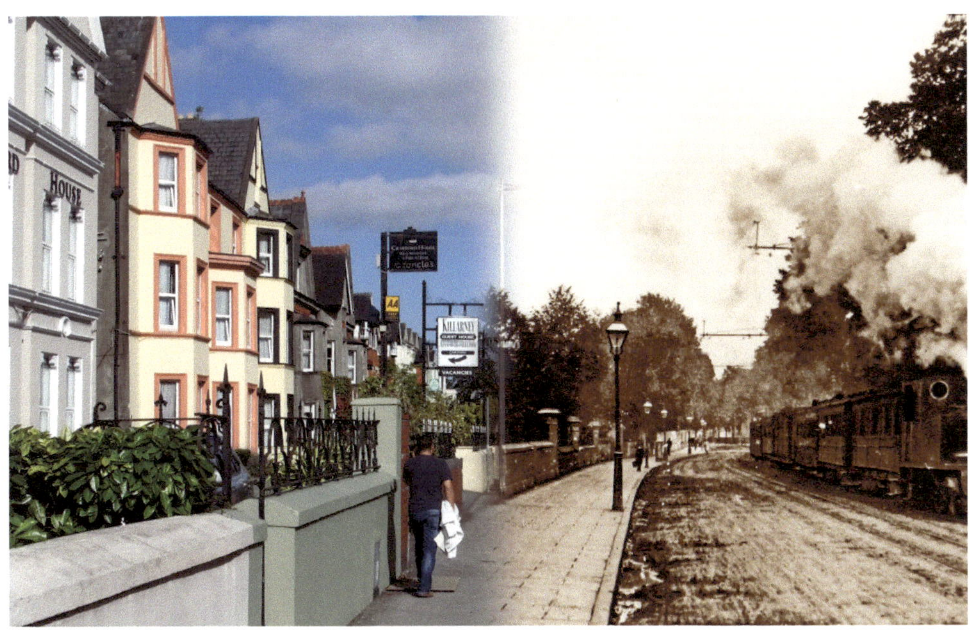

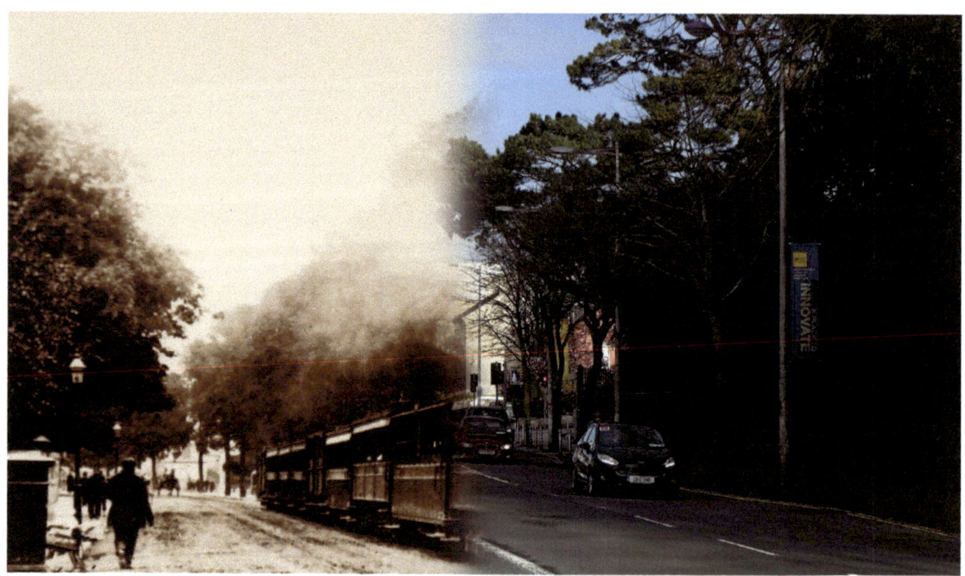

Cork & Muskerry Light Railway

The initial stops were at Victoria Cross, Carrigrohane and then northwards to Leemount, Healy's Bridge and Coachford Junction. There were two branch lines, one to Coachford and the other starting from St Anne's Hydro, near Blarney, which followed the Shournagh valley to Donoughmore. The first-class fare was two shillings and six pence and third class was one shilling and ten pence. The first-class compartment had padded seats covered in red velvet upholstery. In the third-class compartment the seats were of varnished wood and ran the length of the carriage. Whenever an important match was played in Coachford, great crowds travelled on the train. All the freight arrived by train: porter and whiskey, groceries, coal, and yellow meal for Coachford and Carrigadrohid. Pigs were carried to Cork by train for the city's bacon factories.

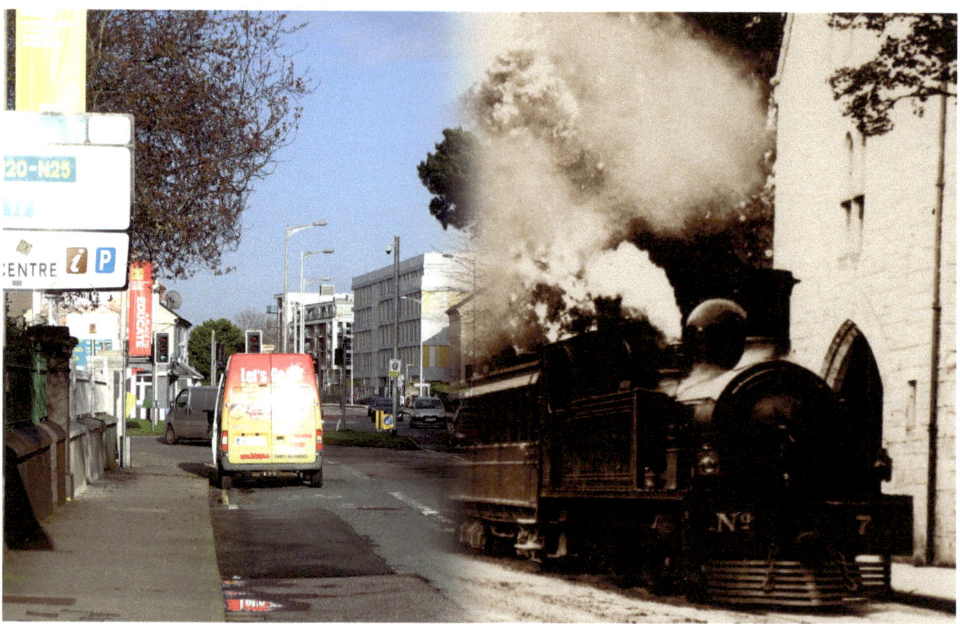

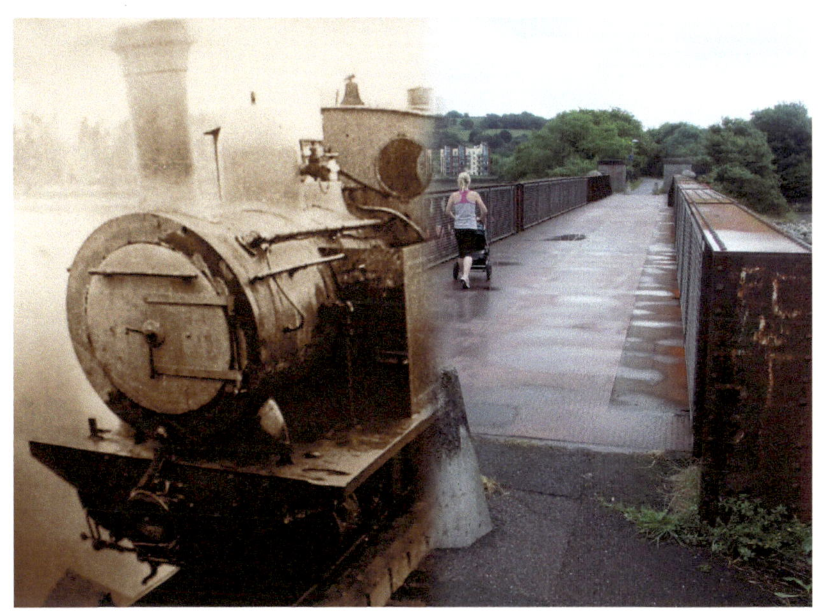

Cork Blackrock & Passage Railway

The Cork Blackrock & Passage Railway opened in 1850 and was among the first of the Irish suburban railway projects. The entire length of track between Cork and Passage was in place by April 1850 and within two months the line was open for passenger traffic. In 1904, the line was extended from Passage to Crosshaven through tunnels and along coastline. In 1886, a contract was given by the railway company to build an iron viaduct across Douglas Estuary. On 8 August 1922, the Irish Free Army blew up part of this bridge, which was duly replaced. Due to competition from buses and to financial losses, the eighty-two-year-old line closed on 10 December 1932. Today, the majority of the elaborate railway line is an amenity walk maintained by Cork City and Cork County Councils, where old bridges, embankments, cuttings and tunnels can be explored at ease and the achievements of the railway line truly appreciated.

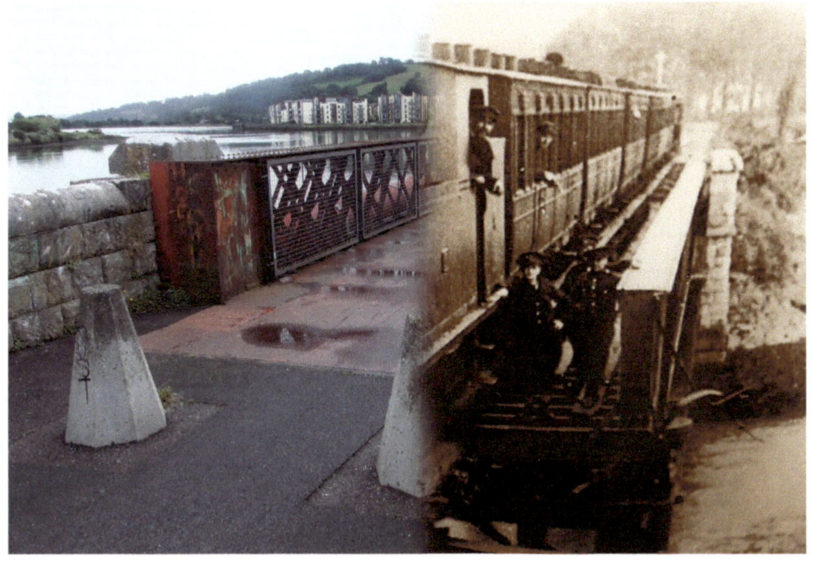

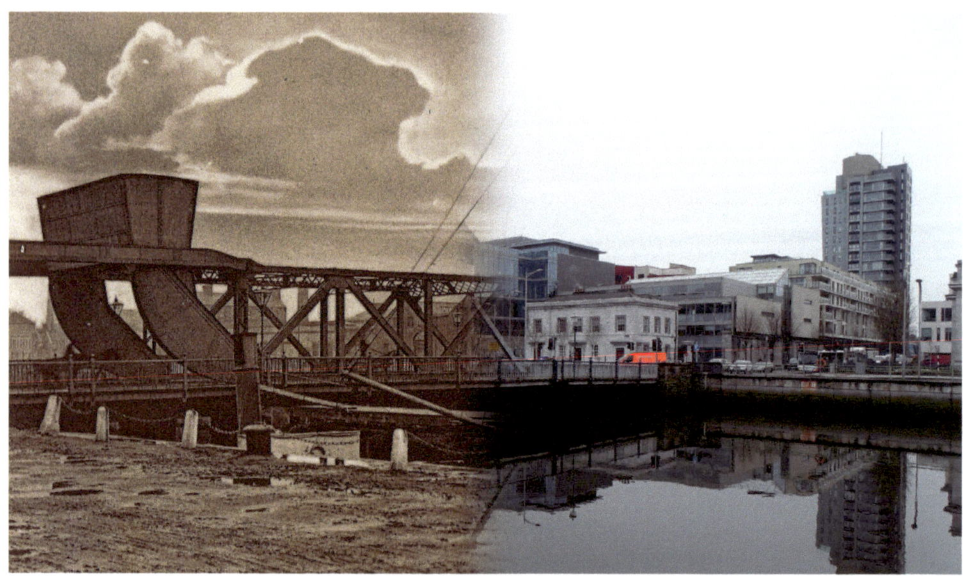

Clontarf Bridge

By 1910, the facilities for dealing with steamer traffic at the port of Cork were unique within Britain and Ireland. The Cork Railways and Works Company provided a link line across the river, which was opened in 1911, between the city termini of the Cork, Bandon & South Coast Railway and the Great Southern & Western Railway. This enabled rolling stocks to run direct from one line to another. The link was forged through the creation of Brian Boru and Clontarf bridges in 1912. They were named after the famous victory by Irish chieftain Brian Boru at the Battle of Clontarf in 1014 over Viking power in Ireland. Providing access between West Cork and Cork City for the general public including visitors and farmers was the Cork, Bandon & South Coast Railway line. The Cork-Bandon line opened to the public on 6 December 1851. The Cork terminus was on Albert Quay, which had three passenger platforms, a carriage storage area, and sidings into Cork Corporation's stone yard and into the adjacent corn market.

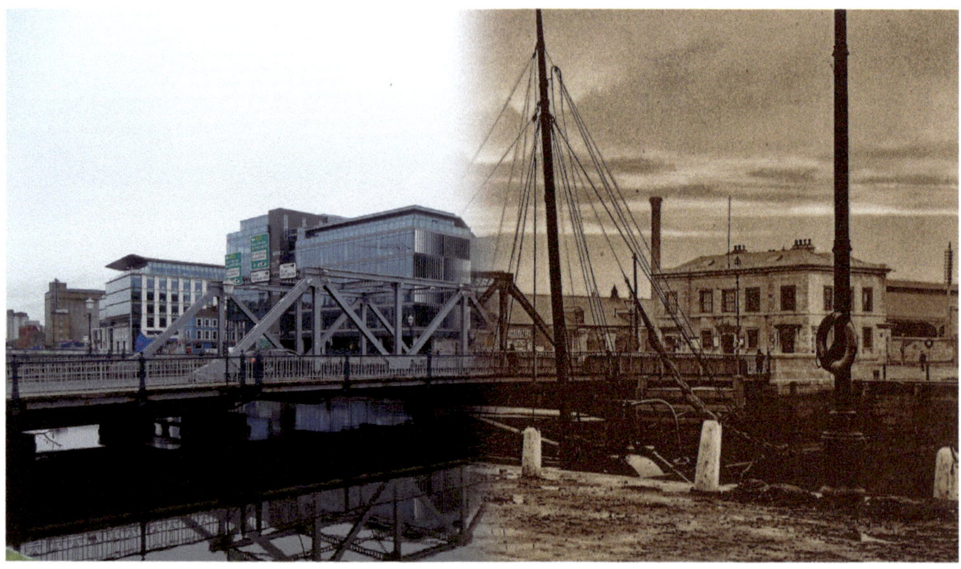

Acknowledgements

The old postcards within this book are archived in the Cork Public Museum. The present-day pictures were taken by the authors. We would like to also thank the staff of Amberley Publishing for their vision with this work. Thanks to Dara McGrath, Digital Officer with Cork City Museum, and Dr Mairéad Mooney for her proofing expertise.

About the Authors

Kieran McCarthy

For over twenty-five years, Kieran has actively promoted Cork's heritage with its various communities and people. He has led and continues to lead successful heritage initiatives through his community talks, city schools' heritage programmes, walking tours, newspaper articles, books and his work through his heritage consultancy business. For the past twenty-one years, Kieran has written a local heritage column in the *Cork Independent* on the history, geography and its intersection with modern-day life in communities in Cork City and County. He holds a PhD in Geography from the National University of Ireland Cork and has interests in ideas of landscape, collective memory, narrative and identity structures. Kieran is the author of twenty-five local history books. In June 2009, May 2014 and May 2019 Kieran was elected as a local government councillor (Independent) to Cork City Council. He is also a member of the European Committee of the Regions. More on Kieran's work can be viewed at www.corkheritage.ie and www.kieranmccarthy.ie.

Daniel Breen

Daniel Breen has worked in the heritage/cultural sector for almost two decades. Having graduated with a degree in History and Archaeology from University College Cork in 2001, he achieved an MA from the University of Sheffield in European Historical Archaeology in 2002. While in college, Daniel spent his summer months working on various archaeological sites throughout Ireland. Since graduation, he has worked in Cork Public Museum where he was appointed Curator in April 2019. In this time, he has managed the museum's ever-expanding collections, covering Cork's rich heritage from prehistoric to modern times. Daniel has also organised hundreds of exhibitions and events to help bring this collection to as wide an audience as possible. Daniel has worked with many local community groups and historical societies to promote a greater understanding of Cork's vibrant past, especially those voices and events that are often overlooked. He co-wrote *Cork City Through Time* with Kieran McCarthy in 2012 as well as *West Cork Through Time* (2013), *Cork Harbour Through Time* (2014), and *North Cork Through Time* (2015). In 2014 he co-authored *The Cork International Exhibition 1902–1903 – Snapshot of Edwardian Cork* with Tom Spalding, published by Irish Academic Press.

The postcards and images shown in this book come from the archives of Cork Public Museum. The current incarnation of the museum has been open since 1945, making it the oldest local authority museum in Ireland. It is housed in a beautiful Georgian building set in the wonderfully landscaped Fitzgerald Park. The house hosted the Fitzgerald Park Municipal Museum between 1910 until 1924. During the turbulent pre-Second World War period, the building was utilised for a variety of civic and municipal functions that resulted in the city having no public museum for twenty years.

Finally, in April 1945 Cork Public Museum was officially opened to the public and it has remained in existence ever since. In 2005, a contemporary and modern extension was added to the existing building making Cork Public Museum one of the most celebrated public buildings in Cork City. The collections of Cork Public Museum are as rich and as diverse as the history of the city itself. The ground floor of the museum has two permanent galleries, each dealing with the historical and archaeological heritage of Cork City and County.

The archaeological section takes the visitor into what life was like in medieval Cork where the finds from all of the city's past excavations are exhibited, highlighting the importance of Cork as a trading and economic centre during medieval times. The historic displays focus on many important industrial, social and political aspects of Cork City's development since the eighteenth century. The visitor will trace the ebb and flow of Cork's industrial past where butter making, glass manufacture and silver working were once dominant but now no longer form part of the city's industrial landscape. Cork Public Museum traces the roles played by many Cork people, from the eighteenth to the early twentieth century, in striving and eventually achieving Irish Independence. The collections and archives of Lord Mayors Tomás MacCurtain and Terence MacSwiney, who both died in 1920 during the Irish War of Independence, are very important historical resources in the study of this period.

From amateur genealogists to university academics, Cork Public Museum proves invaluable to researchers and students alike. The museum houses a vast amount of artefacts and documents in our reserve collection. Though they may never be publicly exhibited, they need to be protected and preserved so that future generations can have access to this material to aid further research or educate the future about our past. Cork Public Museum has served people from Cork and further afield since 1945 and it is our intent and desire to continue to be custodians of Cork's historical and archaeological legacy for the foreseeable future.

Cork Public Museum Digitisation Project

Since 1992, Cork Public Museum has collected thousands of postcards and other images depicting scenes, people and places associated with Cork City and County the mid-nineteenth to the early twentieth century. Though initially focused on acquiring postcards, the museum has also sought and acquired, through donation and purchase, other visual media including glass negatives, stereography views, personal photograph albums, as well as other photographic formats. The museum's image collection includes some of the oldest known images of Cork, showing a city on the cusp of the modern world.

Cork Public Museum is committed to cataloguing and digitising its entire image collections and to making them available to the public through exhibition, publication and online purchase. This project is still in the planning phase but it is envisaged to have the project complete and ready by 2022.